The Theological Moveme
and Its Confessional Writings

LUTHERANISM

ERIC W. GRITSCH
and
ROBERT W. JENSON

FORTRESS PRESS
Philadelphia

To our students,
past, present, and future

"We are not minded to manufacture anything new."

—*The Book of Concord*

Biblical quotations from the Revised Standard Version of the Bible, copyrighted 1946 and 1952 by the Division of Christian Education of the National Council of the Churches of Christ in the United States of America, are used by permission.

Library of Congress Catalog Card Number 76–007869

ISBN 0-8006-1246-9

1-1246

Contents

Preface

> I ask that men make no reference to my name; let them call themselves Christians, not Lutherans. What is Luther? After all, the teaching is not mine. Neither was I crucified for anyone. St. Paul, in I Corinthians 3[:22] would not allow the Christians to call themselves Pauline or Petrine, but Christian. How then could I—poor stinking maggot-fodder that I am—come to have men call the children of Christ by my wretched name? Not so, my dear friends; let us abolish all party names and call ourselves Christians, after him whose teaching we hold. (LW 45, 70–71)

Luther was an ecumenist, not a sectarian. When the Lutheran movement of the sixteenth century was asked to justify its existence at the Diet of Augsburg in 1530, it did so as a theological movement dedicated to expound, to guard, and to celebrate the cheering news that Christ liberates mankind from sin, death, and evil. The Augsburg Confession and subsequent documents of this Christocentric stance have been collected in the Book of Concord of 1580—the authoritative confessional book for Lutherans around the globe.

The title and disposition of our book are determined by the way we understand the Lutheran confessions: as authoritative documents of a theological movement within the church catholic. It is precisely *Lutheranism*, in its formal self-definition, that we wish to describe. We do not, therefore, present a detailed, serial exposition of the Lutheran confessions. Instead, we try to explicate the one article of faith in the promoting of which the Lutheran movement exists: justification by faith apart from works of law. This was the dogma which sixteenth-century Lutheranism proposed to the church catholic as a norm of orthodoxy and orthopraxy. We try to show the difference this proposed dogma makes for the great traditional topics of Christian reflection which became thematic in the Reformation controversies reflected in the Book of Concord. A historical-theological introduction (Part One) and a discussion of critical issues (Part Four) surround the explication of the chief Lutheran article of faith (Part Two) and of its consequences for Christian reflection (Part Three).

What we offer here is a product of long collaboration in teaching the Lutheran confessions to ministerial candidates. We present the fruits of our common teaching experience in the hope that active clergy, laypersons, and students other than our own may be helped to know Lutheranism and be encouraged to read the Book of Concord itself. To that end, we give a list of readings from the Book of Concord at the head of each chapter. Source readings from BC (English) and BS (German and Latin) are listed by "parts," "articles," and "sections" rather than by pages. (For example, instead of citing BC, p. 292, or BS, p. 414, we use SA II, 1:1, "The first and chief article is this . . ."; instead of BC, p. 29, or BS, p. 53, we use AC 2:1, "It is also taught among us. . . .")

The collaboration of a church historian and a systematic theologian is suggested by the subject matter itself: the Lutheran confessions, like the Bible, are at once mandatory objects of historical exegesis and subjects of a claim on our present understanding. It would not, of course, be necessary for this duality to be matched by the professional duality of historian and theologian; but where such a professional collaboration is possible, and in fact works out, that collaboration is clearly appropriate.

Chapters 2 and 4 have been written by the historian, Chapters 1 and 3 by the systematician. The other chapters each contain two parts (simply designated "A" and "B") written by the historian and systematician respectively. In each chapter the two parts cover the same ground: A in more narrative order, B in more systematic order. Readers should not, however, expect a stringent division of historical and systematic reflection between the chapters and part-chapters. We have made no great effort to stay out of each other's professional ways, and have, over the years, appropriated too much from each other to sort it out now. The historian does history in concern for the present thinking and life of the church; this shows in his parts of the book. In the systematician's constructive theologizing, he pursues historical exegesis; this shows in his parts of the book. Each of us contributes to the collaboration not so much a discrete sort of reflection as an emphasis and—we hope—a needed expertise. Our purpose and method also require historical discussions to reach past the Lutheran confessions themselves to the work of Martin Luther and other reformers. Indeed, in Chapter 7—on Christology—where connection to the patristic and medieval theological inheritance is most explicit and positive, we have found it pedagogically necessary to expound that inheritance; the additional historical section on ancient Christology is, in this one case, by the systematician.

This is not a scholarly book in the sense of Teutonic depth and precision. The forthcoming 400th anniversaries of the Formula of Concord (1977) and the Book of Concord (1980) may generate detailed scholarly work on the Lutheran confessions. Moreover, we did not want to burden our book with lengthy footnotes reflecting our debate with other interpreters of the Book of Concord, thus drawing attention away from the sources. Rather, our aim is simpler and more direct: to present the basic tenets of Lutheranism to contemporary Lutheran and non-Lutheran Christians in the hope that they, as we, rejoice in the continuing reformation of the body of Christ on earth.

We are grateful for the challenge of our Gettysburg students to state the succinct Lutheran option in ecumenical Christianity; it is to them—our students, past, present, and future—that we dedicate this book. We are also grateful for the constant critical evaluation of our work by our spouses Ruth and Blanche, the former of whom typed the manuscript in its various stages.

Earlier versions of some material in this book have appeared in other publications: *Lutheran-Episcopal Dialogue*, ed. Peter Day and Paul D. Opsahl, FM Maxi-Books; *Religion and the Dilemmas of Nationhood*, ed. Sydney Ahlstrom, Lutheran Church in America; *Concordia Theological Monthly*; *Dialog*; *Lutheran Theological Seminary Bulletin*; and *Lutheran Quarterly*.

In the sesquicentennial year of Lutheran theological education at Gettysburg,

ERIC W. GRITSCH
ROBERT W. JENSON

ABBREVIATIONS

AC	Augsburg Confession.
AP	Apology of the Augsburg Confession.
BC	*The Book of Concord,* translated and edited by Theodore G. Tappert (Philadelphia, 1959).
BS	*Die Bekenntnisschriften der evangelisch-lutherischen Kirche,* 3d ed. rev. (Goettingen, 1930).
CR	*Philippi Melanchthonii Opera,* vols. 1–28 of the *Corpus Reformatorum,* edited by Carl G. Bretschneider and H. E. Bindseil (Halle, 1834–60).
EP	Epitome of FC.
FC	Formula of Concord.
Inst.	*Institutes of the Christian Religion,* by John Calvin, 2 vols., translated by Henry Beveridge (London, 1957).
LC	Large Catechism.
LW	American Edition of *Luther's Works* (Philadelphia and St. Louis, 1955–).
SA	Smalcald Articles.
SC	Small Catechism.
SD	Solid Declaration of FC.
TR	Treatise on the Power and Primacy of the Pope.
WA	*D. Martin Luthers Werke.* Kritische Gesamtausgabe (Weimar, 1883–).
Walch	*D. Martin Luthers saemmtliche Schriften,* edited by Johann G. Walch. Edited and published in modern German, 23 vols. in 25 (St. Louis, 1880–1910).

PART ONE

THE LUTHERAN CONFESSIONS

Chapter I

An Ecumenical Proposal of Dogma

Readings:
BC or BS I, "The Three Chief Symbols"
FC, "Rule and Norm"

Gospel, Theology, and Dogma

There are a variety of reasons for reading the Lutheran confessions. Some are purely historical. The confessions are main documents of an epochal event: the breakup of medieval Christendom and its replacement by a system of secular states and cooperating, coexisting, and warring "churches." Some of these churches were defined organizationally, some territorially, and some theologically. The Lutheran confessions are the clearest example of a theological definition. Some of the confessions are important also as documents of the work of historically decisive theologians: the Catechisms and the Smalcald Articles are Luther at his most characteristic, and the Apology of the Augsburg Confession is a chief work of Melanchthon, the creator of standard continental Protestantism. As rich works of theology, the confessions may also be used as historical grist for theological systematic mills. We have tried to serve all these interests.

But one may also read the confessions because one takes their *claim* seriously, whether in support or in opposition. It is this reading we wish especially to serve, and for which we have found our cooperation as historical and systematic theologians so helpful. The confessions understand themselves as addresses to the church catholic, making a few allegedly indispensable points about the discourse and life of the church, points that ought always to be observed but must be made explicitly just because they often are not. That is, the confessions are a *proposal of dogma*; it is as such that we wish to discuss them, and much of the rest of this chapter will be explanation of the phrase.

The word "dogma" has an unfortunate connotation, standing for opinion held come what may, in defiance of change. It is just because Christian faith is not at all "dogmatic" in this sense that dogma in the churchly sense is needed.

The church is the community of a certain communication: the story of Israel and its Jesus, told as a message of final destiny. The church is the band of those sent into the world to say by word and action: "Jesus the Israelite is risen, and has death behind him. Therefore, nothing can now overcome his will for you; what will come of the human enterprise, and of your participation in it, is in the hands of this man of hope, and no other. There is reason for all your struggles."

This "gospel" is an unconditional promise, a message of undefeatable hope; and as such it is a permission of freedom from any and every bondage to the past and a static status quo. Just so, it must itself be addressed to the new hopes and struggles, the new ways of participating in the human enterprise, that open whenever history escapes the bondage of the past. It will do no good, for example, to proclaim Jesus' death as the payment of a great indemnity to God, to people freed—partly by the gospel itself!—from the feudal fear of indemnities, and from conceiving of God as supreme feudal master. To be itself, the gospel speaks to the living hopes and fears of its actual hearers; to be itself, the gospel changes.

Sometimes the change is imperceptible, sometimes it is violent. There are great epochs in the gospel's history: when its missionaries bring it to a new civilization—as in the extension from Jews to Greeks in the early decades; or when a civilization with which it has been involved undergoes a crisis that breaks old guarantees of meaning and possibility and calls for new ones—as at the Reformation. At such epochs, whole gospel-languages rise and fall.

To speak gospel to my fellows and myself, I cannot, therefore, merely repeat formulas from my days in Sunday school. I must speak of Jesus as the hope of the new possibilities and new threats that open today and tomorrow in their life and mine. Therefore I must think, and not merely recite. "Theology" is this thinking. We must ask: given that such-and-such *was* said to us (e.g., by missionaries, parents, friends), and that these words functioned in our life as gospel, what are we *now* to say that will function as gospel? We must propose sentences of the form: "To say the gospel now, let us say '———,' rather than '———.'" What goes in the first blank is either a proposed sample of the gospel itself, or some stipulation about it; the whole sentence is a piece of "theology."

If an individual addresses such sentences to the community, we call him a "theologian." But such sentences can also be addressed by the church as a whole, to individuals: "If you want to speak for this community, say '———,' rather than '———.'" In the proper churchly sense, *a dogma is merely a theological proposition addressed by the community to its members, rather than by members to the community.*

The church must from time to time speak in this way to be responsible to its mission. The church understands itself as a community sent into the world to speak there a certain message. But since the church is a real historical community, people will, over the years, affiliate with it for reasons irrelevant to its mission, and those people who are authentically related to the church may partly forget their original purpose. Since there are words other than the gospel which must be spoken in the world, and many more which can and will be spoken, the church is permanently tempted to confuse its gospel with other messages: to proclaim hope in names other than that of Jesus, and to talk about Jesus in ways that evoke despair rather than hope.

From time to time, the possibility of perversion becomes so pressing that the matter must be fought out; this usually happens when an epoch in the gospel's history demands radically new preaching of the gospel, and many in the church are not sufficiently freed by the gospel to take the risk. If the church masters such a crisis, with a good theological word to its members about what the gospel is to be, we call that word a dogma.

Therefore, dogma is always also a political reality: it is the self-definition of a specific community over against the larger society, and will often be first proclaimed in some courtroom or parliament of the larger society (e.g., the Augsburg Confession), or as the manifesto of a conspiratorial group (e.g., the Smalcald Articles). By the "Nicene" Creed, for example, the ancient church said publicly: those committed to a message about the reality of God *himself* in Jesus' crucifixion and resurrection belong to our community; those committed to a less radical claim belong to some other community. Such exclusiveness offends the conventionally religious; but it is necessary to the very existence of any lively community with a specific mission. The church indeed hopes that at the End a redeemed mankind will replace it, so that it will have no boundaries. But it also knows that the End is not yet.

Therefore, also, dogma is always *ecumenical*: it is addressed by the whole church to the whole church. In classical discussions of these matters the point is always made that "reception" is essential to dogma: the vital theological point may originate anywhere—as a bright idea of some professor or a political dictate of a Byzantine emperor—but it becomes dogma in that it is explicitly confessed as self-definition by a community that can with some plausibility claim to be *the* catholic church. It is evident that in the post-Reformation situation no further new dogma can be actual, unless some denomination or territorial church is willing to declare all the others excluded from the church catholic. The church of Rome's post-Reformation attempts to define dogma are presently an embarrassment to it: wishing now to recognize that the church is larger than itself, Rome must either deny these attempts or act hypocritically.

There are not so many dogmas as outsiders suppose. There is the definition of a canon of Scripture as the final norm of the gospel's authenticity. There is the stipulation that those entering the church must affirm some trinitarian confession, on the lines of the "Apostles'" Creed. There is the stipulation of washing in Jesus' name as the way into the church, and of a meal of bread and wine as the center of the church's interior life. There is the "Nicene" Creed's assertion that Christ is not the kind of halfway station on the way to God that is provided by normal religion's various saviors. There is the complementary assertion of the Council of Chalcedon that Christ is not therefore a merely halfway man. There is the proposition of the Council of Orange that salvation is God's work and not ours, and that we should get on with ours. And that is about the list. Dogma is but a tiny part of the church's actual message and teaching.

At the Diet of Augsburg and elsewhere, the Lutheran reformers and their followers proposed further dogma to the church. Many, including groups that the reformers could not simply regard as not-church, did not accept the offer. Thus the Lutheran confessions remain *proposals* of dogma. If the Lutheran proposals had been ecumenically accepted, there would be no Lutheranism. As it is, Lutheranism is a *confessional movement* within the church catholic that continues to offer to the whole church that proposal of dogma which received definitive documentary form in the Augsburg Confession and the other writings collected in the Book of Concord.

Whether this movement is organized as a "church" or not is secondary to its purpose; some times and some places it is so organized, and other times and places it is not. In any case, the Lutheran confessions are not primarily the constitution of an established denomination or territorial church; they are rather the manifesto of a movement whose ecumenical hour—if it has one—is still partly in the future. "The Lutheran Church" is, indeed, an ecumenical movement of its own: it is a fellowship of territorial churches, denominations, and sects that contains within itself nearly every possible kind of church life and organization, and is held together only by common dedication to the Lutheran theological movement.

The Lutheran proposal of dogma has one great theme: justification by faith alone, apart from works of law. This is the heart of the matter; we state it here only as a slogan, the explication of which is the task of the whole book. All else is elaboration.

Dogma and proposed dogma claim *authority*. Dogma is address by the community to the individual, saying: this is how you should speak. A well-known mark of our time, however, is that we have trouble with such dictates; we therefore cannot responsibly continue without some discussion of the whole matter of churchly authority.

Such authority as the confessions claim for themselves is understood by them to be corollary to the authority of the Bible. This matter is rarely discussed, yet everywhere assumed. But not only is the nature of the derivation of dogmatic authority from scriptural authority not specified, but the confessions are also surprisingly reticent about scriptural authority itself, giving neither a theory of the Scriptures' authoritative character nor a rule for their authoritative work in the church. The Formula of Concord typically states only *that* "the prophetic and apostolic writings of the Old and New Testament" are the final authority of the church's teaching. This authority does receive a suggestive double interpretation: (1) "We pledge ourselves to the prophetic and apostolic writings of the Old and New Testaments as the pure and clear fountain of Israel" (FC, "Rule and Norm," SD 3) and (2) "We believe, teach, and confess that the prophetic and apostolic writings of the Old and New Testaments are the only rule and norm according to which all doctrines and teachers alike must be appraised and judged" (FC, "Rule and Norm," EP 1). But also this duality is not developed.

What follows, therefore, cannot claim merely to expound what the confessions say. It can only claim to be *a* Lutheran doctrine of churchly authority. Its most obtrusive feature will be the attempt to make something of the duality suggested in the Formula of Concord.

Two Kinds of Authority

All talk of "authority" is a certain way of talking about the event of communication. When you address me, I come to stand in possibilities—however trivial these, in a particular exchange, may be—which are new to me in just those ways in which you are different from me and open that difference to me in your address. By your utterance you in some way determine my future. This determination is what we mean by "authority." Every human communication, therefore, posits a relation of authority; to encounter authority is not necessarily to encounter heteronomy or a block to freedom, but only to encounter another human existence in its communication.

Ordinarily, of course, we do not especially note this aspect of the event of communication; and we therefore do not speak of "authority" unless the mutual determination is in some way obtrusive. Then we will speak of "an authoritative statement" or "an authoritative impact." Moreover, we do not address each other *de novo*: our ability to address each other depends both on the tradition of language itself and on a tradition of information about each other. These traditions together lead us to *expect* authoritative utterance in certain situations or from certain persons. Thus we come to identify "authorities."

Believing reflection, accustomed to understand reality under polarities such as "old man" and "new man," or "creation" and "redemption," may expect what experience seems to confirm, that there are two possible basic modes of authority. One is much the more usual. When you and I address each other, each of us commonly seeks to *dominate* the other—under however many masking layers this may be concealed. I seek to determine your future in a certain way: by foreclosing your options. I seek to establish for you patterns like "If . . . then . . . ," where what fits in the first blank is an action to be performed, or an attitude to be adopted, or a character to be exemplified by you, and where what fits in the second blank is an event or state of affairs already desired or feared by you, and where I decree the if-then relation between the two. We will call this mode of authority *legal* authority, and by no means wish to denigrate it indiscriminately thereby.

But there could be quite another mode of authority. In our encounter, I could determine your future precisely by freeing you for it. My utterance might not so much foreclose your possibilities as open them to you, or indeed grant possibilities not otherwise yours. Our communication might, instead of having the structure, "If . . . then . . . ," have the structure, "Because . . . therefore . . . ," where what fits in the first blank is a commitment by me, and what fits in the second blank is a future for you—especially one not previously seen by you—and where the relation between the two is the space for your freedom. Such authority was called by the Lutheran reformers the authority of *promise*. A promise is at least as fully an occurrence of authority as the laying down of a law; it is simply different authority from the legal sort we more commonly pursue.

So much for a cursory analysis of the notion of authority. We must next consider briefly how the question of authority arises for the church in particular.

As the community of a story, the church lives by *tradition*. That is, the church depends at any time on being *told* this story, and therefore on those who have already heard it; and the church cares for its own future by in turn telling the story. The reality of the church at any time is the reality of a link in a tradition; the reality of the church is the hermeneutic event of the move from hearing to telling. So also an individual believer belongs to the community as one who hears from others and then speaks to others: faith, too, is a hermeneutic reality, and occurs in tradition. Both the church and the individual believer therefore depend on "the" tradition, on the totality of witnesses from which, at any time, we *have* heard the gospel.

If the church's life is in this way a hermeneutic event, relations of authority must be intrinsic to it. The only question about authority in the church is therefore the question, What *sort* or sorts of authority or authorities are posited in this hermeneutic occurrence? The answer to this question depends on the structure and content of this particular address and response. The question about the authority of Scripture or dogma is the question about their particular unique roles in this hermeneutic event.

The tradition's legitimate authority in the church is fundamentally the authority of promise rather than of law. The determination of my life and the life of the community by the address of the gospel is that it sets the community and me *free*. We are given to hope for that love which is the plot of Jesus' story as the consummation of the human enterprise. We may hope for it because of the utter commitment enacted on the cross. And the relation of this commitment to this future is the space opened for an unquenchable freedom. The gospel-tradition determines my life by giving me a sure and specific hope and by freeing me equally from inhibiting guilt and static security. Three points must be made:

First, either the Scriptures and the rest of the tradition acquire this authority over me, or they do not. If they do, this is a contingent fact; if they do not, there is no other authority by which we could say they *ought* to acquire this authority. If in fact I have heard the gospel story, and if what that story claims has contingently become a determinant in my life, then the witnesses from which I receive the gospel simply *are* my liberators. Then I simply have them as my authorities and there is no further argument to be made. If I have not been freed by the gospel, its witnesses have no authority for me—and there is no way to insist that they should have.

Second, the Scriptures and dogma have—in respect of *this* authority—preeminent places among the witnesses of the tradition because and only because the other witnesses direct us to them. "Authorities," we said, are persons or documents or offices from which tradition leads us to expect authoritative utterance. The other components of the gospel-tradition lead us to expect to hear liberating utterance in the reading and exposition of these particular documents; and in the history of the church this expectation has repeatedly been rewarded. The faith that this expectation will continue to be rewarded is the legitimate content of the notion of inspiration (it is also the *sole* legitimate content of the notion, and one which would probably better be expressed otherwise, given the unfortunate burden the notion has been made to carry). The historical position of Scripture at the beginning of the tradition is at *this* point irrelevant.

Third, where Scripture and the rest of tradition speak authoritatively in the church, their work is *liberation*; they are then the "pure and clear fountain of Israel" (FC, "Rule and Norm," SD 3). Under the authority of Scripture and the whole tradition, the function of theology will *not* be to provide the ideology of an established community; theology will not begin with concern either to "preserve" or "deny" anything at all. Theology will first of all be the activity of critique which discovers new life and new language. Neither can there be any such thing as *the* theology of a church or a denomination. Any attempt to deny time theologically, to decree theological immutability, is an attempt to evade scriptural and dogmatic authority in this its fundamental mode.

Under the authority of Scripture and the whole tradition, we will become free to worship in other ways than we have done, and, in whatever ways, for other reasons than that we have always done it so. The church cannot avoid being a social force; under the authority of Scripture and the whole tradition, the church will be a cell for the future rather than for the past, and be free to alter its own social structure in order to be this. Any attempt to decree that a particular form of government, or of ministry, or of worship, or of social presence, is permanently necessary to the church is a declaration of independence from the Scriptures and creeds.

There is, however, also a "legal" authority of the tradition and its Scriptures, in which they are "letters" that "rule" and "judge" us. This authority arises in this way: under the impact of the primary authority of the gospel-tradition, we are called to reflection on how we are now to tell the church's story, and so also on how we are now to enact it liturgically and act upon it socially. This reflection is freed to be creative: the answers to these questions need not be those previously entertained. Yet it is the same story we have heard which we now wish to tell, and in *its* promise for our future, not in one we might now invent. Theological reflection therefore requires a norm of the gospel's continuity, of its self-identity through history. We must be able to ask,

Is what we are saying *authentic* gospel? where "gospel" has historical meaning. And there must be a norm by which to make this judgment.

Fundamentally, the reality of the gospel's self-identity is the self-identity of the crucified and risen Jesus. As *risen,* he is the final future who ever opens new promises beyond those already made. All gospel address and response is in his name and to him, so that he is the free *subject* of this conversation, who initiates its surprising twists and new beginnings. As the *remembered* Jesus, he is also the *object* of gospel-talk; he is the given about whom we speak, and accurate narration of the facts about him is the objective self-identity of all gospel-talk. He can be at once fixed object and innovating subject because part of what we remember is exactly that he is risen.

Authentic gospel, we may therefore say, is talk of Christ which is (1) faithful to the remembered Jesus and (2) free response to the futurity of the risen Jesus. It is, therefore, under the authority of the tradition. For, with respect to the first criterion, only by tradition do we have historical memory, and only by tradition can we judge our historical memory. Our gospel-talk is authentic only if it is accurate recollection. This same tradition is not, however, merely documentation of a past event. For what is handed on includes that Jesus is risen, that he is free future and not dead past. Thus the tradition is a tradition of proclamation, of that telling about Jesus which is liberating promise. Thus, with respect to the second criterion, our gospel-talk is authentic only if it is an address which does for the hearers' freedom what the proclamation in the tradition has done for past hearers; it is authentic if it opens the hearers' unique future in Jesus' love. These two necessary conditions are together a sufficient condition, and in this double way the tradition is the norm by which we may test our life as the church.

The Legal Authority of Scripture

This doctrine is still incomplete. For "the tradition" as an undifferentiated whole will not function as a norm. As with any actual historical tradition, the boundaries of the gospel-tradition are too indefinite—anything I might feel like saying can find precedent somewhere in "Christian" antecedents. Over against the undifferentiated tradition, I can always justify myself. Only if the tradition is not undifferentiated with respect to authority, only if part of the tradition, a part to which I do not belong, is normative for the rest of the tradition, can the whole tradition be normative for me.

This authority *in* the tradition *for* the tradition is a certain roughly distinguishable set of witnesses, the "apostles." Our gospel is authentic if and only if it is "the same" (*in the way just specified*) gospel as they spoke. Within any tradition, there are multifarious relations of authority: each distinguishable part claims to be normative for the rest in some way. The apostles are normative for all the rest of the gospel tradition in that if we try to get behind them we find no gospel-*tradition* at all; for their witness is that in which this particular story first comes to word.

Nor is this only the usual authority of the beginning of a tradition. Where the tradition is that of an alleged event, it is possible to ask even of the witnesses at the beginning of the tradition, Did it really happen that way? But the particular event witnessed to by the gospel tradition is Jesus *as* his life and fate make a promise to our future. Therefore, if we go behind the witness in which this promise first comes to word, what we will find is not anymore the witnessed event at all, but only one of its presuppositions, the not-yet-risen Jesus: the objective norm of the gospel isolated from the ruling subject of the gospel.

Thus our gospel is authentic if it is—again *in the specified sense*—"the same" gospel as that of the apostolic period. We come to the special role of Scripture; for immediately one set of documents stands out normatively from the tradition: the canonical books of Israel. They stand out because they were normative for the apostles themselves. The apostles' message was intrinsically a word spoken following the record in these writings. The apostles could say what they had to say only with a *text* and only with *these* books as the text: their witness was to what happened with Jesus as interpreted by these books, or, equally, a witness to the teaching of these books as interpreted by what happened with Jesus. Our talk is hermeneutically the same as theirs only if it also submits to a text, and to this text.

The function of the New Testament is quite different. Its existence marks the end of the apostolic period; that is, it marks the point where the church had to note that the identity of its gospel with that of the apostles was no longer tautologous, that the identity of the gospel had to be worked at, that the apostolic proclamation had become something to be *remembered.* The New Testament comprises the literary relics of the apostolic gospel: it collects the literary remains of the gospel's life in the church, up to the point of beginning *recollection.* The New Testament is a substitute for the living voice of the apostles, a substitute for being able to question them and discuss with them and perhaps argue with them. Our talk of Christ is gospel only if it is objectively about the same events as the witness recorded in the New Testament documents, and only if it opens our lives to the future in the same way as did that witness.

The Scriptures—and the whole tradition in its various ways—have this legal authority in the church only because of their liberating authority. Where the Scriptures do not in fact have authority as promise, any attempt to claim legal force for them is an arbitrary imposition. Any theory, interpretation, or practice of the Scriptures' legal authority which obscures this derivation is pernicious. Vice versa, the legal authority of the Scriptures, and of the rest of the tradition, is always somehow misconstrued if it is used to assert a theology or a structure of ministry or a pattern of relation to society as immutably necessary to the church. The legal authority of the tradition can never properly be used to limit its liberating authority—since the fact of the legal authority depends upon the absoluteness of the liberating authority. This does not mean that theological formulation or ministerial order or social-political stance are in any way unimportant; on the contrary, just because these are mutable they are the arena of our existence before God and man, of our free responsibility as believers. Nor does it mean that one solution is as good as another.

One error in this connection is so thoroughly discredited that we mention it now only for old times' sake: any theory of Scripture's propositional inerrancy. An authority of necessarily affirmed propositions is legal in its very form. Applied to the whole content of the Scriptures, it embraces their proclamation of promise in a legal authority and so inverts the proper order. A parallel error sees the Scriptures as one set of the class of "religious" documents, and traces their authority to their superiority within the class. Here again their authority as promise is embraced by a foreign mode of authority. Yet another misinterpretation begins with the notion of the church as a historically continuous community, sees theological reflection as the ideological function in this community, and so gives the Scriptures a sort of *consti-*

tutional function and authority. Whether this constitution is then interpreted by strict or liberal constructionists makes no difference at this point. Also in this way the authority of the Scriptures is made to derive from legal structures.

The Authority of Dogma

That the Scriptures are the final legal authority in the church does not mean they are the only legal authority. The structure is not that on one side of the authority-relation there are the Scriptures, and on the other side are all the members of the church lined up side by side facing the Scriptures. All actual situations of authority are much more complicated than that, and so is this one. Always we find that A is authority for B, B for C—and probably C, in a different way, for A. Final scriptural authority is in no way inconsistent with a rich pattern of other authorities.

Within the network of other-than-final authorities, which operate in the church as in any living historical community, dogma is one kind. Any community which has a final authority and tries to be faithful to it, will from time to time have to speak authoritatively to its members in the attempt to maintain that faithfulness. These attempts will enter the tradition of the community and play their particular role in whatever authority tradition has for the community. We have discussed the way in which tradition generally is authority for the church-community. Within this authority, the particular authority of dogma may perhaps be described so: to reject Augustine's personal doctrine of the Trinity is simply to disagree with a brother, though with one who is very likely to be right; to reject the Nicene Creed's assertion of Christ's full divinity is to rebel against that community by whose tradition alone the gospel has been spoken to me in the first place.

Nevertheless, the fathers of Nicaea—or of Augsburg—are not the apostles. The authority of these fathers can be questioned by the authority of Paul or John; there can be rebellion against the community and its tradition for the sake of the mission of the community and the truth of its tradition.

In one way such rebellion occurs whenever the church lives. The dogmas cannot merely be recited, if they are to be of any continuing use. We ourselves regard the Nicene affirmation as a work of genius and absolutely essential to the faith—and having said that, we must hasten to say that "consubstantial with the Father" is obviously not a phrase that is much help now, and that we are not quite sure we approve of *everything* even the Nicene fathers themselves had in mind when they wrote it. In these matters there is no neat line between the essential point and its formulation; there is no simple formula to guarantee in advance that my attempt to reflect creatively and critically on the gospel will not slip into that proclaiming of some message other than the gospel, against which the dogmas warn. But judgments can nevertheless be made. There is, after all, no difficulty in seeing that a preaching whose talk of "God" is no different than it would have been were Jesus not risen is outside the bounds set by Nicaea; or that a Sunday school that teaches the children what they "must do" to be "Christians" is condemned by "justification by faith alone."

For the rest, everything said above about the two modes of tradition's authority, and about the workings of each, of course applies to dogma and proposed dogma. Dogma too *establishes* its authority as authority of promise, not of law. Dogma is either a word that sets us free or it is not; and if it is not, it has no other authority. Dogma is only one, central part of the gospel-tradition. And its function is not to bind to what has been but to liberate for what is to come. Dogma, too, has also a legal function: it is an authority within the tradition for the rest of tradition, and is law for us in that we listen in the tradition to hear the gospel so that we may speak it.

Chapter 2

Documents of Concord and Reform

Readings:
Prefaces to: BC or BS, LC, SC, AC, SA, FC

Toward a Territorial Church

The Lutheran movement grew rapidly after Martin Luther's condemnation by papal bull and imperial edict in 1521. Apostate priests and monks proclaimed Luther's teachings to a restless laity. Young professors and enthusiastic students carried Lutheran ideas throughout the European continent. Satirical pamphlets and popular songs praised the reformer as the German Hercules eradicating the evils in Christendom. By 1523, the Reformation had spread from Wittenberg to the Hapsburg lands in the south and east, to the Spanish-ruled Netherlands in the west, and to Scandinavia in the north. German knights revolted against the emperor, and peasants rebelled against their feudal landlords; both groups based their actions upon their understanding of Luther's proclamation of Christian freedom.

The emperor, Charles V, who was constantly involved in foreign wars, compromised with the territorial princes favoring the Lutheran movement. The Diet of Nuremberg in 1524—one of several called to quench the Reformation—was unable to enforce the Edict of Worms against Luther and his followers. Lutherans had gained enough territorial power to threaten the political unity of the Holy Roman Empire. When Roman Catholic princes founded the military League of Dessau in 1525 to save the unity of church and empire, Lutheran princes responded by creating the League of Gotha under the leadership of young Landgrave Philip of Hesse. In 1526, therefore, the Diet of Speyer agreed to let German princes deal with the Edict of Worms according to their own best judgment before God and emperor. It was only natural that Lutheran nobles interpreted this agreement as "the right to territorial ecclesiastical reform."

Luther did not oppose the principle of territorial ecclesiastical reform under the auspices of the prince. He had experienced the tyrannical power of the church rather than that of the state. Moreover, Elector Frederick of Saxony, later dubbed "the Wise" by historians, seemed far better suited to run ecclesiastical affairs than Pope Leo X, Cardinal Albrecht of Mainz, or most bishops. Luther expected more Christian daring from the laity than from the clergy in matters of ecclesiastical reform and he appealed to the baptized laity, as the "common priesthood," to preserve the purity of the gospel in a perverted church. In 1520, in his famous open letter "To the Christian Nobility of the German Nation," he had declared, "Since those who exercise secular authority have been baptized with the same baptism, and have the same faith and the same gospel as we, we must admit that they are priests and bishops" (LW 44, 129). Medieval kings and princes had frequently claimed authority over the church in their territories, defying the Roman papacy's argument for the superiority of the spiritual realm over the temporal realm. Luther baptized such claims with his doctrine of the common priesthood of all believers.

When radical reformers (Anabaptists, iconoclasts, and other "left-wingers of the Reformation") proposed separatist, theocratic, and revolutionary solutions to the church-state problem, Luther once again relied on the authority of the princes to preserve law and order. Events such as the Wittenberg disturbances in the fall and winter of 1521/22, the legal persecution of Lutherans in certain territories, and the uprisings of the peasants in 1525 had compelled Luther to develop a political ethic culminating in the so-called doctrine of the two kingdoms. Embedded in Luther's basic theological conviction that creaturely existence is but a reflection, a "mask," of God's reality hidden until the end of time, the doctrine of the two kingdoms interpreted state power as such a mask and was intended to forestall political chaos in territories torn by religious strife.

The salient points of the doctrine were made in Luther's 1523 treatise, "Temporal Authority: To What Extent It Should Be Obeyed." First, Luther defined government in terms of the Augustinian distinction between the spiritual and temporal dimensions of human existence:

God ordained the spiritual government "by which the Holy Spirit produces Christians and righteous people under Christ"; and he also ordained the temporal government "which restrains the un-Christian and wicked so that they are obliged to keep still and to maintain outward peace." The Christian is to serve in both, since he is a citizen in both realms as long as the world, God's creation, exists. Second, Luther defined the power of temporal government in terms of noble officers who are ordained by God to maintain the stability of the world. No prince can impose faith or dispose of heresy by force. "Faith is a free act to which no one can be forced"; and "heresy is a spiritual matter which you cannot hack to pieces with iron, consume with fire, or drown in water." Temporal power cannot rule over conscience. Finally, Luther described the ideal Christian prince as being devoted to his subjects, just to evildoers, and faithful in Christ—a description modeled after Elector Frederick the Wise.

Though controversial (especially in light of subsequent history), Luther's doctrine of the two kingdoms enabled sixteenth-century Christians to maintain a positive relationship to the world without succumbing to the perennial temptation of realizing their belief in the kingdom of God either through a monastic asceticism—separation from the political world—or through a puritan theocracy—total Christianization of law and order. Moreover, Luther's notion of a divinely ordained government (a constructionist interpretation of Romans 13:1–2), combined with his doctrine of the common priesthood of all believers and his monarchic interpretation of political authority, provided a theological rationale for the absolutist tendencies of sixteenth-century German territorial politics. To this extent, the doctrine of the two kingdoms contained the seed from which grew the Lutheran territorial churches under the authority of princes.

Luther himself accepted the territorial prince only as an "emergency bishop." He argued that Elector Frederick of Saxony, Landgrave Philip of Hesse, and other Lutheran princes should, "out of love," take over the reins of the church when no other leadership was available. Luther, of course, presupposed *Christian* princes—men dedicated to the gospel and the church who were willing to withdraw from "spiritual government" (which was not their proper vocation) as soon as ecclesiastical affairs had been normalized.

In the fall of 1525 Luther urged Elector John Frederick, the son of Frederick the Wise, to initiate a program of visitations to assess the religious state of affairs in electoral Saxony. The devastating results of the peasant uprisings, the schisms between radical and conservative Lutherans, and the general confusion over the "new faith" made such an assessment mandatory. In June 1527, the elector issued guidelines for a program of visitations which were based on Luther's advice, and a year later, Luther had his friend Philip Melanchthon draw up Articles of Visitation. After some difficulties were ironed out, systematic visitations were conducted in electoral Saxony, later duplicated in Hesse under the leadership of Landgrave Philip. Visitation teams usually consisted of four members appointed by the prince: two to examine economic conditions and two to diagnose religious affairs. Needy congregations were to receive subsidies from the territorial coffers, and taxes could be collected for the purpose of financing reform programs.

The peaceful years between the Diet of Speyer (1526) and the Diet of Augsburg (1530) enabled German Lutheran princes to initiate various ecclesiastical reforms. Although Luther objected to the confusion between spiritual and temporal authority—he always stressed the need for proper offices in both church and state—territorial princes solidified their episcopal role. With the famous principle "He who is in charge of the region is in charge of religion" (*cuius regio, eius religio*), the Peace of Augsburg in 1555 secured the right of territorial princes to determine the faith of their subjects. Eventually, Luther's demand for "evangelical bishops" or "superintendents" (a Latin translation of the Greek term *episcopos*, meaning "overseer") was met, but only in conjunction with the creation of "consistories" by the territorial prince. The interaction between bishops and consistories determined the course of territorial churches in Germany until monarchical government was dissolved in 1918.

Blueprint for Educational Reform

> Good God, what wretchedness I beheld! The common people, especially those who live in the country, have no knowledge whatever of Christian teaching, and unfortunately many pastors are quite incompetent and unfitted for teaching. Although the people are supposed to be Christian, are baptized, and receive the holy sacrament, they do not know the Lord's Prayer, the Creed, or the Ten Commandments; they live as if they were pigs and irrational beasts, and now that the Gospel has been restored they have mastered the fine art of abusing liberty. (SC, Preface, 1–3)

With these words, Luther diagnosed the state of religious affairs in electoral Saxony after he had participated in Elector John Frederick's official visitation program during the fall and winter of 1528/29. He was convinced that only a long-range program of educational reform would alleviate the miserable conditions of the new "Lutheran" congregations.

Luther had stressed the necessity of catechetical instruction, as a natural consequence of baptism, since the beginning of the Reformation. Accordingly, he consistently preached catechetical sermons based on the Decalogue, the creeds, and the Lord's Prayer. After 1523, it was customary in Wittenberg to preach such sermons twice a year, in May and September; after 1525, such sermons were preached four times a year, for a period of two weeks, four days a week, in addition to the traditional catechetical sermons at the early Sunday services. Baptism and the Lord's Supper were added to the three traditional topics of Decalogue, creeds, and Lord's Prayer. Luther himself preached three series of sermons on the five catechetical topics in Wittenberg during May, September, and December 1528. The sermons are the immediate source of the Small and Large Catechisms—the oldest portion of the Lutheran confessions, preceded in the Book of Concord by the three ecumenical creeds.

Luther's two catechisms—the "German Catechism" (later called "Large Catechism"), published in April 1529, and the "Small Catechism," published in May 1529—are more than doctrinal textbooks. They are summaries of the Christian faith, permeated by Luther's understanding of the gospel as the source of a new life liberating man from sin, death, and the devil. Originally published in the form of charts and posters to simplify use in church, school, and home, each of the five parts (Decalogue, creed, Lord's Prayer, baptism, and Lord's Supper) discloses the center of Luther's theology: the doctrine of justification of faith apart from works of law.

The Decalogue is interpreted in terms of the childlike faith in God commanded by the First Commandment; not to have such faith means sliding into idolatry, which is defined as trust in one's own good works as a condition for God's salvation. The Apostles' Creed reveals what God as creator, redeemer, and sanctifier is prepared to do for men. The Lord's Prayer illustrates how men ought to communicate with God—simply, like children ready to state their needs. Baptism initiates a person into a new life marked by the polarization between good and evil, faith and unfaith, God and Satan; Christian life is penance—a constant "change of mind," in order to be free for God. The Lord's Supper celebrates Christ's "real presence" as the powerful source of Christian fellowship; people abstaining from it are not to be considered Christians.

Although Luther used traditional catechetical materials and pedagogical methods in the Catechisms—usually five topics to be memorized in one form or another—he meant them to be tools for the continuing theological education of the clergy as well as the laity. The memorized words were to lead to the "word of God," the dynamic, liberating force of the Christian life in the world. Subsequent Lutheran orthodoxy, which was permeated by a return to medieval scholastic methods, and Lutheran pietism, which was influenced by humanistic assertions of existential individuality, have used Luther's catechisms (especially the Small Catechism) either as theological *summae* or as tools for converting people. Consequently, Luther's intention to use the catechisms as a first step in the continuing theological education of all church members disappeared in a quicksand of Christian educational theories, which reduced the catechetical portions of the Book of Concord to an ineffective exercise in confirmation classes. Against such misuse stands Luther's *caveat* in the Preface to the Large Catechism:

> Many regard the Catechism as a simple, silly teaching which they can absorb and master at one reading. After reading it once they toss the book into a corner as if they are ashamed to read it again. . . . Yet I do as a child who is being taught the Catechism. Every morning, and whenever else I have time, I read and recite word for word the Lord's Prayer, the Ten Commandments, the Creed, the Psalms, etc. I must still read and study the Catechism daily, yet I cannot master it as I wish, but must remain a child and pupil of the Catechism, and I do it gladly. (LC, Preface, 5, 7)

The Lutheran Magna Carta

The Diet of Augsburg in 1530 was convened to stop the spread of the Lutheran movement. When Emperor Charles V summoned it, he sounded conciliatory:

> to allay divisions, to cease hostility, to surrender past errors to our Saviour, and to display diligence in hearing, understanding, and considering with love and kindness the opinions and views of everybody . . . so that we all may adopt and hold one single and true religion; and may

> all live in one communion, church, and unity, even as we all live and do battle under one Christ. (Walch 16, 622)

Although the Lutherans sensed deception on the part of the emperor—he was devoted to Rome and had promised the pope he would eradicate the Lutheran heresy—they were nevertheless prepared to state their position. Philip Melanchthon, known for his diplomatic skill in the use of theological language, went to work on an "Augsburg Confession." Drawing upon such previously drafted statements as the Schwabach Articles of 1529, and incorporating the advice of a Lutheran conclave in Torgau, he tried to demonstrate (1) an ecumenical stance, (2) a commitment to continuing reform, and (3) a willingness to compromise. The result was a masterfully written confession signed by seven German territorial princes and two city councils, with Elector John Frederick of Saxony heading the list. Luther, who was unable to attend the diet, since he had been declared a heretic, approved Melanchthon's work, admitting that he himself was unable to tread so softly in these matters. The Lutheran layman Melanchthon has been known as the "pussyfooter" (*Leisetreter*) ever since.

On June 25, 1530, at 3:00 p.m., the electoral chancellor Gregorius Brueck read the Augsburg Confession in German to the emperor and the diet. The following outline briefly indicates method and content:

ARTICLES OF THE AUGSBURG CONFESSION

Chief Articles of Faith (1–21)

I. Agreement with Ancient Church (1–3)
- 1. God
- 2. Original sin
- 3. Christology

II. Understanding the Gospel (4–6, 18–20)
- 4. Justification
- 5. Ministry
- 6. New obedience
- 18. Free will
- 19. Cause of sin
- 20. Good works

III. Understanding the Church (7–15)
- 7–8. Definition
- 9–13. Sacraments
- 14–15. Organization

Articles in Dispute (22–28)
- 22. Sacrament in both kinds
- 23. Clerical marriage
- 24. Mass
- 25. Confession
- 26. Foods and ceremonies
- 27. Monastic vows
- 28. Power of bishops

Three Individual Problems (16–17, 21)
- 16. Government
- 17. Second Coming
- 21. Cult of saints

"We have at various times made our protestations and appeals concerning these most weighty matters," Melanchthon declared,

> and have done so in legal form and procedure. To these we declare our continuing adherence, and we shall not be turned aside from our position by these or any following negotiations (unless the matters in dissension are finally heard, amicably weighed, charitably settled, and brought to Christian concord in accordance with Your Imperial Majesty's summons) as we herewith publicly witness and assert. (AC, Preface, 22–24)

The Augsburg Confession was immediately attacked by the forces of Rome. After a lengthy Roman "Confutation" was read to the diet on August 3 (prepared by approximately twenty theologians, elected by Cardinal Lorenzo Campegio, papal legate to the diet), Charles V ruled that the Lutherans had been refuted. They were not even to receive a copy of the Confutation unless they agreed (1) not to publish it, (2) not to reply to it, and (3) to accept its conclusions. To preserve his image as a conciliating arbiter, the emperor then called for theological negotiations between the two parties, but to no avail. The gulf between Rome and Wittenberg could no longer be bridged.

After the Diet of Augsburg, Melanchthon composed a brilliant and scholarly "Apology of the Augsburg Confession," published in 1531 together with the confession. It is one of the most valuable of the many monographs on the doctrine of justification (AC 4), and an incisive critique of Roman Catholic medieval theology.

The Lutheran Magna Carta, the Augsburg Confession, is the work of a lay theologian totally committed to the reform of the church. Melanchthon nurtured the text of his confession for years after the Diet of Augsburg—in 1540 he produced a version known as the Altered Augsburg Confession (because of its stance of compromise toward Rome in the face of left-wing enthusiasm). But it was the Unaltered Augsburg Confession of 1530 which became the foundation for the pan-Lutheran struggle for civil rights in the sixteenth and seventeenth centuries. Those who signed it—and their numbers increased constantly—were willing to defend their signature with their lives, as they proved in the religious wars that led to the political rearrangement of Europe in 1648 by the Peace of Westphalia.

Luther's Theological Testament

Luther had been convinced, before the Diet of Augsburg, that the only effective driving force of the Reformation was the "Word." In March 1522, at the height of political turmoil in Wittenberg, he had preached to the Wittenbergers:

> While I slept or drank Wittenberg beer with my friends Philip [Melanchthon] and [Nicholas von] Amsdorf, the Lord so greatly weakened the papacy that no prince or emperor ever inflicted such losses upon it. I did nothing; the Word did everything. (LW 51, 77)

Luther had difficulty preserving such equanimity after the Diet of Augsburg. When Saxon jurists justified territorial armed resistance to a tyrannical imperial government, Luther and other Wittenberg theologians declared, in a statement issued in October 1530, that such resistance is self-defense and not contrary to Scripture. In "A Warning to His Dear German People"—a best-selling pamphlet printed in the spring of 1531—Luther bullishly spoke his mind on the topic of "word" and "sword":

> If war breaks out—which God forbid—I will not reprove those who defend themselves against the murderous and bloodthirsty papists, nor let anyone rebuke them as being seditious, but I will accept their action and let it pass as self-defense. (LW 47, 19)

Uncertain of the emperor's next move, Lutheran princes expanded the military League of Torgau into the Smalcald League in December 1531. For a while they hoped that Swiss territories might join, since the intransigent Swiss reformer Huldreich Zwingli had been killed in a battle with Roman Catholic forces in October, but theological differences prevented a German-Swiss alliance. Nevertheless, the display of so much political power persuaded Emperor Charles V to grant official toleration to Lutheran territories until an ecumenical council could deal with the schism in the church.

When, in 1536, Pope Paul III agreed to call a council, Luther was pessimistic about its effectiveness. Rome had never been willing to grant heretics voice and vote in ecumenical councils—and Luther had been declared a heretic in 1521. But he complied with the request of Elector John Frederick of Saxony, the most powerful member of the Smalcald League, to draft a summary of his theological position for possible use at the ecumenical council. The result was a "theological testament," written in 1536 during one of Luther's severe illnesses, and published in 1538 as the Smalcald Articles—so-called because many of Luther's friends signed them at a convention of the Smalcald League in February 1537, even though the convention as a whole never officially adopted them.

The Smalcald Articles are Luther's statement of faith for posterity. "If I should die before a council meets," he wrote in the preface, "those who live after me may have my testimony and confession . . . to show where I have stood until now and where, by God's grace, I will continue to stand." (Preface 3)

First, Luther reaffirmed his belief in the trinitarian faith of the ancient church—which neither Lutherans nor Roman Catholics disputed.

Then, Luther restated the doctrine of justification by faith alone—the article of faith upon which the church stands or falls. "Nothing in this article can be given up or compromised, even if heaven and earth and things temporal should be destroyed" (II, 1:5). Convinced of the idolatrous nature of the church's existing hierarchical power structure ("The pope is the real Antichrist"), he called for its condemnation by a truly ecumenical council.

Finally, Luther listed the theological topics he felt should be discussed with "learned and sensible men"—sin, law, penitence, the gospel, sacraments, ministry, and church. But his polemical language cast a dark shadow over the possibility of fruitful dialogue with Roman or other non-Lutheran theologians. To Luther, the Roman church had become a fraud and the world deserved to end.

Forty-three theologians and churchmen joined Luther in signing the Smalcald Articles. Philip Melanchthon "pussyfooted" once again when he added this reservation to his signature:

> I, Philip Melanchthon, regard the above articles as right and Christian. However, concerning the pope I hold that, if he would allow the Gospel, we, too, may concede to him that superiority over the bishops which he possesses by human right, making this concession for the sake of peace and general unity among the Christians who are now under him and who may be in the future.

Melanchthon stated his position on the papacy in a Latin "Treatise on the Power and Primacy of the Pope," officially endorsed in 1537 by the Smalcald League as a supplement to the Augsburg Confession, and printed in a German translation in 1541. The treatise contained (1) a refutation of papal primacy, with arguments based on Scripture and tradition, and (2) a call to revive the ancient practice of having bishops elected by the entire church rather than appointed by the pope. Melanchthon was almost as harsh as Luther in his attack on the papacy. "All Christians ought to beware of becoming participants in the impious doctrines, blasphemies, and unjust cruelties of the pope," he warned, after having collected damaging evidence against Rome. "They ought rather to abandon and execrate the pope and his adherents as the kingdom of the Antichrist" (TR 41). Melanchthon was now convinced that reconciliation between Rome and Wittenberg was no longer a concrete option—even though he had felt obliged to add his personal reservations to Luther's strong views in the Smalcald Articles. It is always difficult to pussyfoot through a revolution.

Formula of Concord

Luther's cause, protected by the Smalcald League, threatened to destroy the fabric of the Holy Roman Empire; and pope and emperor prepared to meet this threat by force. The League of Nuremberg was formed in 1538, with the support of Emperor Charles V, to oppose the Smalcald League; and Pope Paul III summoned an ecumenical council to meet in Trent in 1541, to rally the forces of the ecclesiastical status quo against the Lutheran heresy. No Lutheran was willing to attend such a "papal council"; Luther's wrath was expressed in the treatise "Against the Roman Papacy, an Institution of the Devil," published in 1545 when the council held its first sessions.

Three tragic events decisively weakened German Lutheranism during this period of confrontation, and prepared the way for the eventual defeat of the Smalcald League.

First, Landgrave Philip of Hesse, one of the most powerful leaders of the league, destroyed the moral authenticity of his leadership by entering into a bigamous marriage in 1540—a sordid story that involved Luther, who condoned Philip's behavior on the basis of Old Testament polygamy. Bowing to pressure, Philip signed a treaty with the emperor in 1541 renouncing his opposition to the empire. When the Smalcaldic wars broke out in 1546, Philip ignored his treaty obligations, joined the Lutheran forces, and was imprisoned by the emperor after the defeat of the Smalcald League in 1547.

Second, Maurice of Saxony, Philip of Hesse's son-in-law, resigned from the Smalcald League in 1541 after family quarrels over territorial rights in Saxony. For some time he harbored hopes of becoming a neutral mediator between the emperor and the league. But when Charles V promised him the Saxon electorate, on condition that he desert the Lutheran cause, Maurice sided with the imperial forces.

The third and greatest blow to nascent Lutheranism was Luther's death on February 18, 1546, for Philip Melanchthon was incapable of presiding with Luther's inimitable strength over the multifaceted anti-Roman Catholic theological forces.

When the Smalcaldic wars broke out, the fate of the Lutheran alliance was sealed. Without effective military leadership and hurt by the moral scandals of Philip of Hesse and Maurice of Saxony, the Smalcald League capitulated in 1547. An interim agreement in Augsburg in 1548, between Lutheran princes and the emperor, left the settlement of all major religious issues to the Council of Trent. Roman Catholic theologians agreed to permit marriage to priests and the chalice for laymen in Lutheran territories—token concessions for the sake of maintaining an image of tolerance. The Lutheran cause seemed lost. Pope and emperor were expecting to give Lutheranism the coup de grace with ecumenical conciliar decrees and legal political persecution.

It is one of the ironies of history that German Lutherans survived their darkest hour with the help of the prince who was instrumental in the defeat of the Smalcald League: Maurice of Saxony. In 1551, the "Judas of the Reformation" launched a coup d'etat against Emperor Charles V by waylaying him in Innsbruck, Austria, on his way to Trent. The emperor escaped by a hair, and the Council of Trent was so shocked at the news that it postponed its meeting for two years. A hasty agreement in Passau in 1552, between the emperor and Maurice, postponed all action against Lutheran territories until the next German Diet, and arranged the release of Philip of Hesse. Maurice died shortly thereafter.

The Peace of Augsburg, in 1555, granted the territories subscribing to the Augsburg Confession equal rights in the empire, and thus prevented a major religious war between the German states until the

Thirty Years' War in 1618. But the three principal provisions of the peace treaty contained the seeds for new conflicts over the old religious questions. (1) Only the adherents to the Augsburg Confession were exempt from laws against heretics and from the ecclesiastical ban; "left-wingers," Zwinglians, Calvinists, and other groups not supporting the Augsburg Confession remained subject to persecution. (2) Territorial princes had the right to determine the religion of their subjects, who could emigrate if they disagreed with their prince; religious liberty was tied to feudal class distinctions rather than to the doctrine of the common priesthood of all believers. (3) If a "spiritual prince"—a cardinal or bishop—converted to Protestantism, he would lose all his territorial possessions and revenues; this "ecclesiastical reserve clause" protected Roman Catholic ecclesiastical territories.

The Council of Trent, which sat, with interruptions, from 1545 to 1563, formally condemned Lutheran doctrine. The newly formed Society of Jesus propagated this condemnation politically and pedagogically, and helped to inaugurate an age of "counterreformation." The adherents to the Augsburg Confession had won a major victory on the political front through the Peace of Augsburg, but the battle for the survival of Luther's heritage was by no means over.

Serious internal strife among supporters of the Reformation, as well as among the adherents to the Augsburg Confession, followed the external peace established in Augsburg. As early as 1529, Luther and Zwingli had met in Marburg and had been unable to reconcile their theological differences, especially over the Lord's Supper. After Luther's death in 1546, John Calvin's influence on German Lutherans on the one hand, and Philip Melanchthon's ambiguous position on the other, created a number of theological controversies. In addition, "left-wingers" of the Reformation—Anabaptists, Spiritualists, anti-Trinitarians, and other groups—infiltrated Lutheran territories and advocated various reform programs opposed to existing political and ecclesiastical establishments. Six major theological controversies over the proper interpretation of the Augsburg Confession threatened the unity of Lutherans after 1530.

The Antinomian Controversy, climaxing in 1537 and extending beyond Luther's death in 1546, wrestled with the question of whether or not Old Testament law should have authority over those who live under the New Testament promise. John Agricola, one of Luther's disciples, argued that *nomos* (the Greek term for "law") had ended with the advent of Christ in the year one. Philip Melanchthon rejected Agricola's antinomian position in favor of Luther's law-gospel dialectic. When Luther sided with Melanchthon, Agricola left Saxony in 1537 and propagated his views in electoral Brandenburg.

The Adiaphorist Controversy dominated the Saxon theological scene between 1548 and 1552. Matthias Flacius, Luther's most ardent disciple, headed a super-Lutheran party called "Gnesio-Lutherans" (from the Greek *gnesios*–"authentic") to fight the more liberal Melanchthonian party called "Philippists" in this and other controversies. "Adiaphora" (from the Greek *adiaphoron*, a thing that makes no difference; in German, *Mittelding*) were understood to be "nonessentials" in matters of salvation. When Melanchthon and the Philippists declared liturgical ceremonies and ecclesiastical structures to be adiaphora during the negotiation of the Leipzig Interim in 1548, Flacius and the Gnesio-Lutherans accused Melanchthon of selling out to Rome. They asserted that, in a period of persecution and coercion such as was being carried out by Rome at the time, no concessions whatever ought to be made. Melanchthon softened his position in 1552, and pleaded for peace, but the quarrel lingered on.

The Osiandrian Controversy raged in Prussia from 1549 to 1566 over Luther's doctrine of justification by faith alone. Andrew Osiander, a professor at the University of Koenigsberg, managed to draw the theological wrath of both Gnesio-Lutherans and Philippists when he described justification as the indwelling of Christ's essential nature in the believer, thus abandoning Luther's emphasis on the external "word" as the chief instrument of salvation. The controversy ended in 1566 when the last Osiandric theologian, Court Chaplain Funck, was executed–after an intensive political Prussian power play involving both the ducal court and academic politicians.

The Majoristic Controversy, involving the University of Wittenberg between 1552 and 1558, dealt with the classic Lutheran question of whether or not good works are necessary for salvation. George Major, a Philippist professor at Wittenberg, argued that good works are necessary for salvation. Nicholas von Amsdorf, a Gnesio-Lutheran, declared that good works are detrimental to salvation. Flacius sided with Amsdorf, while Melanchthon cautiously stayed in the background.

The Crypto-Calvinist Controversy started in 1555 in the city of

Bremen when the Gnesio-Lutheran pastor John Timman attacked his Philippist colleague Albert Hardenberg for teaching the Zwinglian interpretation of the Lord's Supper. Since Melanchthon once again stayed in the background, the Gnesio-Lutherans accused him of being a secret Calvinist, a "Crypto-Calvinist." Gnesio-Lutherans used "Crypto-Calvinist" as a battle cry against the intrusion of Swiss Reformed doctrine on German Lutheran soil whenever someone denied the doctrine of Christ's "real presence" in the Lord's Supper. The controversy was partially settled through the expulsion of Hardenberg in 1561, but Philippists eventually predominated in Bremen.

The Synergistic Controversy disclosed all the basic features of future Lutheran academic infighting. From 1556 to 1560, Gnesio-Lutherans from the University of Wittenberg debated a classic issue with Philippists from the University of Jena: the relationship between the providence of God and the freedom of man. A number of theologians from other universities took sides in the controversy, and some of them were arrested by the Saxon court. The climax came during a colloquy in Weimar in 1560, when Matthias Flacius, debating against the Philippist Victorinus Strigel of Jena, declared that human freedom can only resist divine providence (man is, at best, like a piece of wood in the process of salvation) because man's whole nature consists of original sin. Flacius' views were rejected as heretical; and there was general consensus among Lutherans that the fury of the theologians had gone too far.

Melanchthon made a last attempt to reconcile the feuding factions through a union document submitted to Lutheran nobles during the coronation ceremonies for Emperor Ferdinand in Frankfurt in 1558. This *Frankfurt Recess* defined as "pure doctrine" the three ecumenical creeds, the Augsburg Confession, and its Apology. Since, however, Melanchthon used ambiguous language regarding "new obedience" (AC 6) and the Lord's Supper (AC 10), no agreement was reached. Some princes rejected the union document because John Calvin could accept it. When Duke Christopher of Wuerttemberg called a meeting of princes at Naumburg in 1561, Philippists argued for acceptance of the Altered Augsburg Confession of 1540; but Gnesio-Lutherans opposed such a move. Melanchthon had died during the negotiations for the Naumburg meeting on April 19, 1560. Duke Frederick III of the Palatinate, the staunchest supporter of the Philippists, converted to

Calvinism and celebrated the event through the publication of the Heidelberg Catechism in 1563.

Melanchthon's death and Flacius' dismissal from the University of Jena in 1561 (he went to Antwerp and Strasbourg) paved the way for new and more creative ways of seeking Lutheran unity. Duke Christopher of Wuerttemberg and the Swabian theologians of the University of Tuebingen created a "middle party" which eventually succeeded in uniting the major forces of the Lutheran movement behind a formula of concord.

In 1567 Duke Christopher and Landgrave William IV of Hessen-Kassel commissioned the Chancellor of Tuebingen, Jacob Andreae, to produce a union formula. At the same time, Martin Chemnitz, the "superintendent" (bishop) of Brunswick, attempted to transcend the controversial issues in a "Church Order" for Brunswick in 1569. He and Andreae worked with theologians at the universities of Wittenberg, Jena, and Leipzig, hoping for a compromise based upon a series of theological propositions. But a meeting of theologians at Zerbst in 1570, initiated by Elector August, failed to reach agreement.

Andreae did not give up. In 1573 he published six union sermons on what he considered the basic points of confessional Lutheranism emerging from the article of justification. Entitled "Six Sermons on the Controversies Within the Lutheran Church from 1548–1573," they dealt with most of the major issues which the Formula of Concord attempted to settle. When the sermons were favorably received by Chemnitz in Brunswick and by the theological faculties in Hamburg and Rostock, Andreae summarized their content in eleven theological theses known as the Swabian Concord of 1573.

In the meantime, Elector August of Saxony had become quite apprehensive about the fierce theological quarrels and political deceptions of some of his professors at Wittenberg. He commissioned three non-Saxon theologians to evaluate the Wittenberg theologians at a meeting in Maulbronn in 1576. The result was the dismissal of most of the leading theologians in electoral Saxony. Elector August immediately initiated a further step toward Lutheran unity. Persuaded by Andreae's Swabian Formula which had been further revised by Chemnitz and others (the Swabian-Saxon Formula of 1575), the elector assembled leading theologians at Torgau in 1576 where they produced the Torgau Book. Again reactions and revisions were collected during the following year, summarized in the Bergen Book of 1577. Andreae was asked to edit the book with a synopsis of its content. The longer version became known as the Solid Declaration; the synopsis as Epitome (the Greek term for "excerpt"). Both constitute the Formula of Concord published in 1577. Three electoral princes, twenty dukes, twenty-four counts, four barons, thirty-eight imperial cities, and approximately eight thousand theologians subscribed to it. The Formula intended to be, according to its subtitle,

> a thorough, pure, correct, and final restatement and explanation of a number of articles of the Augsburg Confession on which for some time there has been disagreement among some of the theologians adhering to this confession, resolved and reconciled under the guidance of the word of God and the comprehensive summary of our Christian teaching.

A statement on biblical authority and twelve articles of faith, grounded in deep reverence for Luther and the Augsburg Confession, constituted the new Lutheran union formula. The following outline reveals the theological concerns of the Formula of Concord—reflecting the controversies between Gnesio-Lutherans and Philippists—as well as its relationship to the Augsburg Confession:

ARTICLES OF THE FORMULA OF CONCORD

1. Original sin } Synergistic controversy; AC 2, 18 and 19
2. Free will }
3. Righteousness of faith before God—Osiandrian controversy; AC 4
4. Good works—Majoristic controversy; AC 6 & 20
5. Law and gospel } Antinomian controversy
6. Third use of the law }
7. Lord's Supper } Crypto-Calvinist controversy; AC 10
8. Person of Christ }
9. Christ's descent into Hell—controversy with Calvinists
10. Ecclesiastical rites called adiaphora—Adiaphorist controversy; AC 15
11. Eternal foreknowledge and divine election—again with Calvinists
12. Factions and sects which never accepted the AC—Anabaptists, Schwenckfelders, and Anti-Trinitarians

The Formula of Concord is permeated by scholastic language, reflecting the Lutheran movement's theological sophistication. The Formula exhibits a sense of history by adding the three ancient creeds

(Apostles', Nicene, and Athanasian), the Apology of the Augsburg Confession, the Smalcald Articles, and Luther's two catechisms as parts of a Lutheran canon intended as the Lutheran summary of Christian doctrine. This canon appeared on June 25, 1580—exactly fifty years after the submission of the Augsburg Confession to Emperor Charles V—as the Book of Concord. An extensive "catalogue of testimonies" from the Scriptures and the history of the church appeared in an appendix, demonstrating the ecumenical character of Lutheran doctrine. As the preface put it:

> We are not minded to manufacture anything new by this work of agreement or to depart in any way at all, either in content or in formulation, from the divine truth that our pious forebears and we have acknowledged and confessed in the past. . . . On the contrary, we are minded by the grace of the Holy Spirit to abide and remain unanimously in this confession of faith and to regulate all religious controversies and their explanations according to it.

The Lutheran confessions assembled in the Book of Concord represent an exciting phase in the history of Christian doctrine. Luther's existential explosion—triggered by his intensive search for a merciful God behind the walls of monastic seclusion—could never really be transformed into cool, ecclesiastical doctrine; his faith will always be an enigma to theological and sociological architects of the *ecclesia sapiens*. But sixteenth-century Lutherans were forced to make an attempt to cast Luther's burning faith into statutes of doctrine submissible to political assemblies. The Lutheran confessions, therefore, are not irrelevant summaries by esoteric theologians. They are documentary evidence that the Lutheran testimony of the Christian faith in the world is not the product of an otherworldly asceticism or an innerworldly theocracy; Lutheran Christian witness is born in the sociopolitical conflict between God's word and his world.

PART TWO

JUSTIFICATION BY FAITH APART FROM WORKS OF LAW

Chapter 3

A Christological Answer to the Radical Question

The Shift of Language

The single great proposed dogma of the Reformation was "justification by faith alone, without the works of law." It is well-known that the Lutheran reformers proclaimed this as the doctrine by which the church "stands or falls." It is, one fears, not so well-known why they would have done so.

Most of Protestantism worries about the matter not at all, having long since returned to various—bowdlerized—versions of medieval religion, supposing these to be the latest thing. Indeed, for much of Christianity, the Christian substance itself is so thin that such profound matters as "justification" do not at all arise. When they do, and where there are reminiscences of the Reformation, a usual concept is that the church has a list of discrete opinion-items to be accepted, that "justification by faith" is one such item, and that Protestantism has for some reason decreed it the most important. Thus one is to believe that one is justified by believing that one is justified by believing that one is . . . —which instruction classes understandably find hard to grasp.

When "justification by faith" is thus taken for one item on an ideological list, the doctrine itself is interpreted correspondingly. The idea is that there is a list of things which God really wishes we would do—be kind to animals, be generous to the poor, be against war and injustice; that on the list is "believe in God"; and that, as a favor to Jesus, God has decided to let us off the rest of the list if we will do just this one. But this proclamation is the precise opposite of what the Reformation said. For the "believing" that can be one of a list of desirable deeds or characteristics is just what the Reformers called a "work"; moreover, it is the kind of special religious work against which they mostly directed their polemic.

"God will be gracious," we say, "if only you believe," thinking to follow the Reformation. Instead, we thereby usually proclaim a works-righteousness that makes medieval Catholicism seem a fount of pure grace. This "belief"-condition is either too easy or too hard. If, as usually happens, "faith" is psychologized into the holding of certain opinions and/or attitudes, then to offer salvation if only this work is done (never mind others) peddles grace more cheaply than did the worst indulgence-sellers. We usually sense this, and try to patch on a little authenticity by adding a few more conditions such as "love" and "really" believing. Then even the verbal reminiscence of the Reformation is lost, and the pattern of medieval Catholicism is fully embraced.

If, on the other hand, "faith" retains some shadow of its Reformation meaning, it is an impossible condition to put on salvation. Faith, in this sense, is utter and unmixed dependence on God. If I really think I can win ultimate fulfillment by chastity, or civil honesty, or even monastic asceticism, there is no insuperable problem in performing such things, given so overwhelming a motivation. But how do I set out to *believe*? And how would I ever know I had achieved it? Precisely where such Protestantism is taken most seriously, all of life is made into a Sisyphean task, an endless self-examination and urging-onward.

"Faith" no longer means, in ordinary usage, what it did in the usage of the Reformers. Perhaps the abstract best would be to eliminate the vocabulary of "justification" and "faith" from our gospel-language altogether; for, as the words "justification by faith" are *now* almost certain to be understood, they are an exact contradiction of the Reformation proposition. As we shall see, the whole point of the Reformation was that the gospel promise is *un*conditional; "faith" did not specify a special condition of human fulfillment, it meant the possibility of a life freed from all conditionality of fulfillment.

But the words are too deeply rooted in the biblical and liturgical language of the church for their interdiction to be practical. Since we must use them, we need great clarity about their various and sometimes antithetical biblical, Reformation, and modern uses, and great subtlety in deploying them (in some contexts, to use a drastic example, "justification by unbelief alone" could be, now, the only way to make the Reformation point with this language).

The Radical Question

In the original Lutheran movement, the language of "justification" was the locus of an epochal radicalization of the problematic character of human life. There are times in history when precisely the best people of the age suddenly find their own lives a question too terrible to be borne. At the end of the Middle Ages, some of the most devoted children of medieval Christianity found themselves thus threatened with spiritual destruction, by their very Christianity.

The religious, intellectual, and political arrangements of the medieval world had provided a varied and effective repertoire of ways to deal with the meaning-problems of life. If you were trapped by guilt, your confessor had therapies generally far more profound and effective than are modern replacements. If you were threatened by despair, a whole range of certifiably meaningful activities—from a brief prayer to a life-long crusade—were open for your dedication. The "breakdown of the medieval synthesis" was, in large part, that these arrangements lost their plausibility for certain dominant persons.

Why the medieval arrangements lost their force is beyond the scope of this book. For our purposes, it is enough that people like Luther took their ordinary life problems to the constituted religious agencies, did what they were supposed to do, and found no solutions. Some then got along without solutions, some so secularized their experience of life as to eliminate deep problems, and some found solutions outside the Christian community.

Those most decisively caught by Christianity sought to rebuild their lives by renewed attention to Christianity's constituting message, the "gospel." But under the weight of this unprecedented concern, the fundamental medieval understanding and proclamation of the gospel proved unable to sustain itself as *gospel*, "good news." Luther and others encountered in it not good news, but news so bad that it destroyed their grasp on the value of life. Our first main task is to see how this happened.

The gospel, in anyone's version, is a promise that our life will be fulfilled by Christ. Whenever this promise is made, someone will rise and ask, But if *he* is to bring our meaning, what then is *our* role? What is the point of our works of culture and religion?

It was the great task of the patristic and medieval church to conquer and assimilate the cultural and religious heritage of the ancient world. Obviously this could not be done if all cultural and religious works were, in advance, declared irrelevant to the principal meanings of life. Therefore the medieval church sought, with great spiritual and intellectual subtlety and persistence, so to speak and enact the gospel as to reassure the aforementioned questioners. However this might have been done, it was in fact done so: the *availability* of fulfillment was acknowledged as the sole work of Christ, temporally *back there* on the cross; our *participation now* in that fulfillment was made dependent on "cooperation" between God's influence in our lives, "grace," and our "natural" religious and ethical energies. The completion of Christ's past work was defined by Anselm of Canterbury's doctrine of atonement; the exact nature of the cooperation was the great problem of subsequent "scholasticism."

The trouble was, Christian theologians and pastors obviously could not leave the matter quite like that. For since the availability of "grace" is universally guaranteed by Christ's past work, all the practical difference would be made by our present cooperating or not; and God would be left without a role in actual life. Medieval theology and pastoral practice sought to avoid this consequence by what we may call the "anti-Pelagian codicil": If, they said, our religious and ethical response to grace is in fact that we cooperate and so come to participate in the fruit of Christ's work, this fact of our cooperation is itself a work of God's goodwill and grace. If we do respond properly to God's offer, this response itself shows that we are of the "elect," those whom God freely makes his own. The pattern should be familiar, having remained that of most of the best preaching: twenty minutes of ethical and religious exhortation, with the closing qualification, "of course, all this is by grace." It was exactly this codicil that undid Luther, and provoked him to revolt also against the doctrine of "cooperation" which made the codicil necessary.

As an item of academic theology, the anti-Pelagian codicil may appear adequate. But in the situation of a man hearing the church's message in deep concern for the value of his life, it works differently. If I hear of God's offer of fulfillment, and am told that I will receive it only if I do such-and-such, as "accepting" it, it will in most circumstances make no difference whatever to my existential situation to be told that only by grace can I accept it. I must still set out to do the accepting, knowing that salvation depends on this work. I am thrown back on the normal churchly and moral arrangements for becoming religiously affirmable as the real objects of my concern. And so it went throughout the Middle Ages: the anti-Pelagian codicil remained existentially empty, and the religious life of the people, as the Reformers would charge, remained straightforwardly works-righteous.

But if the normal religious arrangements fail, the anti-Pelagian codicil may acquire meaning. And in the actual situation of religious crisis, that meaning must be destructive. Its effect must be to suspend me over the awful question of whether or not God will indeed enable me to cooperate, whether or not I am one of the "elect"*—and there will be no way to answer the question.* The gospel can in this case provide no answer, for it is exactly whether the gospel is meant for me that is in doubt. The person who arrives at this point is asked—and cannot answer—whether his life has any point at all. God, the reality of all possible meaning, has himself become the threat of meaninglessness.

It is this experience of a radical threat to all meaning which, for Luther and his followers, attached to standard theological topics about "justification." In Reformation language, Am I justified? acquired the sense: Have I any justification for existence? What is my excuse for taking up space and time?

This usage, moreover, closely resembled Paul's use of the language, and so opened up a new possibility of understanding Paul. The image behind Paul's talk of "justification" is that of the accused at the bar of a court, awaiting the verdict that will either "justify" him or condemn him; the court in question is that of "the last judgment," the judgment about the value or lack of value of his whole life.

The radical question could, of course, have settled on some other language-complex than that of "justification." Luther might have asked, for example, Is there any hope at all? or, Is God real? (Contemporary atheism is not necessarily a more radical questioning than that of the Reformation—as it in fact happens, quite the contrary.) That "justification" became the place of pain was determined by the tradition: by Pauline usage, by the Augustinian language of the medieval church in general and Luther's Augustinian order in particular, and probably also by the central place of "justifications" in the feudal social and legal order.

The Reformation Insight and Discovery

The Reformers' fundamental *insight* was that the radical question about ourselves can accept as answer only an unconditional affirmation of the value of our life. An affirmation which sets a condition of any sort whatever, which in any way stipulates "you are good and worthy if you do/are such-and-such" only directs me back to that very self that is the problem. The point made by "without works" is: any affirmation of our life which says "if you do/are . . ." is not merely a poor answer to the Reformation question about justification, *it is no sort of* answer to the question being asked; for what is being asked is whether it is worth doing or being anything at all.

We can already see why "justification without works" is a doctrine by which the church stands or falls; in times of meaning-crisis, preaching and teaching which disobeys this rule is not merely inadequate in certain respects, it speaks altogether past any possible issue. Perhaps we can also begin to see why the doctrine might be more relevant to our own time than its desuetude in the church would make it seem.

The Reformation *discovery* was that the message about Jesus, told without the medieval restriction to the past tense, is an affirmative answer to the radical question, and was so intended by its original speakers. *If the gospel is allowed the present tense,* if it is allowed to invade the previous reserve of "cooperation," it says: The Crucified lives for you. This affirmation is unconditional, for it is in the name of one who already has death behind him, and whose love can therefore be stopped by nothing. As Luther usually put it, Jesus died in order that his will to give himself to us might be a "*last* will and testament," and so be subject to no further challenges.

With the present tense, and the transcending of conditions, we come to "faith." In Reformation language, "faith" is *not* the label of an ideological or attitudinal state. Like "justification," the word evokes a *communication-situation*: the situation of finding oneself addressed with an unconditional affirmation, and having now to deal with life in these new terms. Faith is a mode of life. Where the radical question is alive, all life becomes a *hearing*, a listening for permission to go on; faith is this listening—to the gospel.

Again there is a bridge to Pauline usage. With his talk about justification, Paul evokes the situation of the last judgment. He asserts that the gospel is the last judgment let out ahead of time, and as affirmative.

Paul's "faith" is the whole possibility of entertaining daily hopes and making daily choices as persons irrevocably judged worthy rather than unworthy.

According to the Reformation insight and discovery, the gospel is a wholly unconditional promise of the human fulfillment of its hearers, made by the narrative of Jesus' death and resurrection. The gospel, rightly spoken, involves no ifs, ands, buts, or maybes of any sort. It does not say, "If you do your best to live a good life, God will fulfill that life," or, "If you fight on the right side of the great issues of your time . . . ," or, "If you repent . . . ," or, "If you believe. . . ." It does not even say, "If you *want* to do good/repent/believe . . . ," or, "If you are sorry for not wanting to do good/repent/believe. . . ." The gospel says, "Because the Crucified lives as Lord, your destiny is good." The Reformation's first and last assertion was that any talk of Jesus and God and human life that does not transcend all conditions is a perversion of the gospel and will be at best irrelevant in the lives of hearers and at worst destructive.

Moreover, this assertion is itself unconditional. It cannot be agreed to with moderation, as "one legitimate concern" among many, or as a doctrine to be honored on some occasions but not on others. That is what offended such admirable and reform-minded Renaissance moderates as Erasmus or Thomas More or Cajetan: the line the Reformation draws between itself and medievalism allows only the one form of proclamation on its side, and calls all deviations therefrom evil. But that is the very logic of the case. For the only way to *practice* a conditional affirmation of the Reformation position is occasionally to speak the gospel conditionally—whereupon the Reformation discovery is wholly denied. Either we wholeheartedly and exclusively affirm the unconditionality of the gospel-promise, or, in all that was of importance to the Reformers, we join the medieval church against them.

Law and Gospel

We have been talking about language: about versions of "the gospel," tenses, and communication-situations. This reflects the particular kind of proposed dogma that is "justification by faith alone, without works of law." This dogma is not a particular proposed content of the church's proclamation, along with other contents. It is rather a metalinguistic stipulation of what *kind* of talking—about whatever contents—

can properly be proclamation and word of the church. It does not say: Talk about justification and faith. It is perfectly possible to talk about these subjects, even mimicking the Reformers, and proclaim the purest works-righteousness. Rather, it says: Whatever you talk about, do so in such a way that the justification your words open to your hearers is the justification that faith apprehends rather than the justification that works apprehend. Unpacking the words "justification" and "faith," the proposed dogma says: Make the subject of your discourse those points in your and your hearers' life where its value is challenged, and interpret the challenge by the story about Christ, remembering that when this is rightly done your words will be an unconditional promise of value.

It is this metalinguistic character of the proposed "justification by faith" dogma that makes it a doctrine by which the church stands or falls. If justification were a content-item of the gospel, along with other content-items, the question of which was "most important" would always be a matter of silly debate. But the doctrine is instead an attempt to state minimal identifying characteristics of the language-activity we call "gospel." If the attempt is well-taken, then when people discourse in ways not so describable, they simply are not doing gospel; they are playing some altogether different language-game—perhaps a laudable and vital one, but different. The church is the gathering that occurs when it is speaking the gospel that brings persons together. A community constituted by some other communication is not the church at all—though it may well be a useful community of some other sort. And where the discourse is not the gospel-kind of discourse, and the gathering is not the church-kind of gathering, then the other dogmas of Christianity have no application; it is in this sense that "justification by faith," if a right dogma, is the chief dogma.

Since "justification by faith" is a stipulation about identifying language-characteristics of the gospel language-activity, the Lutheran Reformation had an alternative form of the doctrine, more directly as analysis of language. This goes: So speak of Christ that you "rightly divide law and gospel." "Law" and "gospel" are here labels for two fundamental kinds of discourse into which, the Reformers believed, all human communication could be divided.

The "law" is the totality of all human communication, insofar as what we say to each other functions in our lives as *demand*, or, what is the same, poses the future *conditionally*. Literal laws say, "If you do such-and-such, such-and-such will happen." They open a desired or feared future and make that future depend on what the person addressed does or is in advance thereof. The way the Reformers used "law" supposes that explicitly lawlike utterances make up a good deal of the human conversation, and that a strong law-factor pervades the whole. We have already seen why no lawlike word can be an affirmative answer to the radical question about human life.

The direct counterpole to "law" is "promise." If law-communication imposes an "If . . . then . . ." structure on life, a promise grants the pattern "Because . . . therefore. . . ." "Because I love you," I say to my daughter, "I will further your ambitions." The trouble is that this promise and the rest of our promises are implicitly conditional; for by every promise I commit my future, and my future is not altogether mine to commit. Death can always take it from me and turn my promises into law just when they are most needed. "The gospel" is the Reformation label for that promise which, if true at all, is unconditional: the promise made in the name of one who has already satisfied the condition of death and therefore has all the future in his gift.

Our alienated fear of the future will always seek safely conditional evocations of future possibility, that is, "law." "Rightly dividing" the law and the gospel is the knack of so making promises in Jesus' name as endlessly to transcend this turn back to law. "God loves you for Jesus' sake." "Yes, if I could believe that. But I can't." To which the gospel-sayer who knows his job responds, "Just by your unbelief you prove yourself the very man whom God loves, for he chooses above all the *un*godly!" In actual preaching, teaching, liturgical practice, counseling, etc., the game can go on forever. He "rightly divides law and gospel" who always finds the way to make new proposed conditions into so many objects and reasons for the promise; who in the speaking of the gospel discovers how never to take "but" for an answer.

The gospel tolerates no conditions. It is itself unconditional promise. And when it is rightly spoken, it takes the conditions we put on the value of our life as the very occasions of its promise. This is the first and fundamental Lutheran proposal of dogma. When it is practiced consistently, the Lutheran Reformation has succeeded, whatever else may happen. When it is not practiced, other departures from medieval Christianity represent only sloth and lack of seriousness.

Chapter 4

From Experience of Promise to Apology of Doctrine

Readings:
SA II, 1; III, 1–4, 13, 15
AC and AP 2, 4, 18–19

The God Who Justifies the Ungodly

Lutheran doctrine is inextricably linked to Luther's faith; and Luther's faith is rooted in the experience of a God who justifies the ungodly. That is why the doctrine of justification by faith apart from works of law is the cornerstone of the Lutheran confessions.

Luther's entire "God-talk" is permeated by the existential turmoil he called *Anfechtung* over the "righteousness of God," in the sense the phrase has in Paul's Letter to the Romans. Friar Martin's intensive scholarly labor and anxious meditation on this subject, sometime between 1508 and 1518 in his tower room at the Black Cloister, was later dubbed the "tower experience." Luther reported it in his 1545 "Preface to the Complete Edition of Latin Writings":

> I hated that word "righteousness of God" (Rom. 1:17), which, according to the use and custom of all the teachers, I had been taught to understand philosophically regarding the formal or active righteousness, as they called it, with which God is righteous and punishes the unrighteous sinner.
>
> Though I lived as a monk without reproach, I felt that I was a sinner before God with an extremely disturbed conscience. I could not believe that he was placated by my satisfaction.
>
> At last, by the mercy of God, meditating day and night, I gave heed to the context of the words, namely, "In it the righteousness of God is revealed, as it is written, 'He who through faith is righteous shall live'

> (Hab. 2:4)." There I began to understand that the righteousness of God is that by which the righteous lives by a gift of God, namely by faith. And this is the meaning: the righteousness of God is revealed by the gospel, namely the passive righteousness with which merciful God justifies us by faith, as it is written, "he who through faith is righteous shall live." (LW 34, 336–37)

Luther's existential appropriation of the Pauline doctrine of justification signaled an epistemological revolution in the history of Western Christian thought. Medieval scholastic theology unfolded Christian truth as a series of doctrines disclosing rational order rather than existential dilemma. A classic controversy between the British monk Pelagius and the North African bishop Augustine set the stage for a methodological shift from existential to ontological categories at the beginning of the fifth century. Pelagius argued that man has the free will to decide for or against God—sin is an accident of will rather than a dominant part of nature inherited from Adam. Augustine defended the opposite view that man lost his free will in Adam's fall, and can be saved only by God's free grace.

Although Augustine pressured the church into condemning "Pelagianism" at the North African synod of Carthage in 418, "semi-Pelagian" as well as "semi-Augustinian" views prevailed, especially among monastic theologians in southern France. These theologians tried to refine the balance between God and man in the drama of salvation. They argued that men still have the possibility of striving for salvation, even though the grace of God is needed to bring men into full fellowship with God. The controversy was finally ended, at least for a while, by Bishop Boniface II of Rome, who confirmed the compromise position of the Second Council of Orange (529) as a norm for "the catholic faith." Favoring Augustine, the bishops of southern France, under the leadership of Caesarius of Arles, had declared that God himself inspires men to cooperate with divine grace. Thus the bishop of Rome attempted to reconcile the Augustinian doctrine of predestination with the Pelagian view of human freedom.

But "semi-Pelagian" or "semi-Augustinian" views did not disappear in the Western church. By the thirteenth century, speculations concerning the cooperation between human nature and divine grace had once again become dominant. Medieval scholastic theologians described the process of salvation as a complex interaction between the entities God and man: On the one hand, there is the church, God's earthly "institution of salvation" endowed with the full treasure of Christ's redeeming grace available through sacramental channels; on the other hand, there is man, created by God with the ability to accumulate merits for his salvation—casuistically defined as (1) "the merit of fitness or congruity," the effort to do good without the benefit of infused grace, and (2) "the merit of worthiness or condignity," the effort to do good with the benefit of infused grace. Justification before God is in process once the proper balance between institutionalized grace and creaturely moral effort is achieved.

Luther attacked the casuistry of scholastic thought as an idolatrous "theology of glory" proclaiming the deification of man rather than the incarnation of God in Jesus. "The whole of Aristotle is to theology as darkness is to light," he declared in the 1517 "Disputation Against Scholastic Theology"; and in the "Heidelberg Disputation" of 1518 he presented his evangelical alternative to scholastic methodology in forty theses reflecting the epistemological consequences of the "tower experience." These theses laid the groundwork for a theology which views God's revelation exclusively in terms of salvation through Christ. Theses 19 and 20 stated the differences between true and false theology:

> 19. That person does not deserve to be called a theologian who perceives and understands the invisible nature of God, through His works (Rom 1:20).
> 20. But he deserves to be called a theologian who comprehends what is visible and world-oriented in God, through suffering and the cross. (WA 1, 361–62)

True theology is a "theology of the cross," resting on the faith that the source of the most realistic vision of life is the death of God. False theology is a "theology of glory," resting on the speculation that man's effort guarantees divine forgiveness. According to Luther, God has established an order of salvation which seems foolish in the eyes of the world:

> Because men misused the knowledge of God through works, God wished to be recognized in suffering. He wanted to condemn the wisdom of invisible things by the wisdom of visible things, so that those who did not honor God as revealed in His works should honor him as He is hidden in suffering. (1 Cor. 1:21) (WA 1, 362)

God cannot be perceived by mystical introspection or scientific observation—ways by which sinful men try to know what is true; rather, God is comprehended through his self-revelation in the Jesus of Israel.

Luther was a thoroughgoing biblical theologian and took seriously the divine revelation in historical events, whose final meaning remains hidden until the end of time. His intensive study of the Old Testament exposed him to the force of the Hebrew mandate that "to know" means "to relate" in a covenant of existential commitment. "Adam knew Eve his wife, and she conceived and bore . . ." (Gen. 4:1). To know God means to abandon oneself to him in the complete trust that he alone can save from sin, devil, and death. For Luther, to do theology meant to live out, in the totality of human existence, the divine covenant established in the life, death, and resurrection of Jesus. To do theology meant constantly to distinguish between the history of salvation, heralded in the gospel, and the history of condemnation, proclaimed in the law. The decisive epistemological point of Luther's theology was the "correct distinction between law and gospel." Law and gospel are God's ways of dealing with the world. The law reveals sin, and the gospel discloses salvation. They *appear* to be two distinct forces in the lives of man, yet the "mask" of history hides the one God behind both. Thus law and gospel are the ways in which God reveals himself as the god who justifies the ungodly.

Luther held that the proper distinction of law and gospel—the proper distinction between the God of wrath and the God of mercy—was the real business of the theologian for as long as he exists on earth. History is the "carnival of God" and the many masks of history make it difficult for men to detect the God who justifies the ungodly. So the theologian must keep alert against the forces of confusion. In heaven he will be free from the necessity of distinctions and able to praise God continuously as the angels do. But on earth he has to read the signs of the times in order to know the truth which shall make him free. Luther's doctrine of justification was his way of distinguishing the true from the false church of his time. His axiom of judgment is clearly expressed in the Smalcald Articles:

> The first and chief article is this, that Jesus Christ our God and Lord, "was put to death for our trespasses and raised again for our justification" (Rom. 4:25). . . . On this article rests all we teach and practice against the pope, the devil, and the world. (SA II, 1:1, 5)

Melanchthon's Apologia

If Luther was the prophet of the German Reformation, Melanchthon was its scribe. It was no small task to translate Luther's prophetic intensity into theological *loci* suitable for scholastic debate. Nevertheless, Melanchthon tried hard to develop "Lutheran" dogmatic formulations. In 1521, as professor of Greek and Hebrew at the University of Wittenberg—he was only twenty-one when he accepted the call to that post—he published the *Loci Communes*, the first Lutheran systematic theology. In 1530, when he drafted the Augsburg Confession, he presented Luther's theology in a conciliatory tone designed to produce an atmosphere of dialogue between reform and establishment theologians. The doctrine of justification is a case in point (AC 4). Melanchthon did not want to emphasize the preeminence of the "chief article" (as Luther did later, in SA II, 1:1), and so wrote, "Our churches *also* teach that men cannot be justified before God by their own strength . . ." (emphasis added). That is why the article on justification follows rather than precedes the "ecumenical" articles on God, sin, and Christ.

Melanchthon stated Luther's doctrine of justification in the context of a theory of satisfaction, as the Latin version clearly shows:

> [Men . . .] are freely justified for Christ's sake through faith when they believe that they are received into favor and that their sins are forgiven on account of Christ, who by his death made satisfaction for our sins. This faith God imputes for righteousness in his sight (Rom. 3, 4). (AC 4)

Melanchthon also wanted to assure his scholastic colleagues that justification by *faith* does not mean the rejection of *good works* (AC 6 and 20). On the contrary, "faith should produce good fruits and good works" as the result of the "new obedience" which naturally flows from commitment to the merits of Christ. What Luther considered the ecclesiastical "original sin"—the teaching that man can be justified before God through good works—Melanchthon labeled a historical "neglect" which reform theologians wanted to correct.

> Inasmuch, then, as the teaching about faith, which ought to be the chief teaching in the church, has so long been neglected (for everybody must grant that there has been profound silence concerning the righteousness of faith in sermons while only the teachings about works has been treated in the church), our teachers have instructed our churches concerning faith. . . . (Latin AC 20:8)

Melanchthon's conciliatory tone was not shared by the opponents to the Augsburg Confession. On the contrary, the 1530 Confutation set out to prove that the Lutheran theological movement was heretical, particularly in its insistence on "justification by faith alone."

> Anyone who wants to reject the merits of men, which are established with the assistance of divine grace, asserts an opinion which is closer to Manichaeism than to the catholic church. (On AC 4, CR 27, 93)

Manichaeism had been condemned in the fourth century for teaching a metaphysical dualism—the complete separation of matter and spirit—and thus the denial of the Christian creed that God is both creator and redeemer of the world. To accuse Lutherans of Manichaean tendencies was indeed a blow below the ecumenical belt of the Augsburg Confession.

Melanchthon countered with an elaborate treatise on the Lutheran doctrine of justification in the Apology of the Augsburg Confession (AP 4). The treatise disclosed two typical Melanchthonian traits: total familiarity with medieval scholastic methodology, and ecumenical commitment to ecclesiastical tradition. Melanchthon fought his opponents on their own ground, using the scholastic form of debate: (1) the statement of the issue, (2) supporting arguments, (3) opposing arguments, and (4) the convincing answer. These rules for debate are applied throughout the fourfold explication of the article of justification: (1) the definition of justifying faith (AP 4:48–60), (2) the origin of justifying faith in Christ (61–74), (3) the forgiveness of sins as the result of justification by faith alone (75–121), and (4) the relationship of justifying faith to love and law (122–82). Melanchthon summed up the issue and the proper way to deal with it in a final section entitled "Reply to the Opponents' Arguments" (183–400).

The major issue is the main doctrine of Christianity, "the distinction between the law and the promises or Gospel" (2, 183). The two positions in the controversy, according to Melanchthon, can easily be detected. Lutherans accept the biblical dialectic of law and gospel.

> In some places it [Scripture] presents the law. In others it presents the promise of Christ; this it does either when it promises that the Messiah will come and promises forgiveness of sins, justification, and eternal life for his sake, or when, in the New Testament, the Christ who came promises forgiveness of sins, justification, and eternal life. (5)

The authors of the Confutation follow the philosophers whose highest authority is reason:

> They teach only the righteousness of reason—that is, civil works—and maintain that without the Holy Spirit reason can love God above all things. As long as a man's mind is at rest and he does not feel God's wrath or judgment, he can imagine that he wants to love God and that he wants to do good for God's sake. In this way the scholastics teach men to merit the forgiveness of sins by doing what is within them. (9)

The proper way to deal with the issue is to make a correct assessment of Christ (12, 156). Lutherans make this assessment on the basis of the biblical testimony: the gospel promises forgiveness of sins through Christ alone. This promise is free because Christ paid for the sin of man (43, 53). He is the mediator between God and man. Faith in him justifies (69–73); and faith in him sanctifies (162–77).

> Therefore we conclude that we are justified before God, reconciled to him, and reborn by a faith that penitently grasps the promise of grace, truly enlivens the fearful mind, and is convinced that God is reconciled and propitious to us because of Christ. (386)

The authors of the Confutation assess Christ on the basis of philosophical reason rather than biblical testimony: Christ stimulates man's natural disposition to love God and to fulfill his law by an "initial grace." Once man has been sufficiently stimulated by Christ's merit, he is able to complete his salvation through the accumulation of his own merits (17–19). Such a view of salvation is based on an understanding of faith as merely "historical knowledge"—a set of dogmas rather than a power grasping the heart of man (48, 383).

> The only righteousness that reason can see is the righteousness of the law, understood as civic uprightness. So there have always been some in the world who taught only this outward righteousness to the exclusion of the righteousness of faith, and such teachers there will always be. (394)

Melanchthon's entire Apology was designed to show the ecumenicity of the Augsburg Confession and the sectarianism of the Confutation. "These theologians have lost all sense of shame if they dare to smuggle such a notion into the church," he declared concerning the doctrine of good works, which Lutherans regarded as the most intolerable theological contraband (AP 20:4). He hoped that the church of Rome would turn from the anthropocentric speculations of erring theologians to the Christocentric affirmations of the prophets, the apostles, and fathers of the church (388–92).

While Melanchthon had little difficulty finding support from Scripture for the centrality of the doctrine of justification, his argument from ecclesiastical tradition was impeded by lack of evidence. After all, the Western church has accepted, in one form or another, a doctrine of merit based on the assumption that man can earn a part of his salvation by doing good works. Only Augustine defended a radically critical anthropology; most of the other fathers accepted "semi-Pelagian" compromises when they had to wrestle with the question of man's role in the process of salvation. Augustine, therefore, was Melanchthon's chief witness for the indictment of medieval scholastic theology. Other church fathers are hardly cited in AP 4: Ambrose is quoted twice, Jerome and Cyprian once each. Moreover, Melanchthon's own anthropology suffered from a lack of clarity, if judged with the scholastic scrutiny used in the Apology to refute Roman opponents. On the one hand, Melanchthon argued that "to have faith means to want and to accept the promised offer of forgiveness of sins and justification" (4:48); on the other hand, he maintained, " 'to be justified' means to make unrighteous men righteous or to regenerate them, as well as to be pronounced or accounted righteous" (4:72). The first statement stressed the existential restlessness of the human condition—the desire to be liberated from the *Anfechtung* of sin, revealed by the demand of the law; faith is not rational assent to institutionalized grace, "historical knowledge," but trusting hope that the God of the law is also the God of the gospel. The second statement emphasized the force of the divine promise—the acquittal of ungodly man through Christ—disclosed in the proclamation of the gospel; faith is not trust in one's own ability to move toward God, in "proper beginnings," but the recognition that Christ alone satisfied the divine law.

Melanchthon himself favored the "forensic" explication of the Pauline doctrine of justification as the most effective way to refute the Confutation's arguments (4:304–7). But his imprecise and sometimes mingled use of existential and judicial categories confused both friends and foes. Friends and supporters of the Lutheran movement began to quarrel over the relationship of judicial "justification" and existential "sanctification"—a classic Lutheran controversy which threatened to split Lutherans in the sixteenth century and which created theological excitement in subsequent history. Foes of the Lutheran movement and defenders of the church of Rome simply condemned the notion of justification by faith alone, no matter how eloquently it was argued—as did the Council of Trent in 1547 (session 6).

Chapter 5

Faith Seeking Understanding Through Controversy

Readings:
FC 1–6

A.

Forensic Justification

The first six articles of the Formula of Concord disclose theological discord between the followers of Luther and the followers of Melanchthon over the proper interpretation of the chief article of Lutheran faith. The central issue was "the righteousness of faith before God" (FC 3). In addition, there were controversies about the related *loci* of original sin (FC 1), free will (FC 2), good works (FC 4), law and gospel (FC 5), and "the third use of the law" (FC 6). Gnesio-Lutherans claimed to defend Luther's position, and Philippists aligned themselves behind Melanchthon. Both parties were convinced that they were preserving the basic theological thrust of the Lutheran movement.

Two theologians, in their attempts to communicate the doctrine of justification to their generation, exhibited more sound and fury than any others. Matthias Flacius Illyricus (1520–75) stood out for the most conservative reductionist interpretation of Luther's faith in the God who justifies the ungodly; Andreas Osiander (1498–1552) developed the most liberal expansionist doctrine of justification in sixteenth-century Lutheran theology, and was opposed by both Gnesio-Lutherans and Philippists. Yet both theologians were plagued by a classic Christian dilemma—the translation of existential faith into scholastic categories.

Flacius was a Gnesio-Lutheran committed to the most unflinching and uncompromising defense of Luther against both Philippists and Roman Catholics. Embroiled in controversies (specifically the "Adiaphorist," "Majorist," "Osiandrian," and "Synergist" controversies) throughout his academic career in Wittenberg, Magdeburg, and Jena, Flacius continued his nomadic existence after 1561 as a pastor and scholar in Regensburg, Antwerp, Strasbourg, and Frankfort. He died in Frankfort, hated by Philippists, Roman Catholics, and even Gnesio-Lutherans. His two major works are attempts to back his involvement in Saxon ecclesiastical politics with scholarly research: *Key to Holy Scripture (clavis scripturae sacrae)* with a controversial appendix on original sin, and *Ecclesiastical History (ecclesiastica historica)*, known as "The Magdeburg Centuries," a Lutheran view of church history.

Flacius constructed a doctrine of justification against Philippists and Roman Catholics by arguing that man can do absolutely nothing in the process of salvation. He used crude judicial-forensic language with commercial undertones (e.g., in *Key to Holy Scripture*): Men are called into the divine forum to be judged; God presides, holding in his hands a book of accounts containing the debts of men and the treasure of Christ; each man is accused and threatened with eternal torture; then Christ, the mediator, steps forth to plead for the remission of debt on the basis of his own merit. God listens carefully to the plea; finally, he agrees to acquit men by accepting Christ's credit. The "sinner" (*peccator*) has been declared "righteous" (*iustus*) through a divine transaction based on the merits of Christ; God is not only gracious, but also just. To put it in terms of the Flacian theological system, man's justification is based on Christ's redemption which removed "inherited" (original) sin—the wall of separation making it impossible for God to accept men into his fellowship. To be sure, men had always been destined to be with God. But Flacian theology denied a *logical* connection between the *objective* possibility of salvation through Christ and *subjective* conditions for man's reception of salvation. There is no *theological* relationship between God's act of redemption in Christ and man's longing for salvation. God is "active" and man is "passive" in the process of salvation. Using Aristotelian scholastic categories, Flacius even went as far as to assert that man's "substance" is corrupt so that he is totally incapable of doing any good on his own.

This crude doctrine of justification was fiercely debated by Saxon

Lutheran theologians. Philippists, opposed to a totalitarian view of original sin, argued that man is able to cooperate in some way with God in the process of salvation. In 1555, John Pfeffinger of Leipzig, for example, defended the synergistic position that man is not like a "passive statue" during his conversion, but rather has the capacity to cooperate with the will of God. Philippists dubbed Flacius' doctrine of original sin "Manichaean"; Gnesio-Lutherans called Pfeffinger's position "Pelagian"; Lutheran orthodoxy was at stake.

In 1560 Flacius was forced to defend himself against a colleague from the University in Jena, Viktorin Strigel, at a disputation in Weimar on original sin and free will. The disputation represents the climax of the synergistic controversy. Strigel argued that although the Holy Spirit initiates man's conversion, man is henceforth moved to contribute to his own salvation. This is possible because the Word of God adjusts itself to man's creaturely mode of action; God's redemption does not contradict His creation, and man's will is still free enough to cooperate with the Holy Spirit. Word and Spirit persuade man to use his original creaturely freedom to cooperate with God. If this were not so, salvation would have to be a magic transforming power—a view which, according to Strigel, tends to revive the medieval doctrine of sacramental "transubstantiation." Man is not "substantially" corrupt, as Flacius taught, but only "accidentally" corrupt. Once stimulated by God through Word and Spirit, man is capable of using his "substance" (reason and will) to cooperate with God in the battle against sin.

Although Flacius tried to refine his concept of original sin—he even distinguished between two kinds of substances, reverting to medieval scholastic casuistry—he ended by insisting on man's complete passivity in the process of salvation. God *declares man just* through the merits of Christ—this is the cause of justification; and God *makes man just* through the power of word and spirit—this is the effect of justification. God, the judge, does not need the cooperation of man, the defendant. The divine judgment contains enough power to create the disposition of faith in man. To be justified "by faith alone" (*sola fide*) therefore means to be overwhelmed by the word of God. Salvation always comes from the outside. The word has the awesome power to persuade man to accept his salvation through the merits of Christ. This was the way Flacius sought to preserve Luther's faith in the justification of the ungodly.

Inner Justification

Osiander forged a doctrine of justification which shook the very foundation of Lutheran confessional theology in the sixteenth century. One of Luther's early supporters, Osiander used his influence as chief pastor of St. Laurence Church in Nuremberg to win the city for the Reformation; he joined Luther's team against Zwingli in the 1529 Marburg Colloquy on the Lord's Supper; and he participated in the Diet of Augsburg in 1530, eagerly anticipating the establishment of Lutheran territories in the empire. In 1549 Duke Albert of Prussia called Osiander to be the first professor of theology at the newly founded University of Koenigsberg, where he spent the rest of his life embroiled in the Osiandrian controversy over the chief Lutheran article of faith. In the end, only Duke Albert sided with Osiander. Both Gnesio-Lutherans and Philippists refused to support the Koenigsberg professor, and the Formula of Concord condemned his views as "contrary to the Word of God" (SD 3:59–66).

Osiander argued his doctrine of justification most eloquently in a treatise entitled "About the One Mediator Jesus Christ and the Justification of Faith" (*Von dem Einigen Mittler Jesu Christo und Rechtfertigung des Glaubens*, 1551): One must make a careful distinction between two aspects of Christ's office of mediator between God and man. On the one hand, when he died on the cross he satisfied God by taking the punishment for human sin; this is the work of "reconciliation." On the other hand, he makes men righteous by dwelling in them as the risen Lord mediating divine grace, the means for a new life with God; this is the work of "justification." Osiander used the example of redemption from slavery to illustrate Christ's work of reconciliation: just as a slave frees all his descendants when he is freed from bondage, so does the Son of God redeem men from the bondage of sin when they are set free by his sacrifice on the cross. These are the juridical consequences of the act of redemption. The picture of the vine, dominant in the Gospel of John, illustrates Christ's work of justification: just as the creation of wine is dependent on the two natures of the vine, external wood and hidden juice, so man's re-creation is dependent on the two natures of Christ, human and divine. Salvation comes through Christ's life and death on earth as well as through his "indwelling" in the believer. Although the human and divine natures are interrelated (as expressed in the classic doctrine of the "exchange of properties between the two natures"—*communicatio idiomatum*), the *divine* nature effects salvation, just as the hidden juice of the wooden vine produces the wine.

The indwelling of Christ in the believer is the decisive point of Osiander's argument. The proclamation of the "external word" of God about the "objective" justification of mankind through the death of the historical Jesus effects the "subjective" justification of men through the "inner word," the *Logos* making his home in man (John 14:23). Salvation, therefore, means that God himself dwells in the believer, since "the whole fulness of deity dwells bodily" in Christ (Col. 2:9). Thus Osiander greatly expanded Luther's theology of the Word. The external word "declares righteous" and the internal word "makes righteous." While Flacius argued that salvation always comes from the outside, through the awesome power of the external word proclaiming man's acquittal in God's forum, Osiander held that man is overwhelmed by the indwelling Christ.

Flacius and his disciples wrote numerous treatises against Osiander, and the Koenigsberg professor defended himself against all comers. Some theologians tried to mediate the controversy. John Brenz of Tuebingen, for example, submitted an "expert opinion" to Duke Albert in 1552, demonstrating that the controversy was caused by terminological rather than doctrinal differences. Other theologians simply added their own opinions, without regard for Lutheran unity. The Polish theologian Franciscus Stancarus, for example, argued against Osiander that Christ could make men righteous *only* according to his human nature (FC SD 3:3). After Osiander's death in 1552, the controversy took an ugly political turn. Gnesio-Lutherans as well as Philippists undertook to rid Prussia of all Osiandrians. John Funck, Duke Albert's staunch Osiandrian court chaplain, was forced to recant his views at a Lutheran synod in 1563, and in 1566 fell victim to political intrigue and was executed.

An Orthodox Doctrine

The Formula of Concord rejects any attempts to link christological speculations on the two natures of Christ to the doctrine of justification. Accordingly, Luther's and the Augsburg Confession's true defenders held "that Christ is our righteousness, not according to the divine nature alone or according to the human nature alone, but according to both natures" (SD 3:4). Osiander is accused of teaching the former view, Stancarus of teaching the latter (EP 3:2, SD 3:2–3). The orthodox Lutheran doctrine of justification is offered (SD 3:9–43), and Melanchthon's forensic emphasis is upheld (AP 4:305). "'Justify' means to declare righteous and free from sins and from the eternal punishment of these sins on account of the righteousness of Christ which God reckons to faith" (SD 3:17). The relationship between juridical justification and existential sanctification (the chief issue in the Flacian and Osiandrian controversies) is set forth in terms of a dialectic which heeds Luther's advice that the proper distinction between law and gospel (that is, between the God of wrath and the God of mercy) is the real business of an earthbound theology.

> It is indeed correct to say that believers who through faith in Christ have been justified possess in this life, first, the reckoned righteousness of faith and, second, also the inchoate righteousness of the new obedience or of good works. But these two dare not be confused with one another or introduced simultaneously into the article of justification by faith before God. For because this inchoate righteousness or renewal in us is imperfect and impure in this life on account of the flesh, no one can therewith and thereby stand before the tribunal of God. Only the righteousness of the obedience, passion, and death of Christ which is reckoned to faith can stand before God's tribunal. (SD 3:32)

Since Melanchthon had not been all too clear about the role of man in the process of salvation (AP 4:48, 72), the Formula of Concord suggested three ways in which faith and good works are to be distinguished (SD 3:37–41): (1) Human merit is to be totally excluded from the article of justification. (2) Faith only "receives, grasps, accepts, applies, and appropriates" what Christ has done; it excludes "love and every other virtue or work." (3) The process of salvation is the work of the trinitarian God.

> First the Holy Spirit kindles faith in us in conversion through the hearing of the Gospel. Faith apprehends the grace of God in Christ whereby the person is justified. After the person is justified, the Holy Spirit next renews and sanctifies him, and from this renewal and sanctification the fruits of good works will follow. (SD 3:41)

Finally, Roman Catholic and Osiandrian teachings are rejected, and Luther's exposition of Paul's Letter to the Galatians is recommended to those desiring a more detailed explanation of the doctrine of justification (SD 3:45–51, 59–67).

The proposed orthodox Lutheran doctrine of justification (FC 3) was intimately linked with attempts to set norms for a proper Lutheran understanding of sin, freedom, and law. These three major theological *loci* had been hotly debated during the synergist, Majoristic, and antinomian controversies.

First, the Formula of Concord attempted to settle the synergist controversy through the articles on original sin and free will (FC 1–2). Original sin is defined in a twofold way: (1) as the "abominable and dreadful inherited disease which has corrupted our entire nature" (SD 1:5); and (2) as the result of Satan's scheme rather than the will of God (SD 1:7). True Lutheran theology must emphasize the struggle between God and Satan:

> God does not create and make sin in us. Rather, along with the nature which God still creates and makes at the present time, original sin is transmitted through our carnal conception and birth out of sinful seed from our father and mother. (SD 1:7)

> This damage is so unspeakable that it may not be recognized by a rational process, but only from God's Word. No one except God alone can separate the corruption of our nature from the nature itself. This will take place wholly by way of death in the resurrection. (EP 1:9–10)

Consequently, man cannot exercise his free will in the process of salvation.

> We believe that after the Fall and prior to his conversion not a spark of spiritual powers has remained or exists in man by which he could make himself ready for the grace of God or to accept the proffered grace, nor that he has any capacity for grace by and for himself or can apply himself to it or prepare himself for it, or help, do, effect, or cooperate toward his conversion by his own powers, either altogether or half-way or in the tiniest or smallest degree. (SD 2:6, EP 2:1)

Man's only freedom is to turn away from God and toward evil; he is only free to sin (SD 2:17). Salvation is exclusively a divine operation (SD 2:25).

The extreme positions in the synergist controversy taken by Strigel and Flacius at the 1560 Weimar disputation are rejected. Strigel is charged with reviving the ancient Pelagian doctrine that original sin is only a corruption of certain *accidental elements* in human nature, thus still allowing man to cooperate with God in the process of salvation (SD 1:21, 2:60, 77). Flacius is accused of restituting the Manichaean error that after the fall man is *substantially* infused with Satan's sin, thus losing his status as a creature of God (SD 1:26, 2:81). Both positions were based on Aristotelian metaphysics, which tried to unravel all mysteries of the universe by cause and effect. When Melanchthon applied this theory to theological anthropology, claiming "three efficient causes of our good action" in his *Loci* and *Rhetorical Elements*, Philippists soon spoke of the third cause as unregenerated man's power to assist God in the process of salvation. The Formula of Concord found such language confusing to laymen and dangerous to students of theology, since they are apt to simplify Aristotelian categories and thus destroy the complexity of metaphysical issues.

> The young students at our universities have been greatly misled by the doctrine of the three efficient causes of unregenerated man's conversion to God, particularly as to the manner in which these three (the Word of God preached and heard, the Holy Spirit, and man's will) concur. (SD 2:90)

To avoid such aberrations in catechetical and theological instruction, clear definitions of the terms *substantia* and *accidens* are presented: the terms are properly used when a perfect dichotomy is maintained—"every existing thing must either be a substance (that is, a self-subsisting essence) or an accident (that is, an accidental thing that is not self-subsistent but that subsists in another self-subsistent essence and can be distinguished from it)" (SD 1:54). Thus original sin, for example, is not a substance but an accident, since it cannot exist or subsist by itself (SD 1:57). Ultimately, however, the controversy over sin and freedom can be solved not by terminological sophistry but by Holy Scripture, which testifies that sin is an inexpressible impairment of human freedom. (SD 1:60)

Second, the article on good works tries to settle the Majoristic controversy (FC 4). Philippists, led by George Major, stressed existential sanctification with the thesis that good works are *necessary* for salvation. Gnesio-Lutherans, led by Nicholas von Amsdorf, emphasized juridical justification with the counter-thesis that good works are *detrimental* to salvation (SD 4:1–4, EP 4:2–3). The Formula of Concord rejects such a radical distinction between justification and sanctification and establishes four basic guidelines to a proper Lutheran discussion of good works: (1) Good works are "necessary" in the strict Christian sense of obeying God's commandment. "When the word 'necessary' is used in this context [of obedience], it is not to be understood as implying compulsion but only as referring to the order of God's immutable will, whose debtors we are, as his commandment indicates when it enjoins the creature to obey its creator" (SD 4:16). (2) Good works should not be drawn into and mingled with the article on justification and salvation. "Such propositions [those of Major and Amsdorf] are directly contrary to the doctrine of exclusive terms in the articles of justification and salvation (that is, they are diametrically opposed to St. Paul's words which exclude our works and merit completely from the article of justification and salvation and ascribe everything solely to the grace of God and the merit of Christ)" (SD 4:22). (3) Good works do not preserve salvation. Such an assertion is an "Epicurean illusion" (SD 4:31). Salvation is always a gift of God, no matter how many "good works" are done. Thus, it is wrong to assert, as did the Council of Trent, "that our works either entirely or in part sustain and preserve either the righteousness of faith that we have received or even faith itself" (SD 4:35). (4) Christian faith relies on God's unconditional promise of salvation rather than on confidence in good works. "The fault . . . lies not with good works themselves, but with the false confidence which, contrary to the express Word of God, is being placed upon good works" (SD 4:37). Ultimately, the dialectic between faith and works is grounded in the eschatological tension of Christian existence.

> Especially in these last times, it is just as necessary to exhort people to Christian discipline and good works, and to remind them how necessary it is that they exercise themselves in good works as an evidence of their faith and their gratitude toward God, as it is to warn against mingling good works in the article of justification. Such an Epicurean dream concerning faith can damn people as much as a papistic and Pharasaic confidence in one's own works and merit. (EP 4:18)

Third, the articles on the proper distinction between law and gospel and the "third use of the law" seek to settle the antinomian controversies (FC 5–6). Although Luther had managed to avoid a doctrinal schism over the interpretation of Old Testament law during his lifetime, some of his Gnesio-Lutheran disciples--especially Andrew Poach of Erfurt and Anton Otto of Nordhausen—began to argue antinomian positions in 1556. They declared that law and salvation have nothing in common. The law condemns; the gospel saves. Moderate Gnesio-Lutherans as well as Melanchthon and cautious Philippists opposed such antinomian views and insisted that the preaching of the gospel leads to repentance. Accordingly, they could speak of two, or even three, "uses of the law": restriction through government (*usus legis politicus*), conviction through conscience (*usus legis paedagogicus),* and direction through discipline (*usus legis didacticus*). Luther himself had clearly taught the first two uses. The question was whether one could, with a clear Lutheran theological conscience, teach a third use of the law—whether "those who have been born anew through the Holy Spirit, who have been converted to the Lord and from whom the veil of Moses had been taken away, learn from the law to live and walk in the law" (SD 6:1). The Formula of Concord clearly answers in the affirmative:

> We believe, teach, and confess that the preaching of the law is to be diligently applied not only to unbelievers and the impenitent but also to people who are genuinely believing, truly converted, regenerated, and justified through faith. (EP 6:3)

> Believers, furthermore, require the teaching of the law so that they will not be thrown back on their own holiness and piety and under the pretext of the Holy Spirit's guidance set up a self-elected service of God without his Word and commandment. (SD 6:20)

As long as Christians exist on earth they need to be urged on to follow the Spirit of God (SD 6:9). To be antinomian means to fall prey to a romantic view of Christian life, and so the one-sided antinomian position is rejected (EP 6:8). Realistic theologians should know that *both* gospel and law, in their proper distinction, are the driving forces of a faith active in love. Law rebukes sin and gives instruction about good works; gospel promises forgiveness of sins through Christ who bore the curse of the law and paid for human sin (SD 5:18, 20). To confuse these two essential proclamations "would easily darken the merits and benefits of Christ, once more make the

Gospel a teaching of law, as happened in the papacy, and thus rob Christians of the true comfort which they have in the Gospel against the terrors of the law and reopen the door to the papacy in the church of God" (SD 5:27).

B.

The Location of Theology

When the doctrine of justification by faith is observed, theology is done from a specific location. Theology has most often been done from the location of an observer: the theologian observes the realities "God" and "creature" and the relation between them, and tries to describe and partly explain what he sees. It may be doubted that there is any location from which to observe God; but whether there is or not, the doctrine of justification locates the theologian elsewhere. Proper Lutheran theology occurs *within* the event of hearing and speaking the gospel; it is the thinking involved in moving from hearing to speaking. Lutheran theology is reflection within the discourse of the church on how this discourse may be gospel and not only law.

Such reflection is hard to do. The intra-Lutheran controversies described earlier in this chapter are endlessly instructive about its difficulties. They reveal, moreover, two central difficulties: the necessity of contradicting the whole Western ontological tradition, and the necessity of conceiving in a new way the relation between the past and present work of Christ.

The Ontological Problem

Luther himself lived totally in the immediate actuality of preaching and hearing the gospel-story in its saving unconditionality. But the continuing life of the church requires also a certain more-distanced reflection on the gospel, in order to *teach* the craft of this gospel-speaking. As we have seen, Philip Melanchthon was the first to undertake this inevitable schoolroom reflection, the first to try to reduce Luther's direct and explosive addresses to academic form.

Melanchthon developed what we would now call a purely "existential" (they said "logical") statement of the doctrine of justification: a doctrine entirely in terms of the phenomenal effects of preaching and teaching in the lives of the hearers. So long, he said, as we hear only law in God's name, we cannot help but apprehend God as a judge, whether lax or rigorous. Our natural and inevitable attitude toward God will then be self-security, rebellion, or a bit of both. Just these attitudes are what is meant by "sin." But if we hear that God, contrary to our expectation, *forgives,* the cause of this slavish relation to God is removed. Our equally natural and inevitable attitude will then be the love of God—which is the just state of being for a creature of God, and is the psychological possibility also of love for our fellow men.

Medieval theology described the work of God on us by describing alterations of the capacities of a metaphysical entity, the "soul," effected by a supernatural power, "grace." Melanchthon strictly refrained from all such ontological discussions. His approach is reflected in the Apology of the Augsburg Confession, and is typical of one large group within immediate post-Reformation Lutheranism, the so-called Philippists.

Melanchthon seemed to be right in Luther's track. The problem is that we cannot altogether avoid ontological commitments. There are ontological questions that just will be asked, especially in classrooms: What sort of being is man, if such a gospel can be addressed to him? How does the word of forgiveness affect him? How is he different after baptism from before? The very determination of the Philippists not to mix ontological speculation into the doctrine of justification meant that their ontological commitments were unaffected by the new insight, and inevitably remained fixed in the standard Western tradition.

At least since Aristotle, Western thinkers—Christian and otherwise—have seen reality as made up of "substances" with "attributes." A "substance" is a relatively independent something, defined in its independence by certain of its characteristics, those "essential" attributes which it possesses prior to all communication with other substances. If to be a human is to be "rational," then I am and will remain rational so long as I remain at all the human that I am. And I am self-defined in this possession, independently of what may happen to me in my communication with you and the world: I may learn mathematics, come to be loved, or break a leg, but I will stay rational as long as I stay myself.

This ontology is inconsistent with the gospel as understood by the Reformers. For if there is a word which can rightly intervene so decisively in my life as the gospel-promise claims to do, then communication penetrates into me much more deeply than a "substance" could allow. If there can be such communication, then there can be no such thing as a properly human being prior to, and independent of, all communication. If there were such an absolute human entity, its integrity would have to be reckoned with over against any communication addressed to it, even the gospel—and that reckoning would be the works-condition that the radically preached gospel abhors. The standard Western ontology is intrinsically works-righteous.

Thus the Philippists had, on the one hand, a clear doctrine of the unconditional promise and of the transformation which the hearing of such a promise must be; but, on the other hand, they assumed an inherited ontological interpretation of the reality thus to be transformed which defined freedom as independence from any such word from outside. The way this contradiction worked out was that when the Philippists discussed justification directly, they were brilliantly reformatory, but when they discussed related subjects like "original sin" or the "necessity of good works," they always sounded elusively off-key. Insofar as the Philippists won, and became the methodological fathers of the Lutheran intellectual tradition, this same off-key sound persists to this day in standard Lutheran discussions of these matters.

The Gnesio-Lutherans felt this, and some part of the reason for it, and they determined to meet the issue squarely, interpreting the whole reality of God and man by the unconditionality of the gospel. But they allowed their opponents—and so the traditional ontology—to dictate the traditional questions: What is man? What is man's nature? What does man contribute? etc. Their answers *to these questions* had to be harshly paradoxical: "Man is a sinner," "His nature is to be sinful," "He contributes hindrances." If these were to be the questions, these were the right Reformation answers; but the total position that resulted was intolerable. Both sides assumed the basic question, What can man in and of himself do about fulfillment? The Philippists answered: "A little bit"; and the Gnesio-Lutherans answered: "Nothing." But the trouble was the interpretation hidden in the question, that there is any such reality as man-in-himself.

The Osiandrian controversy reveals the same kind of problem. The common Lutheran doctrine of justification interpreted the event of justification as a judgment by God that we are righteous. Osiander worried: "God *says* we are righteous, but how does this make us *really* righteous?" What we *hear* and what we *are in ourselves* are again assumed to be independent; and the Reformation's understanding of the gospel again becomes an insoluble conundrum.

Past and Present

The second pervasive problem is closely related: the relation between the past and present work of Christ. The second generation of reformers adopted the Anselmian doctrine about the past work of Christ to make grace universally available, precisely in order to conceptualize the completeness of his work. But thereby they saddled themselves all over again with the great problem of medieval theology: How do we now come to participate in the benefits of Christ's past work? They could not adopt the medieval solution: that we participate by our *cooperation* with grace. So the regular Lutherans created the doctrine of justification "in the heavenly court": we participate in the fruit of Christ's past work by a sort of bookkeeping entry in which God omnipotently reckons Christ's merits to our account. Osiander, who found this as unsatisfactory as most contemporary persons will, proposed instead that we come to participate in the work of the past human person Jesus by the spiritual indwelling of the divine person united with him.

Clearly, neither solution will do. The problem is that the question repristinates the medieval pattern of thought, which relates past, present, and future by a scheme of foundation, appropriation, and fruition. The gospel cannot be clearly interpreted by this scheme. If what I *am* is decided by what is *said* to me, then the essential determinants of my life are not set by a foundation at my beginnings, but may very well enter my life later, as repentance and forgiveness and new birth.

An Enduring Task

It cannot be said that the Formula of Concord contains solutions to these problems. Instead, the theologians negotiated formulas that set boundaries for the conflicts—which was, of course, a considerable achievement, enabling the consolidation of Lutheran territorial churches as the only then-viable carriers of the movement. But—by hindsight—what could have happened was nothing less than a radical break with the whole traditional Western ontology, with our whole inherited way of speaking of such realities as "man" and "freedom." The possibility of such a conceptual revolution is still contained in the Lutheran insight.

The doctrine of justification by faith alone implies that human reality is not a substance given prior to all community. Rather, humanity happens *in* the event of communication, in the speaking and hearing of the word. The word—the actual, ordinary human word—is the active initiation of human reality. What I am is not defined in advance by some set of timelessly possessed attributes; it is being defined in the history of address and response in and by which you and I live together. So also, past, present, and future are related other than by the traditional schemas. The doctrine of justification will be secured only when the ontology so sketched is worked out. In the years since the Reformation, this has been seen and attempted repeatedly (the most notable attempts were Hegel's and Kierkegaard's), but never, perhaps, quite radically enough.

The word is the locus of the creation of humanity. The lawlike word creates life with one structure: in which the future that opens to us depends on our fulfillment or nonfulfillment of prior conditions. The gospel-word creates life with a different structure: in which the unconditionality of Jesus' self-giving opens an otherwise unthinkable, endlessly new, and unconditionally given future. If the gospel is true, this second human life is the true human life; in the Bible and the Reformation, it is called "faith."

Am I right? Or am I merely *declared* right? There is no difference. I am the first precisely in that I am the second. Speech in the church is to be *the declaration that creates* faith's humanity rather than a humanity of works—this is the instruction the catholic church should give its members, according to the first and main Lutheran proposal of dogma.

PART THREE

THEOLOGICAL ELABORATIONS

Chapter 6

Sacraments—The Visible Word

Readings:
Baptism: SC IV–V; LC IV
SA III, 5; AC and AP 9, 13
Lord's Supper: SC VI; LC V; SA II, 2; III, 6
AC and AP 10–12, 22–25; FC 7

A.

Exodus from Babylonian Captivity

The first and most enduring theological battle of the Lutheran Reformation was fought over the proper understanding of the sacraments. Luther himself had to confront two lines of battle: the medieval church's sacramental system, most powerfully displayed in the celebration of the mass as the climax of priestly power, and the "sacramentarianism" of the "left-wingers" (dubbed "Schwaermer" by Luther), who either relegated sacraments to the status of nonessential externals or rejected them altogether.

Controlled by his experience of a God who promises righteousness without human merit, Luther launched his first major theological attack against medieval sacramentology in "The Babylonian Captivity of the Church" (1520): just as the Jews had been carried away from the sanctuary in Jerusalem into the captivity of Babylon, so a tyrannical papacy had abducted Western Christendom from the freedom of the gospel into the bondage of a sacramental system claiming to have power over life, death, and eternity.

With the aid of decrees issued by ecumenical councils under the domination of popes, a process of doctrinal solidification of theological speculation had molded the church into an institution of salvation in which the priest, through a programmed dispensation of sacramental grace, became the mediator between God and man. In 1215, at the height of papal power under Innocent III, the Fourth Lateran Council formulated the doctrine of transubstantiation: whenever a duly ordained priest consecrates bread and wine, the "substance" (an Aristotelian category describing the essential being of something) of those elements becomes the true body and blood of Christ while their "accidents" (properties such as quantity and chemical nature) remain the same. This transubstantiation occurs when the rite is properly performed, imparting grace regardless of the faith of the priest or of the recipient of the sacrament (*ex opere operato*). The Council of Constance in 1415 promulgated the doctrine of concomitance based on the teaching of Alexander of Hales (d. 1245): only the priest is permitted to consume the wine during mass, since the *whole* Christ is truly present in *one* element or "species." Consequently, the laity need receive only "communion of one kind"—a rejection of the Hussite demand for the "lay chalice," a symbol of common priesthood in the church. In 1439, under the leadership of Pope Eugene IV, the Council of Florence decreed that there are seven sacraments: five for the "spiritual perfection" of the individual Christian (baptism, confirmation, eucharist, penance, extreme unction) and two for the "government and increase in the entire church" (priestly orders and matrimony). These sacraments are valid only if they are correctly dispensed: with "matter" (such as water in baptism), with "form" (words), and by a priest who intends to do as the church does. Three sacraments—baptism, confirmation, and priestly orders—confer an "indelible sign" on the soul and cannot be repeated. The other four sacraments do not imprint such a sign and can therefore be repeated.

Luther's main target was the sacrament of priestly order, because it had become the cornerstone of medieval ecclesiocracy. Ultimately, he could accept only the sacrament of baptism as being necessary to salvation (LC IV, 6). Baptism alone contains God's unconditional promise to forgive sin, and it is the oldest sacrament in the church. The only other "sign" which should properly be called a sacrament is the Lord's Supper, instituted by Christ himself as a source of strength in this mortal life and as a bridge to the new life to be fully realized after death ("The Babylonian Captivity of the Church," 1520). Baptism ordains into priesthood. "For whoever comes out of the water of baptism can boast that he is already a consecrated priest, bishop and pope" ("To the Christian Nobility of the German Nation," 1520; LW 44, 129). There could be no compromise between Luther's doctrine of the common priesthood of all believers, grounded in the sacrament of baptism, and the Roman sacrament of priestly order. While the former reflected the fundamental article of faith, "justification by faith apart from works of law," the latter exhibited the height of human works-righteousness. In his theological testament (SA II, 2:1) Luther stated:

> The Mass, in the papacy, must be regarded as the greatest and most horrible abomination because it runs into direct and violent conflict with this fundamental article [of justification]. Yet, above and beyond all others, it has been the supreme and most precious of the papal idolatries, for it is held that this sacrifice, or work of the Mass (even when offered by an evil scoundrel), delivers men from their sins, both here in this life and yonder in purgatory, although in reality this can and must be done by the Lamb of God alone.

While "right-wing" Rome held Christendom captive with its materialistic sacramentology—salvation requires submission to the priest's indispensable dispensation of holy substance—the "left-wing" reformers introduced the tyranny of a spiritualistic view of the sacraments—the invisible word of the Holy Spirit must be substituted for the visible, bodily means of grace. Although Luther did not know many details of left-wing doctrine, he detected the basic weakness of that position. He argued, in his most elaborate treatise against the left-wingers ("Against the Heavenly Prophets," 1525) that they had a perverted view of God's order of salvation. They see God revealed in the inner man through the Holy Spirit, rather than in outward signs testifying to the incarnation of the Jesus of Nazareth. But "God has determined to give the inward to no one except through the outward" (LW 40, 146). Not even the confession of faith testifying to God's work within man may serve as the norm to determine the validity of baptism and the Lord's Supper. When certain groups began to teach "believers' baptism"—the doctrine that the validity of the sacrament is dependent on the human confession of faith—and thus eliminated infant baptism, since children cannot make such a confession, Luther forcefully argued that faith is never reliable enough to guarantee salvation. Consequently, Luther stated, it is safer to follow God's command to baptize, rather than worry about human response ("Concerning Re-Baptism," 1528). Concentration on human reaction to divine action usually leads to some sort of works-righteousness. The true believer trusts the unconditionality of God's promise and lets God be God.

Baptism

Lutheran sacramentology moves within the dialectic of "promise" and "faith": God made his word of promise visible in specific rites; and man participates in these rites by faith alone, without the condition of human merit. "The Word and the rite have the same effect, as Augustine said so well when he called the sacrament 'the visible word,' for the rite is received by the eyes and is a sort of picture of the Word, signifying the same thing as the Word" (AP 13:5).

Luther's Large Catechism of 1529 elaborates three basic features of a sacramentology centered in baptism: (1) A sacrament is "a holy, divine thing and sign," instituted by a word promising salvation independent of human merit (LC IV, 3–22). (2) Its specific purpose is to save man from sin, death, and the devil, and to establish man's eternal fellowship with the resurrected Christ (LC IV, 23–31). (3) The saving power of the sacrament is mediated by faith in the external word and sign (LC IV, 32–36). Infant baptism is the classic sacrament: it signifies the power of God's mandate rather than the human merit of faith (LC IV, 52–59); and it initiates a life of penance by which the "old Adam" is daily drowned and the "new Adam" is daily raised up (LC IV, 74–79, SC IV, 12). The entire Christian life is clothed in the garment of baptism—a penitential struggle between good and evil (LC IV, 84). The liturgy of infant baptism needs to express this struggle ("Order of Baptism," 1523).

In the Augsburg Confession, Melanchthon reaffirmed Luther's position that baptism is necessary for salvation, and condemned the Anabaptists for rejecting infant baptism (AC 9). Sacraments are "rites which have the command of God and to which the promise of grace has been added" as distinguished from "rites instituted by men" (AP 13:3). Consequently, there are only three genuine sacraments: baptism, the Lord's Supper, and absolution, which is the sacrament of penitence (AC 13:4). It is possible to call other rites "sacraments" if they are directly related to the word of promise, the gospel. Ordination, for example, could be interpreted in such a way, since it is related to the "ministry of the word" (AP 13:11–12). But the *use* rather than the *number* of sacraments is important (AP 13:18). They must be used in faith, for "a promise is useless unless faith accepts it" (AP 13:20).

Baptism itself was not at issue at Augsburg, but the relationship between baptism and penance was. How are *post-baptismal* sins forgiven? The medieval church taught that penance is achieved through a threefold process: "contrition of the heart," "oral confession"—a casuistic enumeration of sin, required by the Fourth Lateran Council in 1215—and "satisfaction in deed." The process of oral confession leads to the absolution from sin through the sacrament of penance, which is administered by the priest. Melanchthon rejected the three "parts" of the medieval sacrament of penance and affirmed only two, following Luther (LC V: "A Brief Exhortation to Confession"): contrition, understood to be the terror of conscience on account of sin, and faith, centered in the absolution of sins through the grace of Christ (AC 12). According to Melanchthon, "private confession" should remain a rite in the church, since it is an act of pastoral care to repentent sinners as well as an instrument of discipline against unrepentent ones (AC and AP 11). Consequently, penance reflects "the two chief works of God in men, to terrify and to justify and quicken the terrified. . . . One part is the law, which reveals, denounces, and condemns sin. The other part is the Gospel, that is, the promise of grace granted in Christ." (AP 12:53) Melanchthon accused the opposition of establishing legalistic conditions for the forgiveness of sin by making the enumeration of individual sins obligatory and thus making gospel into law (AP 12:172–73).

At Augsburg Melanchthon made the conciliatory move of accepting penance as a third sacrament along with baptism and the Lord's Supper (AP 13:4). Luther considered such a move, but could not live with it ("The Babylonian Captivity of the Church," 1520). But neither Melanchthon's appeal to Scripture and tradition nor his critical analysis of scholastic theological speculation changed the minds of the authors of the Roman Confutation. They could not accept a Lutheran sacramentology which regarded baptism rather than the priesthood as the royal sacrament in the church—in Luther's words:

> To appreciate and use Baptism aright, we must draw strength and comfort from it when our sins and conscience oppress us, and we must retort, "But I am baptized! And if I am baptized, I have the promise

that I shall be saved and have eternal life, both in soul and body." (LC IV, 44)

The Lord's Supper

"Baptism leads us into a new life on earth; the bread [the Lord's Supper] guides us through death into eternal life" (LW 35, 67). This laconic summation of the sacraments, offered to the laity by the young pastor-theologian Luther, was soon overshadowed by a prolific sacramentology, for the Wittenberg reformer had become embroiled in bitter controversies over the proper understanding of the Lord's Supper. But despite his lengthy polemical arguments with right-wing Roman scholastics (especially before 1525) and Huldreich Zwingli of Zurich (mainly after 1525), Luther consistently adhered to the basic position he sketched in the two catechisms of 1529 and stated confessionally in the Smalcald Articles of 1537.

According to Luther, the Lord's Supper, like baptism, is ordained by God in the historical Christ's word of promise (LC V, 1–7; SC VI, 1–4; SA III, 6:3). As "sacrament of the altar" the Lord's Supper is the true body and blood of Christ "in and under" the bread and wine (LC V, 8). Christ's true presence is guaranteed by the words of the institution rather than by man's worthiness, "even though a knave should receive or administer it" (LC V, 16; SA III, 6:1). The words "for you" and "for the forgiveness of sins" are the "chief thing in the sacrament" (SC VI, 8–10). Speculations as to *how* Christ is present only lead to "subtle sophistry"—such as the doctrine of concomitance and transubstantiation (SA III, 6:2–5). Luther saw the Lord's Supper as the event whereby God nourishes and strengthens his people, the church, in their daily struggle against sin, the world, and the devil (LC V, 24). No Christian can survive without it (LC V, 42). Every Christian needs it like daily bread. To wait until one feels "prepared," as some do in their anxiety to please God, is only the "old Adam's" temptation to collect merit for salvation. "If you choose to fix your eye on how good and pure you are, to work toward the time when nothing will prick your conscience, you will never go" (LC V, 57). Only people who are truly shameless and unruly should be excluded from the Lord's Supper, "since they do not desire it and do not want to be good" (LC V, 58). The Lord's Supper is the combat ration of the church struggling to do God's will in the world. "If you could see how many daggers, spears, and arrows are at every moment aimed at you, you would be glad to come to the sacrament as often as possible (LC V, 82). Even children should partake of the Lord's Supper, "for they must help us to believe, to love, to pray, and to fight the devil" (LC V, 87). In the sacrament of the altar, Christians not only remember Christ's sacrifice, his historicity, and anticipate his victorious return and his futurity, but also enjoy his "real presence" in bread and wine.

Luther, in his controversy with Rome, consistently stressed the pastoral significance of the Lord's Supper. "Communion" means to partake in the fellowship of those who cling to the word which promises forgiveness without human merit. The Lord's Supper is not just a *rite* guaranteeing grace when correctly performed by a priest (*ex opere operato*), but an *event* celebrating the existential relationship between God's word and man's faith. The word creates faith and faith in turn creates the fellowship of those who with grateful hearts celebrate new life with God. In short, the Lord's Supper is:

> a ford, a bride, a door, a ship, and a stretcher by which and in which we pass from this world into eternal life. Therefore everything depends on faith. He who does not believe is like the man who is supposed to cross the sea but is so timid that he does not trust the ship; and so he must remain and never be saved, because he will not embark and cross over. This is the fruit of our dependence on the senses of our untrained faith which shrinks from the passage across the Jordan of death; and the devil has a gruesome hand in it. (LW 35, 66)

The Roman mass lacks the mutuality of divine word and human faith. It limits intimate communion with God to priests by the practice of secret masses and the denial of the cup to the laity. Rome thus violates the true meaning of Christ's first mass, his last supper. Christ's last meal with his disciples was the new testament between the caring God of Israel and the descendants of sinful Adam; Christ, the testator, bequeathed remission of sins to Christians, the heirs of the testament. The true "sacrifice of the mass" is not the celebrating priest's good work offered to God, but man's response of praise and thanksgiving (*eucharistia* in Greek) to Christ's death on Calvary. Rome has made a mockery of Christ's testament.

> Just as the mass is not properly explained to men, but is understood as sacrifice and not testament, so, correspondingly, that which is and ought to be offered—namely the possessions of the churches and monas-

> tic houses—is never offered; neither are they given with thanksgiving to God and, with his blessing, to the needy who ought to be receiving them. This is why God is provoked to anger and permits the possessions of the churches and monastic houses to become the occasion of war, of worldly pomp, and of such abuse that no other blessing is so shamefully and blasphemously treated and destroyed. . . . What sacrifices, then, are we to offer? Ourselves, and all that we have, with constant prayer. . . . And although such a sacrifice occurs apart from the mass and should so occur, it is more precious, more appropriate, more mighty, and also more acceptable when it takes place with the multitude and in the assembly where men encourage, move, and inflame one another to press close to God and thereby attain without any doubt what they desire. (LW 35, 96–98)

When Luther fought the left-wing reformers and the Swiss faction led by Zwingli of Zurich, he emphasized the authority of God's word as against man's faith. Zwingli had argued that God is present through the Holy Spirit, which cannot be chained to the sacrament. The sacrament of the altar is the congregational rite whereby believers confess their faith before the God who saves without human merit. Moreover, "spirit" and "flesh," "spiritual" and "physical presence" are incompatible. For "it is the spirit that gives life, the flesh is of no avail" (John 6:63). Thus Zwingli rejected any "real presence" of Christ in the sacrament if "real" meant eating the body and drinking the blood of the Lord even if the recipient has no faith (*manducatio impiorum*, Luther called it). According to Zwingli the words "this *is* my body" really mean, "this *signifies* my body." The church *remembers* Christ's sacrifice on Calvary in the sacrament of the altar, and the individual members of the church publicly confess their commitment to the Lord when they participate in the meal. Zwingli and his followers maintained this position against Luther and a Wittenberg delegation at the Colloquy of Marburg in 1529. Luther declared that "*is*," in the biblical words of the institution of the Lord's Supper, meant the "real presence" of Christ: he is "ubiquitous" in the sense that he can be both "seated at the right hand of the father" (as the creed asserts) and in the bread and wine. The "real presence" is neither dependent upon human faith nor on the laws of physics. Thus Luther stuck to the authority of the word *that* Christ is really present in the Lord's Supper, while Zwingli (and later John Calvin) insisted on some explanation of *how* Christ could be present.

To Luther, the difference between the two positions was profound. He defended the mystery of God's incarnation in Jesus of Nazareth as an event to be adored rather than explained. The Swiss tried to explain the mystery, and ended up worshiping the power of human faith. "I would eat rotten apples or dried-up pears if God would place them before me," Luther told Zwingli in their colloquy at Marburg.

> Where the Word of God is, there is spiritual eating. Whenever God speaks to us, faith is required, and such faith means "eating." If, however, he adds bodily eating, we are bound to obey. In faith we eat this body which is given for us. The mouth receives the body of Christ, the soul believes the words when eating the body. . . . If we knew his [God's] ways, he who is marvelous would not be incomprehensible. (LW 38, 21–22).

Melanchthon was much more conciliatory toward Roman Catholics and other reformers than toward Luther. In the Augsburg Confession of 1530, he deliberately used "catholic" language. Luther's doctrine of the "real presence" is presented in German as presence "under the form of bread and wine," a phrase appearing in the Fourth Lateran Council's Latin version of the doctrine of transubstantiation; the Latin version of the Augsburg Confession avoids such language and speaks of the body and blood as "truly present" (*vere adsint,* AC 10). "We defend the doctrine received in the whole church that, in the Lord's Supper, the body and blood of Christ are truly and substantially present and are truly offered with those things that are seen, bread and wine" (AP 10:4).

But although Melanchthon stated Luther's position rather loyally in 1530, his concern for peace with the Swiss Protestants later drove him to theological formulations which earned him and his disciples the designation of "Crypto-Calvinist." By 1540, Melanchthon could speak of Christ's presence in the supper as "*with* bread and wine" (cum *pane et vino* [emphasis added], Altered AC 10), an interpretation which did not deny Calvin's position, known as *extra Calvinisticum,* "that because of the property of the human nature it is impossible for Christ to be present at the same time in more than one place, still less to be present with his body everywhere" (FC, EP 8:30). Some of Melanchthon's disciples injected casuistic speculations about the ubiquity of Christ into the Lutheran movement, and by 1571, Paul Crell, a Wittenberg theologian, posed these questions:

(1) When and how does the body of Christ come to the bread or into the bread?

(2) How near to, or how far away from the bread is it?

(3) How is it hidden under the bread?

(4) How long does the sacramental union last?

(5) When does the body of Christ leave the bread again?

(6) Does the body of Christ which we receive orally enter our body or stomach, and is it digested there?

(7) Is it crushed and chewed with the teeth?

(8) Is it a living body or a dead corpse, since we receive the body under the bread separately from the blood under the wine? (BC 591, n. 4)

When the Swiss, with some support from mediators like Martin Bucer in Strasbourg, united behind the *extra Calvinisticum* in the *Consensus Tigurinus* of 1551, Gnesio-Lutherans such as Joachim Westphal in Hamburg and John Timman in Bremen initiated a violent polemic against all "Crypto-Calvinists" which lasted for a decade (1552–62). Melanchthon's unwillingness to join in these crude polemics, which he called "the wrath of theologians," was interpreted as a betrayal of Luther, who had died in 1546. Melanchthon's death in 1561 made matters worse, since he had been the only cool head left above a sea of confusion over what should be truly "Lutheran."

In 1577 the Formula of Concord tried to settle the controversy over the Lord's Supper by using the formula "under, with, and in the bread" (FC, SD 7:35). Neither "transubstantiation" nor "consubstantiation"—the papistic error explaining Christ's presence in terms of "matter," and the humanistic mistake of seeing the presence of the Lord only in terms of "spirit"—are true Lutheran options. Christ is present *both* spiritually and bodily (FC, SD 7:61–65). This happens whenever Christ's command is obeyed in the liturgy of the Lord's Supper (FC, SD 7:75). The "sacramentarians" are wrong when they claim that Christ is present only internally, by faith, and that those who do not believe do not receive him. "Oral eating" (*manducatio oralis*) and "sacramental eating by the unworthy" (*manducatio impiorum*) are essential parts of the Lutheran doctrine of the Lord's Supper since they affirm the efficacy of the word (FC, EP 7:15, 37). "It is not our faith which makes the sacrament, but solely the Word and institution of our almighty God and Saviour, Jesus Christ, which always remain efficacious in Christendom and which are neither abrogated nor rendered impotent by either the worthiness or unworthiness of the minister or the unbelief of him who receives the sacrament" (FC, SD 7:89) Casuistic speculations, such as those of Paul Crell, are rejected as "presumptuous, scoffing, blasphemous, coarse, fleshly, and Capernaitic"; this is not the way to approach "the supernatural and heavenly mysteries of this Supper" (FC, SD 7:127).

Questions about the "real presence" of Christ in the Lord's Supper are questions about Christology: the person of Christ, the two natures of Christ and their properties (FC, EP 8:1). Indeed, what is at stake is the foremost of all Christian articles of faith: the dogma of the triune God.

B.

The Embodiment of the Gospel

What the Lutheran Reformation says about sacraments follows directly from its doctrine of justification. The basic position is that since the spoken word of the gospel unconditionally grants what God has to give, there can be no rival institutions of grace; if the sacraments justify (or do something else godly), this blessing must be worked by the word. As the Small Catechism says about baptism, "it is not the water alone that does such great things, but the Word of God with the water. . . ."

Therefore Lutheran sacramental teaching is in the first place polemic. As we will see, "word" and "sacraments" are fundamentally but two inseparable aspects of the one event that Reformation theology calls "*the* Word." But considered as religious phenomena, there is this difference between them: the performances we call "sacraments" are more *obviously* something *we* do than are verbal words; they are more directly to be grasped as religious works of the believers. It would be difficult to suppose that we were justified by the preacher's work at getting his point made; but it is easy to suppose that we are justified by attending the eucharist, or by reciting our sins in confession. Our impulse to works-righteousness, seeking to find security in our religiousness, therefore regularly seeks to separate the gospel-promises from the sacraments, in order to claim the sacraments as its own. Lutheran sacramental doctrine is first of all an attack in advance on any doctrine or practice that makes sacraments and the gospel-promise rivals to each other.

Medieval doctrine tended to make sacraments not only rivals but superiors of the word. Medieval doctrine described the sacraments as the actual events of "grace," of God's affirmative presence to us, and regarded preaching, teaching, and the like as the communication of information *about* them. The usual "catholic" viewpoints still show the same tendency. But thereby the word of promise necessarily becomes conditional: "If you will betake yourself to the sacramental event (mass, penance—or group event), you will there find God's blessing." The word becomes directions about what is to be done sacramentally, and insofar as it remains at all promise, necessarily becomes promise conditional on so doing. It was this conception of the relation between word and sacrament that the reformers saw sloganized in the medieval teaching that the sacraments work *ex opere operato*, just because they are done, and insofar independently of the word of the gospel and the possible gospel-meanings of the act. The particular works-justification posited in this conception was the initial target of Reformation polemic.

One way to reject the medieval conception would be simply to reverse it: to praise the word as the real event of grace and devalue sacraments to the level of accompanying ceremonies or gestures of response. All that part of Protestantism that came from Zwingli or the spiritualists made this move; and it has remained popular. But this could not be the Lutheran move, not only because the Lutherans were conservative about the tradition, but because it involves a conception of the gospel-word itself utterly opposed to theirs.

Justification by my own righteousness is overcome only by a word that both declares my justification and is clearly and permanently not my own word. Justification by faith can only be opened by a word addressed *to* me, from outside of me. The gospel is intrinsically an "external" word; it is a word with a home out there in the world that stands against my subjectivity, and that is to say, out there in the world of objects, of bodies and places for bodies. It is, therefore, intrinsically a word "with" a body, with an undetachable nonverbal or more-than-verbal manifestation: a word "with" a bath or a meal or a finger-sign. Thus in baptism it is indeed the spoken promise of a new and pure life that washes the heart; but this promise maintains the externality by which it can be promise of *new* life, of life different from what is already in me, by being a word also about that tub of water over there and about what this other person here therewith does to my body.

Words that are mere words, that could in principle get along without objects and bodily performances, are too mental to open the righteousness of faith. If all the word of promise does is convey the *information* that, let us say, Jesus lives, then once that information is in my head, I can forget the way I learned it. Then the bit of knowledge becomes my knowledge, that I can henceforth tell myself—and if hearing it justifies, I can justify myself. Thus the word that Jesus lives does not occur as a mere conveyance of information, but as a word that includes such addresses as, "This piece of bread is the living Jesus; take it," thereby pinning me each time anew to what does not come from me, but is out there in the world and comes to me from it. In the estimate of the Lutheran reformers, however earnestly Zwingli and those like him set out to praise the justification brought by the gospel, their "spiritual" understanding of the gospel-event invariably perverted that praise into praise of our faith and into talk of the interior conditions we must fulfill.

Visible Words

Therefore the Lutherans prevented rivalry between word and sacrament by a move quite different from that of Zwingli and the spiritualists: the Lutherans interpreted the sacraments as *themselves* "words," as themselves communication-events. Augustine had defined a sacrament as a "visible word," and this definition had become standard in the medieval tradition; the Lutherans adapted it to their purpose. A sacramental act, *as a whole event*, just *is* a word, a mutual address of those involved, an event that says something—which something is, of course, to be the gospel.

Lutheran teaching about the sacraments merely specifies Lutheran teaching about the gospel, for this form of it. This view has three immediate corollaries, the understanding of which is vital for understanding the way the Lutheran confessions talk about sacraments.

First, the critical question about any performance intended to be sacramental performance of the gospel is the same as about an utterance intended to be verbalization of the gospel: What in fact gets said? About all verbalizations in the church the Lutheran movement exists to ask, Is it really the gospel that is being spoken? Just so the Lutheran movement exists to ask about performances in the church: Is the gospel really being enacted?

It was in pursuit of this question that the Lutheran reformers conducted their polemic against the "abomination" of the medieval mass. No doubt many medieval theologians gave *explanations* of the mass that are quite acceptable, or not worth dividing the church about. But what was actually done in the services, to the very architecture and prayer-book instructions, said clearly: "The church makes atonement here, the benefits of which you may have on fulfillment of certain conditions." So also the objection to the "sacrifice" of the mass was not to every use of the concept in theology of the mass, but to a *practice* of the mass that made it our work to placate God.

Insofar as the Lutheran movement still lives, this must still be its question. And if we look at the sacramental practices of contemporary congregations and denominations, including those called "Lutheran," we will find that occasions of the question have not diminished. When the heart of the service consists of the briefest possible "consecration"—an incantation of the "words of institution" with minimal accompanying prayers or remarks, followed by a procession of individuals to the altar, what does this say to those who participate? Not the gospel-promise, surely! Or when, bidden by Scripture to share the cup of blessing, we return to the medieval withholding of the cup from the "laity," distributing private little glasses instead? Or when, having baptized infants, we do not admit them to the community's chief gathering until they have qualified by such-and-such achievements of understanding or maturity? The last question cuts back also at the practice of Lutherans of the confession-making period, which is just what the Lutheran question should do.

Second, within the total enactment that is a sacramental event, verbal utterances must on this view retain a certain primacy. A sacrament is sacrament in that it—in its own irreplaceable way—says something; and to say something is always to say something specific. The specificity of the gospel is a historical specificity; the gospel is a word about the historical individual Jesus. But a dramatic enactment stripped of all discursive language can say nothing historically specific. A meal shared in silence could not be the Lord's Supper, for it would not specify itself as anybody's supper in particular. Nor will it help that specifying propositions are on other occasions made about the meal, or that participants carry them in their minds; for a sacrament is sacrament in that it, as a particular event, says the specific gospel-something. To sacrament, incorporated speech is therefore essential, language the uttering of which is part of the performance itself. Thus the verbal remembrance of Jesus is part of the action that is the eucharist itself; it is part of the act that obeys "Do this," just as the eating of bread or drinking of wine.

Third, just as the word of God is in general both law and gospel, so the word that establishes a sacrament is both command and promise. Thus the apostolic missionary command includes, "Wash your neophytes with invocation of Jesus' name," and this mandate establishes baptism. It is obedience to such commands that provides the referents of the sacramental promises by which the gospel establishes itself as a visible, embodied communication.

What Sacraments Are There?

Given the sort of communication-event the gospel is, it can be argued a priori that there must be some more-than-verbal speakings of the gospel. But what performances we in fact have, out of endless possibilities, is historically contingent. If the church had begun in the Sahara, initiation into it would not be by washing. Since the gospel is historically specific, this historical contingency is appropriate to it.

The Lutheran Reformation radically affirmed the historically specific gospel-message as the sole locus of God's gift; therefore it also radically affirmed the historical contingency of the sacraments. The confessions attempt no argument as to why, for example, the central performance should be a meal, or ordination be done by laying-on of hands. They simply register that the tradition which brings the gospel says "Do this" about a variety of performances. Some of these commands are spoken by the canonical strata of the tradition, in disobedience to which there can be no speaking of the gospel; these we simply obey. Others come from the fathers or councils or custom; upon these we should reflect critically. So also, the Lutheran confessions refrain from speculating about, for example, whether it would "have to" be bread and a cup of wine that communicated the fellowship of Christ's body. If we share bread and the cup, giving thanks to God for his blessings and especially for Jesus, we obey Scripture's command—and theological reflection about such matters as "the real presence" is reflection about the promises that refer to this event. If we do not share bread and a cup with such thanksgiving, we disobey the command, which is great sin—and the sacramental promises lack a referrent.

For the same reason, the Lutheran confessions make little fuss about how many sacraments there are—they are not even quite consistent on the matter. There are a great many enactings of the gospel that may rightly be practiced in the church; which of these you call "sacraments" depends on why and so where you want to draw a line. The Reformers did not always draw the same line. Their primary concerns were to eliminate altogether certain performances that were, in their view, not of the gospel, and to see that among those remaining those with canonical authority retained the special trust they deserved.

"Real Presence"

A mark of confessional Lutheranism is its insistence on the "real presence" of Christ in the Supper, and on its analogues in the other sacraments. The Lutheran confessions' discussions of these matters have a complicated background, and are done in an Aristotelian conceptual framework which sometimes obscures their point. The main thing to remember is that what Lutheranism says about sacraments is always a specification of what it says about the gospel-communication-event in general. About the gospel, the doctrine of justification claims that the gospel does what it says; about each sacrament Lutheranism makes the same point in a way appropriate to that sacrament as a particular embodiment of some part of the gospel.

If the gospel is an unconditional promise, three things follow. First, the gospel promises personal communion. The only thing that can be promised unconditionally is the promiser's own love. However it may be possible to explicate the content of the gospel, in political or cosmic or other terms, its shortest form must be: "I will give myself." Second, this promise grants a present reality. If I promise you something other than myself, you may for the present still lack that something. Or if I promise you myself, but conditionally, we may for the present lack community. But if I could unconditionally promise you myself, the making of the promise would itself be an act of self-giving, and your hearing of it an experience of communion. Third, the subject of the gospel-promise is the risen Jesus himself; it cannot be the momentary witness who speaks in his name. For the witness, with death still before him, does not have his future unconditionally, and so cannot promise anything unconditionally. Either the promise is false, or Jesus is the subject of it.

If we put these three propositions together, we have: The speaking of the gospel is the event of Jesus' own giving of himself into communion with the hearers thereof. *The event of gospel-speaking is the event of the risen Jesus' personal presence to those who hear.*

Next step: a disembodied person, a "Jesus" whose presence was a merely "spiritual" presence in our "inner" selves, would be, for Lutheranism, no person at all; for the doctrine of justification defines personhood as being-in-communication, and also insists, as we have just seen, that all gospel-communication is embodied. Indeed, the urgency is even more deeply theological. If Jesus is the presence of God, a disembodied presence of Jesus would be a disembodied presence of God: a "naked," sheer presence of God, a presence not mediated by human speakers and human words—and it was Luther's first and fundamental experience that such a presence of God can only mean death.

If the Lord is present as the speaking of the gospel, his presence is, therefore, embodied. Which is to say, the bodies that belong to gospel-speaking—the bread and wine and water and even the signs and gestures and our mere physical visibility and tangibility to each other—are the present body of the present Lord. This is the basic Lutheran affirmation of Christ's "bodily" presence in the sacramental life of the church. The affirmation is not that somewhere or other there is an object, the body of the risen Christ, and that there are also the objects involved in the gospel-event, and that somehow the one gets into the others. The confessional writers' Aristotelian substance-language made it hard for them always to avoid such ways of speaking; they break through their language by heaping up incompatible prepositions: "in," "with," "under." Their aim is, we suggest, a very simple affirmation: If what happens in the believing community is Jesus' presence, then the body-side of what happens there is the body-side of Jesus' presence.

The Lord's body-presence is variously modulated in the various sacraments, and is in each case identical with a specific soteriological meaning of the sacrament. That I once inwardly heard the gospel and first believed it is an endlessly ambiguous matter of interpretation that will become uncertain whenever I most need to be sure of it. But the bath of baptism is a physical fact as unexpungeable from my biography as the breaking of a leg; and if this bath was the Lord's reception of me, that reception can be recalled and known and rested upon in times of doubt. Inner repentance and the remembered truth of forgiveness are complicated and dubious matters. The sound of the confessor's voice and his hand on my head, are not; and they are the address and pressure of the Lord. The confessions will speak of a "sacrament," in this sense, wherever they find biblical warrant for such assertions.

"This Is My Body"

The content of the Supper's biblical warrant—"This is my body; this cup is my covenant"—draws special attention to this sacrament's body-side; and around this centered the sacramental controversies of the Reformation period. The Lutherans insisted that Christ is present by the bread and cup in a way that is not merely different from his embodied presence in other speakings of the gospel, but is, as it were, more bodily. They drew the distinction so: only in the Supper is he received "orally," by eating and drinking. This reception is, in the Reformers' discourse, the reception of a more specifically bodily presence than reception by one of the senses merely. The distinction is profound; but it could be worked out in ways that would violate the basic Lutheran understanding of sacraments as visible *words*, and is, in fact, almost always so worked out in the piety of our congregations.

Perhaps we may understand the matter so, and be faithful to the old Lutherans. Gospel-speaking, we have seen, must be embodied to be authentic. That the gospel *is* embodied, is, therefore, part of what the gospel itself must say, in claiming our lives absolutely and so claiming its own truth and authenticity. "See, I—the whole real I, body and spirit—am with you," is an essential utterance of the gospel. And it is this assertion of the gospel's embodiment for us that is the particular aspect of the gospel that is itself specifically embodied in the distribution and physical taking of bread and the cup. The gospel's assertion of its own necessary embodiment is here itself embodied.

The confessional writers understand the canonical "Take, eat, this is my body," and the parallel words about the cup, as addressed not merely to members of the primitive church, but to us. When we obey the commands, an eating and drinking occur to which something is promised: that they shall be reception of the Lord. In that, and if this promise is true, the bread and wine that are *to be* eaten and drunk *are* the Lord's reality promised to that eating and drinking. And since the promise is the word of God, no further justification is required for the sacramental "is."

We may understand it so, as Luther did: of course it is faith that receives the Lord, and if the symbol is of eating and drinking, we must say that it is faith that "devours" the Lord. But faith devours the Lord in that it is the hearing of the gospel-word; and the particular gospel-word in question says, of bread and a cup, "Consume these, they are the coming of the Lord." How do we believe *this* word? Obviously, by consuming. Thus in this case the act of faith and the act of the mouth and gullet are one act; and just so the Christ devoured by faith and the food and drink devoured by the mouth are one reality.

With this way of thinking, the medieval explanation of "This is my body" is rejected in advance. The Lutheran reasoning begins with Jesus' personal presence as the truth of the word, and moves *from* there to the sacramental identification of the objects bread/wine and Jesus' body; whereas the medieval reasoning begins with an identity of the objects, worked by a fiat of divine omnipotence, and establishes thereon the Lord's personal presence. For the medieval church, the bodily presence of Christ in the elements is directly worked by a ritual consecration, and brings with it his personal presence; for the Lutherans, the personal presence of Christ in the gospel necessarily includes his bodily presence, which is, by a particular promise of the gospel, localized as the elements.

In medieval teaching, the churchly hierarchy is the agency of the divine sacramental fiat; ordination authorizes the priest to call on God to work the miracle named by "This is my body." In Reformation teaching, no such fiat of divine omnipotence occurs, and therefore no authorized agents thereof are needed. Here is the fundamental break with the medieval understanding of church and ministry.

Lutherans Versus Calvinists

A slight modification of the Lutheran propositions gives quite another sort of Reformation doctrine. The Western philosophical and theological tradition had separated "spiritual" and "material" reality in a way that makes it impossible to talk of believing with the mouth, or of Christ's personal presence necessarily including his bodily presence. Lutheran sacramental teaching implied a rejection of traditional metaphysics at this point; the Calvinists regarded such a move as a rejection of reason itself, and modified Lutheran sacramental teaching to avoid it. Yet they wished to assert with the tradition that our communion with the Lord includes bodily communion; and they wished to avoid the medieval explanation. They found a way to satisfy all three interests.

Calvinists taught that Christ comes spiritually to the soul by the word of the gospel. Within the gospel-event, the bread and wine have no role christologically different from the role of other, audible words; they are "symbols," material adaptations of the gospel message to the material conditions of our perception. Christ's spiritual presence does not necessarily involve his bodily presence; the latter remains, as is proper to a body, at one place at one time, now "with the Father" to whom he ascended. Our communion with Christ can nevertheless be bodily, because of the space- and time-transcending character of spiritual realities; stirred to faith by Christ's spiritual presence in the words and symbols, our souls are carried to God, there to receive the blessing also of his bodily self-giving. Since the bread and wine, as symbols, mean the body and blood of the Lord, and since the faith in which that meaning terminates is indeed a reception also of his true bodily presence, the bread and wine can truly be said to "be" his body and blood.

So far so good, apparently: the Reformation point is made without radical conflict with the philosophical tradition. But according to this teaching, Christ gives himself into bodily communion only with those who in fact are moved to faith by the symbolic bread and wine. The Lutherans objected that this does the same thing to the visible word that medieval doctrine did to the audible word: if these propositions enter the reflection that is internal to someone's experience of the sacrament, the gift of the sacrament must become conditional for him. To know if the gift is there, I must know if I believe it is there—which makes faith a condition and a work, and must also generate an endless dialectic. The "eating by the unbelievers," affirmed by the Lutherans and denied by the Calvinists, became and remained the main point by which the two movements divided.

The difference between Lutheran and Calvinist teaching is that what Lutheranism attributes to the word that is spoken, Calvinism attributes to the faith that hears. The matter can also be stated christologically;

and this is how it appears in the Formula of Concord. That the risen Christ, by his trinitarian inclusion in God, can be present "spiritually" to believers of all times and places was confessed by all parties. But are flesh and spirit, the man Jesus and God the Son, *so* united in Christ that his spiritual presence simply includes and brings with it his embodied presence? The Romans said no, and posited the power of the church to bring Christ's humanity to the altars. The Calvinists said no, and posited the power of faith to bring the communicants to Christ's humanity. The Lutherans said yes, and needed no such powers—but thereby they opened the christological problematic discussed in the next chapter, and were driven to christological propositions that openly offend the whole Western metaphysical tradition.

Chapter 7

Christology—God Deep in the Flesh

Readings:
SC and LC II, 2
SA I
AC and AP 1, 3, 17
FC 8–9

A.

The Ancient Christology

The Lutheran Reformation's christological discussions, including that in the confessions, used the language of the traditional Christology inherited from the ancient church. This language had three pivotal words: "nature," "hypostasis," and "communion." On this subject, it is necessary to reach beyond the normal limit of this book and give some explanation of this ancient terminology and of the traditional assertions made with it.

A "nature," in the traditional language, is an "essence" in action. About any real thing an indefinitely long list of true assertions can be made: of the author of this paragraph it can be asserted that "Jenson is brown-haired," "Jenson is mammalian," "Jenson is lazy," etc. Of these assertions some are "inessential," in that they could cease to be true without their subject losing identity: Jenson could cease to be brown-haired without ceasing to be Jenson. Others are "essential": an other-than-mammalian Jenson would be nothing at all. The "nature" of a thing is the complex of its essential attributes, insofar as this is an actual teleology, the complex of reasons why the thing behaves as it does.

Thus, "human nature" is the set of characteristics a man or woman must retain in order plausibly to be still regarded as human, and insofar as these are reasons of his or her actions and fate. God's "divine nature" is the set of characteristics by virtue of which we call him "God," and insofar as these give some understanding of his creative and saving work. It is obvious that there are great difficulties in using the "nature" concept of God, but these do not yet concern us.

The Christology of Nicaea (325 A.D.) and Chalcedon (451 A.D.) asserted that Christ has both a human nature and the divine nature, and both entire. That is, Christ is whatever Jesus of Nazareth must be to be this particular human; and he is whatever God the Son is to be God. The two sets of propositions predicating these characteristics of him together state the context of goals and reasons within which his deeds and sufferings can be understood. The Christology of Nicaea and Chalcedon also asserted that this simultaneity of a human nature and the divine nature in Christ in no way mixes the two together. Neither is Christ a little bit of both, so as to be almost and not quite either God or man; nor do semi-divine characters, blending divine and human characters, arise.

If, in Christ, God and man do not mix, how are they one? The Greek theologians of the ancient church answered this question by means of the word "hypostasis." The divine nature and the human nature were said to be one in Christ in that they are the same "hypostasis"; the hypostasis of God the Son became the hypostatic reality also of the man Jesus.

"Hypostasis" became equated with the Latin "persona," which was later anglicized as "person"; both steps can be misleading. Most of what "person" means in modern usage belongs rather to "nature" in christological language: being "personal," as contrasted with being a "thing," belongs to both "human nature" and "divine nature." We will therefore use the Greek word.

Ancient Christology's "hypostasis" may be explicated by our word "identity." If "hypostasis" is detached from associated explanations of what *makes* a hypostasis, it covers much the same functions as "identity"; and just this separation is what happened when the ancient church adapted "hypostasis" from its previous philosophical and mythological uses. There are at least three functions common to the old christological "hypostasis" and the modern "identity"; the first two were covered also by prechristological use of "hypostasis" in late-antique philosophy, the third emerged only in the history of the christological use itself.

First, a thing's identity is its *identifiability*, the possibility of picking it out from the maelstrom of actuality, so as to be able to make assertions about it. The enumerability of the world—whereby we can say "this thing . . . and then this thing . . . and then this thing . . ." is one of its deepest ontological characteristics. The same characteristic, as a characteristic of each such "this thing," is that thing's identity—the Greeks said, its "hypostasis." We identify in three ways; the most fundamental is perhaps the pointing gesture that must accompany "this." But most often we cannot point. We then have two linguistic resources. We use proper names: in the sentence "Jones is a bounder," the word "Jones" serves to pick out which item of actuality we wish to make the subject of ". . . is a bounder." Sometimes a proper name will not work—suppose I say "Jones is a bounder" and you do not know who Jones is. Then, and often for other reasons as well, we use identifying descriptions: "the one who worked at Macy's, sang baritone in St. Mary's choir . . . ," continuing with such "who" clauses until the identification succeeds.

That God the Son and a man are one hypostasis in Christ thus means, first, that when we identify the one we identify the other. If we "point" to the man Jesus, with that proper name or with such descriptions as "the one crucified under Pontius Pilate," we thereby point to God the Son, and vice versa. The heart of the matter is that if a Christian is asked to identify his God, to say which reality it is that he worships, his proper answer is, "Whoever or whatever raised Jesus the Nazarene from the dead." There are many claimants to the Godhead; Christians have to identify which claimant they believe in by descriptions formed from the same narrative material from which would be formed the identifying descriptions of the man Jesus. Jesus' identifiability is this God's identifiability; any reality is somehow identifiable; *so* are God and man one reality in Christ. That this identity of identifiability is not a mere mask put on for us, as the theologians of ancient Antioch were suspected of thinking, can be assured by stipulating that also *God* identifies himself by Jesus.

Second, to identify something is also to identify it *as* something otherwise known and identifiable, and necessarily on some other occasion (this is connected to the first; nothing could be identifiable if some things were not reidentifiable). I identify Jones as the Macy's clerk we already know. Thus, in this use, something's identity is its self-continuity through some palpable stretch of time; I "retain my identity" in that I am somehow or other the same now as I was. The Greek "hypostasis" was a word for that somehow-or-other. We may say that something's hypostasis is its capacity to be described by narrative: "It was green, and then it was brown, and I suppose it will be purple next." The hypostasis is the possibility of the repeated "it."

That God the Son and a man are one hypostasis in Christ thus means that they have one capacity for being narratively describable, that any sequence of events predicable of one must be formulable as predicated of the other. If "Jesus died" is a true assertion, then, so and only so, is "God the Son died." If "God the Son shares the Father's universal rule" is a true assertion, then so, and only so, is "The man Jesus shares the Father's universal rule." Indeed, the historical development was from the other way around: the pervasive presence in the New Testament of such God-narrative with Jesus as subject was a principal reason for working out the doctrine of the one hypostasis.

Third, "identity" is now often used to interpret personal existence in a particular way: as we say that someone is "seeking his identity." This sense is connected to the other two: this "identity" is the mode of self-continuity through time proper to certain things, those we call "persons." As person, I am what I am only in that I have been what I have been; and this persistence of the past is not only causation and material reidentifiability, it is memory and interpretation. As person, I am what I am only in that I will be what I will be; and this anticipation of the future is choice and dream and fear and hope. If Jones is a person, the "is" in "Jones is lazy" is not a normal copula; it is something like a transitive verb, the word for an *act* of positing oneself in and through time, of being what one is not yet, and of relating to what one already is. The modern existentialist tradition has invented words like "existence" or "*Dasein*" for this act. In its prechristological use, "hypostasis" did not have this sense; but in the often tortured ways in which the christological tradition went on to use "hypostasis," just this sense for the peculiar identity proper to person-realities struggled for expression.

That God the Son and a man are one hypostasis in Christ thus means that the time-positing act in which God the Son is himself, and the time-positing act in which Jesus is himself, are one occurrence. In all Jesus' deeds as a man, he does the one deed of being Jesus. In all God's deeds as the Son, he does the one deed of being God the Son. These two deeds are one event, specifiable by us with the historical reminiscence "Crucifixion and Resurrection." God *happens for us* as Jesus' act of existing.

Finally, "communion." The christological tradition uses the word to make a variety of christological points, many of which we have already noted. Most of the previous discussion of the oneness of God and man in the "hypostatic union" was stipulation of what is to be said and not said about Christ. God is identified by descriptions that are also about Jesus, we are to assert "God the Son died," etc. But if the stipulated kinds of assertions are *true*, something is going on between God and man in Christ for which "communion" or "sharing" is a very reasonable word.

The tradition speaks of a "communion of natures" and a "communion of attributes." The point of the first expression should be clear. The second refers to the way in which the allowed and demanded christological language posits a sort of sharing of the characteristics by which the two natures are defined: thus "God the Son died" predicates mortality, a defining character of human nature, of God the Son, and "Jesus sits at the right hand of the Father" predicates universal rule, a defining character of the divine nature, of the man Jesus. Theological reflection worked out elaborate and subtle interpretations of, and restrictions on, this cross-predication; some of these became important for the Lutheran innovations.

Luther's Reinterpretation

Luther unhesitatingly accepted the christological affirmations of the Greek fathers as "articles [which] are not matters of dispute or contention" in the controversy with Rome (SA I). He published expositions of the Nicene, Athanasian, and Apostles' creeds in 1538; and he worked his way through almost all the available sources dealing with the christological controversies in the first four centuries ("On the Councils and the Church," 1539). Luther was also quite familiar with the traditional differences between the Greek and Latin theologians who wrestled with the mystery of God's incarnation in Christ. While the ancient Greek Christology was moved by the quest for divine immortality and envisaged Christ as its mediator, Latin medieval theologians struggled with the question of how man could be freed from the power of sin. Consequently, theologians such as Anselm, Abelard, and Thomas Aquinas elaborated "theories of satisfaction" dealing with the life, death, and resurrection of Christ.

These theories, as well as the entire body of scholastic theology, became the sources for Luther's intense *Anfechtung* during his stay in the monastery. He no longer sought just God's immortal life or the power of His satisfying grace. Instead, the struggling friar asked for "God's Godness," for His heart, for what makes God God. He found the answer in the liberating "tower experience," while studying Paul: God discloses his "hypostasis" in the "person" of Jesus Christ. God is the one who "justifies the ungodly." To know Christ, therefore, means to know "the cheerful exchange" of death for life. The exchange is the true mystery of the relationship between Christ and his church (Eph. 5:31–32). As Luther put it in his treatise "The Freedom of a Christian" in 1520:

> Here we have a most pleasing vision [Eph. 5:31–32] not only of communion but of a blessed struggle and victory and salvation and redemption. Christ is God and man in one person. He has neither sinned, nor died, and is not condemned, and he cannot sin, die or be condemned; his righteousness, life, and salvation are unconquerable, eternal, omnipotent. By the wedding ring of faith he shares in the sins, death, and pains of hell which are his bride's. As a matter of fact, he makes them his own and acts as if they were his own, and as if he himself had sinned; he suffered, died, and descended into hell that he might overcome them all. Now, since it was such a one who did all this, and death and hell could not swallow him up, these were necessarily swallowed up by him in a mighty duel; for his righteousness is greater than all the sins of men, his life is stronger than death, his salvation more invincible than hell. Thus the believing soul, by means of its faith, is free in Christ, its bridegroom, free from all sins, secure against death and hell, and is endowed with eternal righteousness, life, and salvation of Christ its bridegroom. (LW 31, 351–52)

Thus Luther existentialized the ancient Greek and Latin dogmatic formulae for the two natures of Christ, which had been stated in terms of "interpenetration" (*perichoresis* in Greek) or "communication" of the "properties" of the two natures (*communicatio idiomatum* in

Latin). The second article of the trinitarian creed means that God "has completely given himself to us, withholding nothing" (LC II, 26). Jesus Christ "is *my* Lord, who has redeemed *me* . . . not with silver and gold but with his holy and precious blood and with his innocent sufferings and death, in order that *I* may be *his*" (SC II, 4). So Luther could affirm with the tradition that Christ: (1) satisfies, not because of man's ability but because God *wanted* to save man; (2) overcomes the powers of sin, death, and evil; and (3) is present already in the "word" here on earth, pointing to the end-time when sin, death, and evil shall be no more.

Luther united Pauline and Johannine thought: God is the god who justifies the ungodly (Rom. 4:5), and "I and the Father are one" (John 10:30). "St. John and St. Paul bind Christ and the Father so to each other that one learns to think of God only in Christ" (WA 45, 519:22). In Christ we can see the height of divine majesty as well as the depth of human suffering. The mystery of the incarnation can only be expressed in paradoxical language. Luther, therefore, did not develop a properly systematic Christology. He only asserted, again and again, that God's "work" in Christ—His "proper work" of salvation, as over against his "strange work" of creation—is present in word and in faith. "The first and chief article is this, that Jesus Christ, our God and Lord, 'was put to death for our trespasses and raised again for our justification' (Rom. 4:25). . . . Inasmuch as this must be believed and cannot be obtained or apprehended by any work, law, or merit, it is clear and certain that such faith alone justifies us. . . . (Rom. 3:28)" (SA II, 1:4, 4).

The Lutheran-Reformed Discord

In the Augsburg Confession Melanchthon repeated the ancient christological confessions, using traditional metaphysical language to demonstrate agreement with the catholic tradition (AC, AP 3) and disagreement with Anabaptist universalists and millennialists who denied the traditional doctrine of Christ's return as judge (AC, AP 17). But after 1530 he softened Luther's doctrine of the ubiquity of Christ in his effort to unite Protestants. Philippists, therefore, felt quite comfortable about supporting the *extra Calvinisticum* during their negotiations with the Zwinglian-Calvinist wing of the Reformation.

The "Crypto-Calvinist" interpretation of the Lord's Supper led to christological controversies between Gnesio-Lutherans and Philippists in Saxony, Wuerttemberg, and the Palatinate. At issue was the proper interpretation of the "communication of properties of the two natures of Christ (*communicatio idiomatum*), specifically the question of whether "the divine and human natures, together with their properties, *really* (that is, in deed and truth) share with each other, and how far does this sharing extend?" (FC, EP 8:2). Some Philippists tended to view the assertions of the *communicatio idiomatum* as figures of speech, in order to preserve the independent realities of each nature, a position Calvin strongly defended (Inst. II, 14:1; FC, EP 8:3). Gnesio-Lutherans stressed the real interpenetration of Christ's human and divine natures, a position Luther had strongly defended against Zwingli.

Two theologians tried to preserve Lutheran unity during the heated controversy: John Brenz (1499–1570), one of Luther's close friends and the architect of the Swabian reformation; and Martin Chemnitz (1522–86), Melanchthon's close friend and a leading churchman from Braunschweig. Brenz signed Luther's Smalcald Articles (BC 317); Chemnitz' signature appears among the drafters of the Formula of Concord (BC 636).

Brenz argued his Christology in two major treatises: "On the Personal Union of the Two Natures in Christ" (*De personali unione duarum naturarum in Christo,* 1561), and "On the Divine Majesty of Our Lord Jesus Christ" (*De divina maiestate domini nostri Iesu Christi,* 1562). His argumentation is based on the Chalcedonian creed, which affirms that the two natures are united in one person, and on Luther's doctrine of the eucharist, which asserts that the full person of Christ is present in the Lord's Supper. Concerning the "real presence" of the two natures in one person, Brenz argued that if one understood the body of Christ in terms of "substance" its ubiquity can be explained in terms of (1) locality (*localis,* an "accidens" of local extension), (2) repletion (*repletiva,* an "accidens" belonging to divinity), and (3) personhood (*personalis,* an "accidens" derived from the personal union of the two natures). There is, then, a ubiquity of two "substances," one human and the other divine, with "accidental" features belonging to both. If the *communicatio idiomatum* is understood as the interpenetration of two substances, the Gnesio-Lutheran and Philippist positions are transcended: we can assert the presence of Christ in the Lord's Supper without worrying about his bodily "real" presence in either the eucharistic elements (as the Gnesio-Lutherans did) or in heaven (as the Philippists did). The humility of the earthly Jesus, as well as the majesty of the risen Lord, can be affirmed in the doctrines of the incarnation and the eucharist.

Although a number of Gnesio-Lutherans and Philippists were persuaded by Brenz' argumentation (including the highly influential Tuebingen theologian and author of the Swabian Concord of 1574, Jacob Andreae), the 1564 Colloquy of Maulbronn did not produce unity. It did, however, remove much of the polemic sting from the controversy and prepared the way for FC 8.

Chemnitz' Christology, expounded in "The Two Natures of Christ" (*De duabus naturis in Christo*, 1571), emphasized "energy" rather than "substance" in its attempt to explicate the Chalcedonian formulae. Chemnitz described the *communicatio idiomatum* in terms of a "true and real" penetration of the human nature by the divine nature, just as iron is brought to glow by fire. The fire is the divine "logos" and the iron is the "soul" of Jesus who revealed God's love for the world. There is, then, a complete and concrete "interpenetration" (*perichoresis*) of the divine and human in the God-man Jesus, willed and realized by God. The union of the two natures, therefore, is to be conceived as a union of willed existence, rather than as a union of "substances." Thus the "real presence" of Christ in the Lord's Supper is based upon the power of the God-man to be present wherever and however he will: he can be simultaneously in heaven and on earth.

Chemnitz summarized his christological speculations in a trinitarian doctrine of the *communicatio idiomatum*: (1) the properties of each of the two natures are to be ascribed to the whole person; (2) the whole person, rather than just one of the two natures, effects salvation; and (3) the human nature participates fully in the work of the divine. The Formula of Concord and later Lutheran systematic theology adopted this summary by speaking of (1) *genus idiomaticum*–"*to ascribe to the entire person what is the property of one nature*" (FC, SD 8:38); (2) *genus apotelesmaticum*—"the person does not act *in, with, through,* or *according to* one nature only, but *in, according to, with,* and *through* both natures" (FC, SD 8:46); and (3) *genus maiestaticum*—"for the exercise of Christ's office, the human nature in Christ is employed after its own fashion along with the other, and has its power and efficacy not only from and according to its natural and essential properties, or only as far as their capacity extends, but primarily from and according to the majesty, glory, power, and might which the human nature has received through the personal union, glorification, and exaltation" (FC, SD 8:51).

Although this doctrine of the *communicatio idiomatum* in three *genera* united many Gnesio-Lutherans and Philippists, it did not create union with the Reformed wing of the Reformation. Zwinglians, Calvinists, and some Lutheran "Crypto-Calvinists" could not affirm the *genus maiestaticum*—that Christ is "present in the Holy Supper, *not according to the mode or property of the human nature*, but *according to the mode* and property of God's right hand" (FC, EP 8:17). Instead, they affirmed the *extra Calvinisticum*: "because of the property of the human nature it is impossible for Christ to be present at the same time in more than one place, still less to be present with his body everywhere" (FC, EP 8:30). FC 8 insisted that the *genus maiestaticum* is orthodox ecumenical doctrine.

> The Holy Scriptures, and the ancient Fathers on the basis of the Scriptures, testify mightily that, because the human nature in Christ is personally united with the divine nature in Christ, the former (when it was glorified and exalted to the right hand of the majesty and power of God, after the form of the servant had been laid aside and after the humiliation) received, in addition to its natural, essential, and abiding properties, special, high, great, supernatural, unsearchable, ineffable, heavenly prerogatives and privileges in majesty, glory, power, and might above every name that is named, not only in this age but also in that which is to come [Phil. 2:5–11; Eph. 1:21]. Accordingly, for the exercise of Christ's office, the human nature in Christ is employed after its own measure and fashion along with the other, and has its power and efficacy not only from and according to its natural and essential properties, or only as far as their capacity extends, but primarily from and according to the majesty, glory, power, and might which the human nature has received through the personal union, glorification, and exaltation. (FC, SD 8:51)

These careful words are designed to make absolutely certain that Chalcedonian Christology–forged in bitter controversy among the Greek fathers of the church, and preserved in the creed of 451–is clearly reaffirmed in the Reformation. God is "*in, with, and through*" Christ–he is, above all, deep in the flesh: his majesty is hidden in the humanity of Jesus of Nazareth. Thus the strong Lutheran confessional emphasis on the *genus maiestaticum*:

> During the time of the humiliation the divine majesty was concealed and restrained, but now, since the form of a slave has been laid aside, it takes place fully, mightily, and publicly before all the saints in heaven and on earth. . . . Thus there is and remains in Christ only a single divine omnipotence, power, majesty, and glory, which is the property of the divine nature alone. But it shines forth and manifests itself fully, though always spontaneously, *in, with, and through* the assumed exalted human nature of Christ. (FC, SD 8:65–66)

God's incarnation in Christ, his divine majesty humbled in the flesh, consoles troubled consciences. Christ can neither be "materialized" (as the Romanists did, in their sacramental system), nor "spiritualized" (as the Swiss Reformed did, in their dualistic Christology). Preoccupation with the "how" of Christology tempts man to be like God, and such temptation leads to law rather than gospel. What the Lutheran reformers said about the article of the creed "He descended into hell" was meant to apply to Christology as a whole:

> We are not to concern ourselves with exalted and acute speculations about how this occurred. . . . We must only believe and cling to the Word. Then we shall retain the heart of this article and derive from it the comfort that neither hell nor the devil can take us or any believer in Christ captive or harm us. (FC, SD 9:3)

B.

From Justification to Christology

The Lutheran reformers affirmed all the classical formulae of Christology. They also made certain characteristic innovations of their own. These had some precedent in earlier theology, but in this situation they had the effect of novelties, and became for generations centers of controversy with Roman Catholicism and Calvinism. The Lutheran affirmation of tradition and the Lutheran additions to it had the same purpose: to achieve a Christology that could carry the burden of "justification by faith alone."

If the gospel-promise is unconditional, it must be God's word and not man's only; God must be the promiser. For only God can make an unconditional promise, a promise in spite of death. Indeed, that is what the Bible means by "God": the Lord of life and death, who as such can be faithful to his word. To make an unconditional promise that is true, is to have future, and to have future is to be the one the Bible calls "God."

But if the gospel-promise is in this sense God's word, its occurrence is the personal presence of God; just as if I address you, this address brings me into your life. It is in and by their words that persons are present to each other. Again, if there is a promise which is God's promise, it is a revelation of his will. But a revelation of God's will is a self-revelation, for God is not, except merely conceptually, distinguishable from his will.

Therefore, if the gospel promise is true and unconditional, then the event of the living word, of one person speaking the gospel to another, is the locus of God's reality for us. Where is God? He is where one man is promising good unconditionally to another, in Jesus' name. The assertion of justification by faith has three corollaries in the doctrine of God; this is the first (the second follows immediately, the third is in Chapter 9). Medieval theology failed so to locate the reality of God because it understood actual human preaching of the gospel not as itself unconditional promise, but as mere information about promise otherwise and wordlessly made, in the sheer action of the sacraments and in mystical experience.

Moreover, an unconditional promise is one not relativizable by any other authority. Translating into terms of God: God's reality for us in the occurrence of the gospel-word is not relativized by any other reality of God. There is no way to move on from hearing the gospel to some other more complete or profound experience of God. Nor is there an unexperienced reality of God which could in any way call into question the truth or final reliability of what is known in the gospel. These assertions are the second doctrine-of-God corollary of justification by faith; and they contradict all normal religion, which invariably treats the temporal phenomena by which divinity reveals itself as mere *clues*, to be used and left behind in the search for "God himself."

But now—this "gospel," which the assertions of the previous paragraphs seek to characterize, is a word *about* something. It is about Jesus, what he did and will do. The promise is made only if this narrative about Jesus is true. Indeed, a dialectic parallel to that of the last paragraphs works with "Jesus" instead of "God," as we saw in the chapter on sacraments. If the gospel promise is true, *Jesus* must be the speaker, for what the gospel promises is Jesus himself as the fulfilling partner of our End; and only he can thus legitimately promise his own life and work. Therefore, if the gospel-promise is true, Jesus is present to us in and by it. A human, *this* human, is real for us at the same place and in the same way that God is real for us. Or rather, vice versa. Therewith the whole christological matter and problem is before us, in the way it arises for Lutheranism.

All the inherited christological formulae are an attempt to work out the logic of this discourse that is at once word of God and word of and about the man Jesus. What is going on in Christology is not, as it may at first appear, an attempted description of a sort of God-man mechanism inside Christ. The gospel's talk of Christ *interprets the reality of God in terms of the reality of the human Jesus*; and the technical formulae of Christology try to show the logic of this interpretation. Normal religion brings God's reality to word by abstracting from his involvement in human actuality: he is the one who "knows—only not as we do"; who "loves—only not as we do," etc. Christian discourse reverses the religious pattern, and seeks to bring God's reality to word exactly in terms of a particular human life and the role that life has in the total human story. The christological formulae analyze this discourse.

The Gospel Versus the Metaphysical Tradition

The Western philosophical tradition has worked, from its beginning in Greece to the present, with one great ontological distinction: there is *material* reality—temporal, therefore divisible, therefore accessible to the senses; and there is *spiritual* reality—timeless, therefore indivisible, therefore inaccessible to the senses. The distinction presupposes that all realities are "substances" in the sense described in Chapter 5: self-contained possessors of attributes. The ontological classification distinguishes between "material" substances that meet only imperfectly the ideal of substance, in that their self-possession can be interfered with because they are subject to time's dissolutions, and "spiritual" substances in which this defect is remedied. The sensible universe and the human body are the great "material" substances, God and the human soul the great "spiritual" substances.

We posit "spiritual" reality in order to abstract from the threat given with temporality and mortality. Since "spiritual" reality is thus an abstraction from "material" reality, reflection cannot leave the two merely side-by-side; it must think of some relation between them. From Parmenides to the most recent existentialist, various expedients have been tried. But however the relation between "spiritual" and "material" reality may be conceived, it cannot in this tradition be conceived in any way that makes the classification less than exhaustive: all realities must be classifiable as belonging—perhaps "fundamentally" or "originally"—to the one ontological sort or the other.

Reflection about Christ inevitably ran afoul of this tradition from the start. Christians were compelled to say of one whom the tradition must classify as a "material" being that he is in some more than metaphorical sense *God*, that is, the very one who is supposed to be the primary exemplar of "spiritual" being. Nor was the time-tested expedient in such cases available. Late-antique religion regularly deified religious virtuosi; this was possible because the body could be regarded as the mere temporary manifestation of the in any case immortal and so God-like soul. But Jesus' public and notorious death belongs to the very definition of his mission as God; this core of the gospel's soteriology blocked the standard sort of deification. The risen Jesus is a true human, soul and body.

Christology cannot be worked without damage to the metaphysical tradition; and the ancient church finally resolved itself to this. The christological concept of "natures" remained within the tradition; but those of the "hypostasis" and of a "communion" of natures did not.

The word "hypostasis" began its philosophical-theological career harmlessly enough as a near-synonym for "substance" (*ousia*). It was used particularly to emphasize two points about a substance: that it can be distinctly enumerated, and that its enumerable distinctness is not merely a matter of conceptual distinctions in the mind. Third-century Christian theologians adopted this use, first into trinitarian discussion—in the East to one purpose, in the West to the opposite purpose. In the East, Origen taught three "substances" or three "hypostases," meaning that there is a real, extra-mental basis for *counting* "Father, Son, and Spirit"; in the West, Tertullian taught one "substance" or one "hypostasis," meaning that there is really only one God.

Decades of discussion led to a compromise: "one substance of God, in three hypostases." The formula was partly a terminological trick; but it was not only that. "Substance" and "hypostasis" were thus distinguished. When they parted, all the old metaphysical baggage went with "substance": it is as one "substance" that God was now thought to be a self-contained possessor-of-attributes. Therewith "hypostasis" loses its old meaning, and comes to mean what it was said to mean earlier in this chapter—but talk of "identification," "narrative," "event," and "personal identity" is a completely different ontological discourse from that of the philosophical tradition. And within this new discourse, the question about temporality versus timelessness need not arise at all.

It was this new trinitarian use of "hypostasis" which was then adopted also for the christological problem: If in the Trinity there are three hypostases but only one nature, in Christ there are two natures but only one hypostasis. The event of the incarnation, the reality of God as what happens with the man Jesus, was thus named by a word that had been sprung loose from the whole old metaphysical framework: whatever a hypostasis is, it is by definition no kind of substance, and there is no call to ask whether it is timeless or temporal. In the clash between what faith must say of Christ, and what traditional metaphysics says about God and humans, faith had won a battle.

From the Lutheran perspective, the victory, however, was incomplete. Alongside the new trinitarian and christological language, the ancient church also continued late antiquity's usual ways of thinking about God and the world. One way in which this ambivalence manifested itself was in certain qualifications of the radical christological assertions, worked out by the post-Chalcedonian thinkers and by the medieval scholastics. These tried to preserve what could be preserved of the separation between a supposed timelessly substantial Son of God and the temporal human substance Jesus. There are two such separations we must consider.

First, there was the doctrine the Lutherans labeled the "Calvinist extra," but which was not in fact original with the Calvinists. This was a stipulation that while it is true that to encounter Jesus is to encounter God the Son, the converse is not true. The Son is also "outside" the incarnation. We must, it was said, not "limit" God—an injunction that is still popular.

Second, there were certain restrictions on the "communion of attributes." The gospel requires such propositions as "God the Son was crucified," or "Jesus rules universally." So long as the subject-phrase is taken as a mere proper name for the one hypostasis (which is not here conceived as a moral agent anyway), no one is alarmed. But if the descriptive content of such subject-phrases is made thematic, as "God the Son *as* God . . . ," or "Jesus, *qua* man . . . ," traditional theology begins to worry. Such propositions as "God the Son, *as* God, was crucified" are disallowed altogether, from antecedent conviction of God's "impassibility." Propositions such as "Jesus, as man, rules universally" predicate God's characters of the human Jesus. This, too, worries traditional theology; for chief among God's characters are some which are understood to involve timelessness: omnipotence, omnipresence, omniscience. Traditional theology felt unable "really" to assert these of a human, embodied person. So it was said that such characters are only "verbally" predicated of the human Jesus. That is, such a proposition as "Jesus, *qua* man, is omnipotent" is to be understood as an abbreviation for "The man Jesus is hypostatically united to God the Son, who is omnipotent," which latter proposition is alone "really" true.

Lutheran Radicalization

As the doctrine of justification radicalizes the proclamation of the gospel, so appropriate Christology must radicalize understanding of the one proclaimed. The Christology of the entire church is an assault on inherited pagan ways of conceiving God and his relation to us; it seeks to interpret the reality of God by what happens with Jesus: by his "flesh," the historical actuality of one man. Christology in the Lutheran movement works to put God "deep" in that flesh: to assert without qualification that as God meets us in the human Jesus, so God is. It assures us that God has not reserved any part or aspect of his character or will from his involvement with us as Jesus.

It lies at the roots of Lutheran insight that God outside the flesh would be indistinguishable from Satan—at least, if this God were otherwise like the biblical God. God not interpreted by the human story of Israel and by what happens with this one Israelite would be a God of pure "law," a God of naked sovereign demand. God as abstract but otherwise biblical deity, apprehended by rescinding from the actualities and relations of our lives, would be the destructive negation of our lives, a flame engulfing all being but itself. Whether such an experience of abstracted deity were of overpowering condemning presence, or in modern fashion, of utter absence, would make little difference at this point.

Christologically, the gospel is the message that God meets us otherwise than as abstract deity. Thus, christologically, the *unconditionality* of the gospel is the assurance that God does *not at all* meet us as abstract deity. Christologically, the unconditional promise is that in all earth and heaven there is no other God than "the baby at the breasts of his mother." The Lutheran christological innovations labored to secure this assurance conceptually.

Given the traditional christological formulae, the Lutherans made their move simply by dropping the cautions and qualifications. The case with the "Calvinist extra" is relatively simple. The Lutherans said that just as wherever Jesus is, there is the Son, so wherever the Son is, there is Jesus. The Son is the trinitarian reality of God's self-communication; the Lutherans said that there is no self-communication of God other than such as can bring with it the humanity of the Crucified. There is no word of God as sheer law that does not lead to the gospel.

Calvinists correctly said that this amounts to attributing God's omnipresence in time and space to the human Jesus; and since God's presence cannot be separated from his power, or his power from his knowledge, this in turn amounts to attributing omnipotence and omniscience to Jesus. All of which brings us to the "communion of attributes," where the Reformation-period trouble broke out.

Among Romans, Calvinists, and Lutherans, it was agreed that propositions attributing God's attributes to Christ's one divine-human hypostasis itself cause no problem—e.g., "The Christ is omnipotent." Where traditional theology worried was about such propositions as "The man Jesus is omnipotent," where it is the human person—or "nature"—to whom the attribution is made. Here Romans and Calvinists insisted on maintaining the traditional qualification; Lutherans had to drop it, to maintain their rejection of the "Calvinist extra." The heading in textbooks for discussions of the matter was "*Communicatio idiomatum, genus majestaticum*"; and the phrase became a slogan for Lutheran/Reformed controversy.

The gospel-motivation for the Lutherans to drop the "extra" is clear. But Romanists and Calvinists pointed to the consequences for the communion of attributes: What, they asked, could an omnipresent, omnipotent, and omniscient human body and soul possibly be? Indeed, is there not here an idolatrous blurring of the difference between God and creatures? From their viewpoint, they were right: so long as God is defined by timelessness, and creaturehood is understood as inwardly akin to "materiality," the Lutheran christological innovations were indeed intolerably paradoxical. So long as the discussion is conducted in the traditional metaphysical language—and it mostly was, by all parties—the Lutheran concerns indeed create a metaphysical monstrosity.

But it was exactly the traditional metaphysical language against which the Lutherans were struggling. Their paradoxical propositions can be read as reinterpretations of what it means to be God and what it means to be man. Given our intellectual history, we will indeed need to say that God is "omnipresent," etc. But God present "deep in the flesh" of Jesus is not, e.g., "omnipresent" because time and space mean nothing to him; of such a God, "omnipresence" is rather a slogan for the assertion that "neither death, nor life . . . , nor things present, nor things to come, . . . nor height, nor depth, . . . will be able to separate us from the love of God in Christ Jesus. . . ." And so for all the "attributes of majesty": by attributing them to Jesus, we say they must be so understood as to fit him; and thus the deity of God comes to be interpreted by Jesus' human story. Equally, if a human can share in God's omnipresence, etc., even as so interpreted, then the embodied character of human creaturehood is not primarily to be defined by "materiality" as the label of a kind of substance and so by Newtonian rules about where and when such substances can be. Rather, it is to be defined by just the sort of historical and existential characters connected to the word "body" in our chapter on the sacraments.

The Philippists and Gnesio-Lutherans fought also about Christology, and their conflicts show clearly how the Lutheran christological demands must explode the old language and its built-in assumptions about deity and humanity. Melanchthon's followers attempted to retain the sensible old Christology, while also pressing Lutheran understandings of the word and sacraments. The attempt was a failure, and the more consistent Philippists were driven into Calvinism. Their opponents, like John Brenz, who set out to carry Lutheran christological insight to its conclusion, produced profound speculative systems that, within their language, were finally too paradoxical to be believed. Here, too, the Formula of Concord, based on the work of mediating theologians like Martin Chemnitz, produced ecclesiastical peace by formulae that in large part only covered over both the difficulties and the opportunities.

If the metaphysical revolution in the Lutheran Reformation's christological innovations were carried through, the terms of Christology itself would also, of course, change. We would have a Christology not in terms of "natures" and "attributes," but in terms of Jesus' history, the ultimate promise made by the resurrection of that history, and the reality of God's inclusion of and in this span of destiny. A doctrine of God "deep in the flesh" of Jesus remains to be fully achieved. Providing such a Christology is much beyond the scope of this book. Here we have only to show the purpose and tendency of the original Lutheran christological innovations: to work toward a Christology adequate to the doctrine of justification without works, thereby inaugurating a reinterpretation of the deepest concepts of metaphysics.

Chapter 8

Ministry—Serving the Gospel

Readings:
SA II, 3–4; III, 7–11, 14
AC 5
AC and AP 14, 27–28
TR

A.

The Power of the Living Word

Luther asserted that the spoken or "living word" is the "proper function of the gospel," surpassing all other functions in the church (SA III, 4). Ministry, therefore, is the "office of preaching" (LC I, 86). The spoken and visible gospel—word and sacrament—mediates God's gracious forgiveness through the life, death, and resurrection of Jesus, without whom no man can be saved. The ministry of the gospel creates, maintains, and guards the church in its mission to be the proleptic community of God's new world, in the interim between the day of Jesus' ascension and the time of his final return. The word creates faith (AC 5), faith creates new life (AC 6), and the new life creates the church (AC 7–8).

Luther's view of ministry as "ministry of the word of God" grew out of his understanding of the incarnation itself as God's order of salvation: the "revealed God" ultimately remains a "hidden God," because of the word of God. For the word of God is simultaneously the word of man.

Luther stressed the *task*, or function, of ministry rather than its form. Roman medieval doctrine had established the view that the priest has an "indelible character"—that is, that he is endowed with the never-failing power to mediate God's grace to a laity distinguished from the clergy by divine law. Luther destroyed this medieval Roman doctrine of priesthood in 1520, when he developed the concept of the priesthood of all believers by virtue of baptism. "Whoever comes out of the water of baptism," he declared in "To the Christian Nobility" in 1520, "can boast that he is already a consecrated priest, bishop and pope" (LW 44, 129). Luther no longer interpreted "ministry" in terms of a "holy order" metaphysically secured by an infallible sacrament. Rather, he considered it an essential *function* ordained by the sacrament of baptism and protected by a Christian community's proper call at a given time and place. Luther clearly distinguished between the "spiritual estate" of baptism and the various holders of a special "office." Consequently, there are secular and spiritual offices, such as the secular function of princes and the spiritual function of priests; both princes and priests have their different duties.

> There is no true, basic difference between laymen and priests, princes and bishops, between the religious and secular, except for the sake of office and work, but not for the sake of status. They are all of the spiritual estate, are all truly priests, bishops, and popes. But they do not all have the same work to do. (LW 44, 129)

There is, then, a "common" ministry, exercised by all who are baptized, and a "special" ministry, carried out by those who are called to the public office of the word. In his theological battle with Rome, Luther stressed the common ministry; in his controversy with the "left-wingers" of the Reformation, he emphasized the special ministry. When Andreas Bodenstein of Carlstadt, former dean of Wittenberg University, advocated complete equality between "private" and "public" ministry, Luther vehemently defended the divine institution of the public office of the word. "The spiritual estate [the clergy] has been established and instituted by God, not with gold or silver but with the precious blood and bitter death of his only Son, our Lord Jesus Christ [I Peter 1:18–19]" (LW 46, 219). In the face of an almost total lack of theological education on the part of both clergy and laity, Luther created new catechisms (LC and SC "Prefaces") and a new order of ordination for ministers in 1539, and called the public office of ministry "the fifth distinguishing mark of the church" (along with gospel, baptism, Lord's Supper, power of the keys, worship, and suffering) (LW 41, 154).

Luther held neither a "theory of transference"—the derivation of the special, public ministry from the common priesthood of all believers, as represented by the congregation—nor the idea of a "holy priestly order" as a superior spiritual estate instituted by God. He believed that there is *one* "ministry of the word," instituted by God and exercised by both common and special ministers in private and in public. Every Christian is a priest by virtue of baptism, which is the sacrament of ordination; and some Christians are "priests of priests" (bishops of congregations, as it were) by virtue of their calling into the public ministry of the word. They are called into this office either by God himself (especially in times of emergency) just like the prophets of old, or by a congregation of Christians at a particular time and place. The authority of the public office ceases with its function. Therefore "ordination" into the special ministry is a *rite* to be celebrated in worship, rather than a *right* to be secured as a special status.

Luther consistently kept his reflections on the two ministries in dialectical tension, avoiding the temptation of deriving the one from the other. Neither the promise of salvation in Christ, nor its communication through the ministry of the word, can be reduced to the question of the political relationship between congregation and pastor, between "common" and "special" ministry. Both remain in creative tension with each other as organs of the one body of Christ in the world. When Luther shifted the emphasis—before 1525 to the "common" and after 1525 to the "special" ministry—he did so in the face of particular historical circumstances: his struggles with Rome and with the extremists he called *Schwaermer*. Ultimately, Luther's view of the ministry was intimately linked to the turmoil and joy of being a Christian and a priest in search of the ecumenical essence of the Christian faith in his own time. In the sacrament of baptism he found the foundation for both public and private ministry, instituted by Christ as the "visible word of God" by which the salvation of the sinner is celebrated and made real in the life of the church.

Melanchthon, like Luther, defined ministry in terms of "office of preaching" (AC 5:1). The authority of the ministry is based on its faithfulness to the gospel of justification by faith alone apart from works of law; and the word and sacraments are the "means" whereby the Holy Spirit is given, so as to produce faith. But Melanchthon left open the question of whether a "common" or "special" ministry was instituted to obtain faith. He simply stressed the externality of the gospel ministry, condemning the view (ascribed to Anabaptists and other left-wing factions) that salvation occurs not with the external means of word and sacraments, but through an internal, mystical appropriation of the Holy Spirit (AC 5:4). Melanchthon refers only once to the "common priesthood of all believers": all baptized Christians represent the "royal priesthood" (1 Pet. 2:9) when they exercise their right of electing and ordaining ministers (TR 69). On the whole, he seems to favor a definition of ministry in terms of the "special," public, and ordained ministry; ordination may even be called a "sacrament" if it is interpreted "in relation to the ministry of the word," for "the ministry of the word has God's command and glorious promises" (AP 13:11–12).

Neither Luther nor Melanchthon spelled out exact rules for the election, ordination, and installation of ministers. They did believe that since medieval bishops no longer ordained suitable people ("they ordain crude asses," AP 28:4, German version), "it is necessary for the church itself to retain the right of calling, electing, and ordaining ministers" (TR 67).

The Office of the Keys

The Lutheran concern for ministry, as the task of serving the gospel, goes hand in hand with care to limit the authority of the minister—especially episcopal power. Both Luther and Melanchthon agreed that the existing canonical polity for ordination could be maintained by Lutherans, provided that the bishops exercise their duty to ordain priests "for the sake of love and unity, not of necessity" (SA III, 10:1) and that they "stop raging against our churches" (AP 14:5).

Melanchthon argued very strongly that the ancient and ecumenical rite of ordination by bishops represented good ecclesiastical discipline. But he disagreed with Rome's assertion that the existing ecclesiastical hierarchy was divinely instituted. The various hierarchical ranks were created by "human authority," and as such they are proper instruments of ecclesiastical law and order (AP 14:1). For "nobody should preach publicly in the church or administer the sacraments unless he is regularly called" (AC 14).

Melanchthon carefully spelled out the limitations of episcopal power or the "power of the keys": "According to the Gospel the power of the keys or the power of bishops is a power and command of God to preach the Gospel, to forgive and retain sins, and to administer and distribute the sacraments" (AC 28:5). Such power is "spiritual," not "temporal"; that is, it is a power of the word and not of the sword (AC 28:8–20). The office of the keys, embodied in the episcopal office, has the biblical promise to be the judge of what is and what is not "gospel" at any given time.

> According to the gospel (or, as they say, by divine right), no jurisdiction belongs to the bishops as bishops (that is, to those to whom has been committed the ministry of Word and sacraments) except to forgive sins, to reject doctrine which is contrary to the Gospel, and to exclude from the fellowship of the church ungodly persons whose wickedness is known, doing all this without human power, simply by the Word. Churches are therefore bound by divine law to be obedient to the bishops according to the text, "He who hears you hears me" [Luke 10:16]. However, when bishops teach or ordain anything contrary to the Gospel, churches have a command of God that forbids obedience [Matt. 7:15; Gal. 1:8; 2 Cor. 13:8]. (AC 28:20–27, Latin version)

Melanchthon made it clear that "gospel" means the promise that man is saved without any human merit. Consequently, no bishop (or local pastor, the "bishop" in his congregation of "common priests") may set any regulations aimed at earning God's grace, be they laws about food and drink or about going to church on Sunday (AC 28:39–60). Christians must not be coerced to sin (AC 28:78). Melanchthon accepted the old medieval canon-law distinction between two kinds of episcopal power, "the power of the order, namely, the ministry of Word and sacraments" and "the power of jurisdiction, namely, the authority to excommunicate those who are guilty of public offenses or to absolve them if they are converted and ask for absolution" (AP 28:13). Worship, for example, is not to be legislated by bishops (AP 28:14). In short, the power of the keys is the "function and power given to the church by Christ to bind and to loose sins" in terms of Matthew 16:19 and 18:18 (SA III, 7:1).

According to Melanchthon, the papacy goes far beyond the biblical power of the keys when it claims that: (1) the pope is "by divine right above all bishops and pastors," according to canon law; (2) "by divine right he possesses both swords, that is, the authority to bestow and transfer kingdoms," according to the Bull *Unam Sanctam* by Boniface VIII in 1301; and (3) "for such reasons the bishop of Rome calls himself the vicar of Christ on earth," a designation used by popes after the death of Innocent III in 1216 (TR 1–3).

Melanchthon demonstrated, in lengthy arguments attached as a supplement to the Augsburg Confession, that both Scripture and tradition reject the Roman papacy as a proper teaching authority in the Christian church (TR 7–38). "Since this is the situation, all Christians . . . ought rather to abandon and execrate the pope and his adherents as the kingdom of the Antichrist" (TR 41). Temporal magistrates and princes should make the decisions about life and reformation of the church whenever the pope and the bishops become negligent or even betray the gospel (TR 77).

Although Melanchthon essentially affirmed Luther's view of the papacy as the Antichrist (SA II, 4:10), he felt compelled to add an irenic clause to Luther's polemic Smalcald Articles before he signed them in 1537: if the pope would allow the gospel, his superiority over the bishops, which he has by human right, might be conceded to him for the sake of peace and unity (SA III, 15:5). It seemed wiser to make concessions to Rome rather than to the left-wing *Schwaermer* who were, after all, innovators without the ecumenical experience of historic tradition.

When theological controversies plagued the Lutheran movement between the time of Luther's death in 1546 and the acceptance of the Book of Concord in 1580, norms were developed in the Formula of Concord for the proper exercise of the power of the keys and the teaching authority of the church: (1) Scripture, (2) the first three ecumenical creeds—Nicene, Apostolic, Athanasian—and (3) the summary of Lutheran doctrine in the Book of Concord (FC, SD "Rule and Norm," 1–13; EP 1–8). Whatever these documents affirm is "orthodox" doctrine, and whatever they reject is to be considered "heretical" teaching. But no ecclesiastical doctrine per se—the affirmation of orthodoxy at a given time and place for the sake of Christian unity and mission—can take the place of the word of God.

> The prophetic and apostolic writings of the Old and New Testaments are the only rule and norm according to which all doctrines and teachers alike must be appraised and judged. . . . Other writings of ancient and

> modern teachers, whatever their names, should not be put on a par with Holy Scripture. Every single one of them should be subordinated to the Scriptures and should be received in no other way and no further than as witnesses to the fashion in which the doctrine of the prophets and the apostles was preserved in post-apostolic times. . . . Holy Scripture remains the only judge, rule, and norm according to which as the only touchstone all doctrines should and must be understood and judged as good or evil, right or wrong. (EP "Summary," 1–2, 7)

B.

The Office of the Gospel

The sequence of the Augsburg Confession is precise and noteworthy. The first three articles state ecumenically agreed contents of the gospel-word; the fourth states the proposed new dogma about the special linguistic character of this word; the fifth is suddenly about the church's ministry. What happens is that the confession shifts from the logic of gospel-saying to the human event of it—and therewith we have preachers, and, in the following articles, Christian life and the church (AC 6–8). New understanding of the gospel's logic must bring new understanding also of all these matters.

Merely with this sequence, the medieval doctrine of ministry is already rejected, and the main Lutheran point about ministry is already made: the ministry's fundamental reality is simply that if the gospel is spoken, and if this speaking is an external word, some actual human being will be talking, and in that official character which belongs to the external arrangements of communication. That the gospel-speaking *is* an external word is, we have seen, demanded by the doctrine of justification; thus, AC 5 condemns "the Anabaptists and others who think that the Holy Spirit reaches men without the external Word, through their own preparations and works" (Latin AC 5:4)—note that "without the external Word" and "through . . . works" are taken as equivalent. The speaking in question is the total meaning-with-embodiment, "word and sacrament"; the German text's "office of preaching" is represented in the Latin text by "office of teaching the gospel *and* administering the sacraments."

That God arranges for this speaking to occur is the instituting of an "office." This office is not primarily an office in the church, deriving from the necessities of its organization—the Augsburg Confession does not discuss the church until two articles later. It is an office within God's fundamental relation to us, an office within his rule of creation: "office," or "ministry," has the sense it has in such phrases as "ministry of defense" or "office of the budget." A "minister" in this sense is one who *takes responsibility for* some part of the work of rule. In the view of the Lutheran reformers, God's rule uses, basically, two such human ministries: the office of preaching the gospel and the office of "worldly government."

Both offices aim at a "righteousness": the preaching of the gospel at the righteousness of faith, worldly government at the righteousness which enables men to live together at all. Both are offices of a word: one of the gospel, the other of the law. Both offices have power. The gospel's power to unlock man's captivity to fear and death and guilt is called, in the Lutheran confessions, the "power of the keys." The government's power is the power of physical compulsion, which in this age is always needed both to combat evil and to promote good; this is the "power of the sword."

To exercise the office of the gospel and actually to speak (in the comprehensive sense) the gospel are the same thing. Thus God's institution of this office occurred at the call of the apostles, the first actual speakers of the gospel, and was identical with the appearance to them of the risen Lord Jesus. And the office continues in that the gospel, when actually preached, calls its hearers to preach in turn. Therewith we have before us all the fundamental determinants of the Lutheran confessions' doctrine of ministry.

Ministry by and to the Word

But now we are indeed talking about the church, and about its necessities and its structure. For this chain of witnesses *is* the church, as a reality temporally extended through history. The call into this office is but the voice of the church going about its mission, and anyone who responds to the call merely thereby enters the church and so assumes some role in its life.

From everything we have seen so far, it is clear that the office of God's gospel-rule is the ministry which the whole church as a community has to the world. To be in the church is to be appointed to responsibility for the speaking of the gospel in the world; baptism is the appointment. But it is also clear that the Lutheran confessions, at the same time that they talk about this ministry *of* the whole church, are also talking about a "ministry of the gospel" in the sense of a particular office *in* the church, indeed, *to* the church: a ministering to the community of believers. The Lutheran confessions regard provision for this service as the chief and only indispensable part of the church's organization as a community.

As soon as we ask about the precise relation of the office *in* the church to the office *of* the church, we raise a set of very difficult problems. What is more, these are problems which have been debated through the whole history of the Lutheran movement, and which are no closer to solution now than at the beginning: commissions of Lutheran denominations continue to prepare documents on "the ministry" which prove useful to no one but the members of the commissions, and Lutheran participants in ecumenical conversations continue to strike agreements in the name of "Lutheran teaching," only to find them repudiated or ignored by their sending bodies. This is so, it seems, because Lutheranism, in the confessions as well, has been unclear from the start about certain basic matters.

We will try to identify and work through three such matters. We will offer one Lutheran way of achieving clarity. We cannot claim it is *the* Lutheran way, for it is the Lutheran confessions that define Lutheranism, and the whole difficulty is the confessions' indefiniteness at this point. First we will take up the matter of the distinction between the ministry *in* the church and the ministry *of* the church.

The Lutheran confessions clearly assert that there is a ministry of the gospel which is a special ministry in the believing community. At the same time, their fundamental description of a Christian, any Christian, is of one called to speak the gospel. This situation has repeatedly led Lutherans to propose theories of representation or delegation: all Christians have the right and responsibility to speak the gospel, but for certain purposes, of "public" speaking or to satisfy "good order," they delegate their right and thereby create the special "office of preaching." Such theories are attractively simple, but it does not seem that they can be squared with the New Testament language about offices in the church, or with the actual phenomena of Christian history. Moreover, they clash with the independence which the Lutheran confessions—as well as Luther—suppose in the special office. For the Lutheran confessions discuss this office *before* they discuss the church, and they make the apostles the *common* origin of both the special office and the church.

We can avoid such theories if we will notice the ambivalent function of "of" in "ministry of the word." Notoriously, any use of the preposition "of" can run two ways. The confessional "of" runs both ways at once, and the conflation of two quite different phenomena under one formula is responsible for much of our historic difficulty in understanding the ministry "of" the gospel. On the one hand, "of" introduces the agent of the ministry ("subjective genitive"): there the "ministry of the gospel" is the ministry done *by* the gospel, the service done to the world by the gospel proclamation. It is *this* ministry "of" the gospel which is identical with the Christian community's mission to the world, and to which every believer is appointed. On the other hand, "of" introduces the object of the ministry ("objective genitive"): here the "ministry of the gospel" is a service performed *to* the gospel proclamation. It is *this* ministry "of" the gospel which is the function of—let us now introduce the usual technical term—the "ordained" ministry.

The ordained minister of the gospel is one called by the congregation to a quite specific function in the congregation. He is called literally to "minister" to the gospel itself, as the word upon which the community depends: he is called to *tend* the life of the gospel in the congregation, to care for its vivacity and authenticity. The congregation's ministry is a ministry by the gospel to the world; the ordained ministry is a ministry by an appointed member of the congregation to the gospel.

Once this is sorted out, we can go further. For the Lutheran Reformation, it is clear that the gospel calls the church into being, not vice versa. The existence within the church of a gospel-office *not* held by all is the way this priority appears in the structure of the church. The existence of an office of gospel-speaking not held by the community at large represents to the community at large the gospel's independence and priority over against it. The ordained members of a congregation are those members of the congregation appointed to say to the congregation, when need be: "Indeed, this is what we would like to say to each other and the world, and call it the gospel; but the gospel is specifically about the risen Jesus, and we shall have to consult external norms to test whether this favored word of ours is really appropriate to him." The ordination oath is to preach, not in accordance with the wishes of the community, but in accordance with Scripture and dogma; the very purpose of the ordained ministry is that there shall be in the community some whose commitments are so ordered. The appointment and existence of the ordained ministry thus *says* something to the church. It is a "visible word," and we may call it a sacrament; but it is a sacrament performed not on the one ordained but on the community—the ordained one is more like the bread and wine or the water.

In this view, the ordained ministry is an inward-directed function of the Christian community. Persons are not ordained to be general-purpose leaders of the community, or to represent religion to the world, or to do the gospel's mission instead of the "laity." The outward-directed gospel-mission is the task of the whole community; "ordination" to it is baptism.

Of course, ordained ministers do not fulfill their function in abstraction from the work of the community to which they belong. Rather, they carry their specific function by the *way* in which they, as believers, participate in the community's mission. Thus the ordained member of a congregation is neither the only preacher in it nor a sort of abstract critic of preaching. He is to be a paradigmatic preacher. He is neither the only teacher, nor yet no teacher at all. Rather, he is to be a teacher of teachers. An ordained minister must work in his community's mission in whatever ways, and with whatever authority, are necessary in a particular situation for him to fufill his special function.

The Ministerial Succession

The very nature of the gospel creates tradition; this story exists only as A tells B who tells C, etc.—from the apostles to us. The very nature of the gospel involves a *succession* of witnesses. If ordained ministers are merely delegates of the community at large, the succession of witnesses is solely the succession of all believers, who at each specific time create the ordained ministry for certain tasks. Much of Protestantism has often seen the succession in this way. But if the ministry is in a certain way independent of the community at large, the question arises whether there is not also a succession of ordained ministers parallel to the succession of believers. Most of the church has said there is; and, we believe, rightly.

If the Reformation attack on the medieval doctrine of hierarchy is to be sustained, the succession of ministers must be understood as a succession of function *within* the personal succession of all believers—so much is clear. But since the ministry's function is to represent the independence of the gospel over against the community, the ministers of any one time do not derive their exercise of this function from the community at large, but rather from their predecessors in that function—or so, it seems, the New Testament speaks of these matters. There is a parallel descent of believers and of ministers among the believers from a common beginning in the first apostolic preaching of the gospel.

The ecumenically divisive form of the problem is the question: Who ordains? The whole community, or the predecessors in office? We choose the second answer as a probable Lutheran position.

On this understanding, the community at large calls individuals to the office; their predecessors in office grant it. Neither act is more important than the other. For the Lutheran reformers, it is entirely clear that the "call" to ordination is not an interior event of any sort, but the verbal and legal summons of a community of believers, a local congregation or some other manifestation of the church. Prior to this call, there are at most volunteers for it. Ordination is induction into the ministerial succession, performed by predecessor incumbents of the ministerial office acting through some publicly acknowledged organ of their succession.

Function and Order

The Reformation has a *functional* understanding of the ordained ministry. Protestant theology has often contrasted this understanding with an alleged Roman Catholic understanding of the ministry as an "*order*." This contrast is not so easy to state clearly as Protestants often assume. But perhaps we may do it in this way: we pick out the class of ministers by a description of what ministers *do*, not by making a list of names.

It follows from this that someone not actually engaged in tending the gospel is not a minister, even though he may once have been. It does not necessarily follow that, should he return to the ministry, he should be reordained; any more than that a lapsed and newly repentant believer should be rebaptized. An ordained person has been given, and has sworn to fulfill, a specific responsibility. The permission and the commitment remain, whether the person honors them or not; the community will always have the right to hold the person to them. And this vested right of the community in the person may well be thought of as a permanent alteration of his life.

From its refusal to call the ministry an order, Protestantism has usually concluded that there are no orders in the church. This conclusion is obviously hasty and has had disastrous results. Every human community or movement needs what we have lately called a "leadership cadre," a pool of persons whose circumstances are so arranged that they are available to serve the community's needs in a way most members cannot be. Through most of the church's history, "orders"—of monks, nuns, widows, couples committed to mobility and subsistence-economics, "deacons," etc.—have been the church's cadre, its pool of persons for shock-troop service in the mission and for service to the endlessly varying internal needs of the community. These orders have been distinct from the ordained ministry; some ministers have belonged to orders and some have not, and some ordered persons have been ordained and some have not. In Protestantism's pretense that it has no orders, its normal communal needs have driven it, in practice, to treat the ordained ministry as a general-purpose cadre. Thus Protestantism has in practice embraced the doctrine it attributes to Roman Catholicism, that the ministry is an order rather than a particular function. Moreover, it has distracted its ministers from the much-needed special function that is in fact theirs. Sooner or later, the Reformation's functional understanding of ministry must compel us to rethink radically the whole question of leadership in the church.

The Organization of the Ministry

The ministry, as a group of persons appointed to a function, must and will have some organization of its own. Not all ministers do exactly the same things. The differentiation is of two sorts; both are recognized in the Lutheran confessions: ministers are *functionally* and *hierarchically* differentiated.

Since ordained ministers fulfill their function in and through their participation in the general life and mission of the community, their possible role-differentiation is as various as is the life and mission of the community. Every ordained minister will play a variety of roles, but the normal development of human organization will, in most situations, lead to specialization. A particular minister in a particular situation may be mostly a rabbi, or mostly a paradigmatic preacher, or mostly a liturgical leader, or mostly a counselor of troubled believers, or a specialist in the skills needed to minister to the believing population of a hospital or an army camp, etc.

The lines and the degree of specialization, and the organization of the specialties among themselves, are historically variable; and this variability is by God's will. If it were not, the undeniably occurring historical variability would mean that we had to bring the organization of the ministry into conformity with God's will, and that the rightness of the community before God depended on this effort—a set of propositions denied by the article on justification.

The hierarchical differentiation of the ministry results from the ecumenicity of the church; the Lutheran confessions mostly assume it without discussion. Each actual gathering of believers is the church, yet is so only *with* all other such gatherings. This mutual dependence of the gatherings will find organizational expression in some form or other; as it does, some ministers will acquire responsibilities that transcend the separate congregations. A chart of the ministers' organization will look like a pyramid: there will be a "hierarchy." Occasionally various branches of Protestantism have tried to deny these necessities, in the name of spiritual equality before God, but never with success in practice. Again, the sort of hierarchy the ministry has is historically variable; and Lutheranism affirms the variation.

Finally, a particular overlap of functional and hierarchical differentiation leads to the much-argued question of "episcopacy." Historically, this has been the most important and most divisive organizational issue in post-Reformation Christianity, dividing Protestants from Roman Catholics, and Protestants from each other. We will discuss it later, under "adiaphora" (Chapter 14).

Chapter 9

Church—Body in Conflict

Readings:
SC and LC II, 3
SA III, 12
AC and AP 7–8, 21
FC 12

A.

The Creature of the Gospel

> Thank God, a seven-year-old child knows what the church is, namely, holy believers and sheep who hear the voice of their Shepherd [John 10:3]. So children pray, "I believe in one holy Christian church." Its holiness does not consist of surplices, tonsures, albs, or other ceremonies of theirs [the papists] which they have invented over and above the Holy Scriptures, but consists of the Word of God and true faith. (SA III, 12:2–3)

This statement, from Luther's theological testament of 1537, discloses the dialectic so characteristic of the reformer's theology as a whole: childlike faith clinging to the word of God, and theological sagacity tracking down the weakness of the word of men. He summed up his position during the 1519 Leipzig debate on the power of the pope: "Where the word is, there is faith; and where faith is, there is the true church" (LW 39, xii). The Word of God, the gospel, mediates the Holy Spirit who "calls, gathers, enlightens, and sanctifies the whole Christian church on earth and preserves it in union with Jesus Christ in the one true faith" (SC II, 6).

Luther stressed the noninstitutional character of the church. He disliked the word "church" (*Kirche*) and preferred terms such as "assembly" (*Sammlung*) and "community" (*Gemeinde)* (LC II, 48–49). The church is both a hidden community (in the sense of Paul's statement in 1 Cor. 2:7–15) and a visible fellowship. It is hidden because faith is "the conviction of things not seen" (Heb. 11:1); and it is visible because of the preaching of the gospel and the administration of the sacraments. Luther maintained this dialectic between the hidden church and the visible fellowship with a fundamental consistency throughout his career as a reformer. Thus he could say that, on the one hand, "God does not want the world to know when he sleeps with his bride" and, on the other hand, "the assembly of the church is visible for the sake of the confession of faith" (Rom. 10:10) (LW 39, xiii–xiv). The constitutive element of the church is the word:

> Neither you nor I could ever know anything of Christ, or believe in him and take him as our Lord, unless these were first offered to us and bestowed on our hearts through the preaching of the Gospel by the Holy Spirit. . . . For where Christ is not preached, there is no Holy Spirit to create, call, and gather the Christian church, and outside it no one can come to the Lord Christ. (LC II, 38, 45)

Word and spirit belong together. The church is neither an invisible Platonic reality—as some of the *Schwaermer* argued—nor an infallible, unchanging institution, as the papal church claimed. Rather, like the individual Christian, the church is continually struggling, and is to be constantly re-created and sustained by the word of God.

> Now we are only halfway pure and holy. The Holy Spirit must continue to work in us through the Word, daily granting forgiveness until we attain that life where there will be no more forgiveness. (LC II, 58)

The Holy Spirit, mediated through word and sacrament, "sanctifies" and "makes holy." The Holy Spirit "first leads us into his holy community, placing us upon the bosom of the church, where he preaches to us and brings us to Christ" (LC II, 37).

Luther's dialectic between the hidden and visible church drove him to the question of whether the Roman church was a true or a false church. His studies in the history of the church (especially "On the Councils and the Church," 1539) convinced him that the Roman church could no longer claim to be the true church. On the contrary, Luther argued, those who are "evangelical" are the true church, which bears the marks of the ecumenical communion of saints: the word, baptism, Lord's Supper, the power of the keys, public ministry, worship, and suffering. "Outside the Christian Church, where the gospel is not, there is no forgiveness and hence no holiness" (LC II, 56). Accordingly, for the sake of its faithful mission to the gospel in the world, the church may excommunicate "manifest and impenitent sinners from the sacrament and other fellowship of the church until they mend their ways and avoid sin" (SA III, 9).

Melanchthon's Augsburg Confession (AC 7) defended Luther's ecclesiological position that the church is a creature of the gospel. It did so in terms of three doctrinal assertions designed to demonstrate the ecumenicity of Lutheran ecclesiology.

(1) The gospel *must* be embodied in a visible community of believers as long as the world exists. "One holy Christian church must be and must remain forever" (AC 7:1). The Lutheran movement had been accused of "dreaming of a Platonic republic"—of teaching a doctrine of the invisible church as the "true" church (AP 7–8:20). Melanchthon assured his Roman opponents that the promise of the gospel is bound to a church which "actually exists, made up of true believers and righteous men scattered throughout the world" (AP 7–8:20).

(2) The gospel, heralded through preaching and the sacraments, is the only necessary mark of the church. The church is "the assembly of all believers among whom the Gospel is preached in its purity and the holy sacraments are administered according to the Gospel" (AC 7:1). The church is an event rather than an institution. Luther liked to call the church a "mouth house" (*Mundhaus*)—an acoustic phenomenon rather than a constellation of impersonal forces. Melanchthon insisted that the gospel be preached *and taught* in its purity. He, like Luther, stressed the wholistic aspect of the gospel: its concrete history disclosed in the witness, suffering, and death of the followers of Christ, the body of the church in time. What is to be preached and taught, once again, is the sanity and integrity of the gospel, according to the prophetic and apostolic witness of Holy Scripture. The homiletical and didactic life of the church is to be "re-formed" according to the gospel, which becomes powerful when it addresses human despair and brings hope for new life.

(3) The unity of the church is given in the gospel event itself rather

than in ecclesiastical uniformity. "It is sufficient for the true unity of the Christian church that the Gospel be preached in conformity with a pure understanding of it and that the sacraments be administered in accordance with the divine Word" (AC 7:2). Melanchthon carefully distinguished between the "gospel" and "ceremonies, instituted by men, . . . uniformly observed in all places" (AC 7:4). "Human traditions" are not the *ecumenical* marks of the church. "The church catholic" consists of those "who agree on the Gospel and have the same Christ, the same Holy Spirit, and the same sacraments, whether they have the same human traditions or not" (AP 7–8:10). The issue between Rome and Wittenberg was quite clear:

> With a very thankful spirit we cherish the useful and ancient ordinances, especially when they contain a discipline that serves to educate and instruct the people and the inexperienced. Now, we are not discussing whether it is profitable to observe them for the sake of tranquillity or bodily profit. . . . The question is whether the observance of human traditions is an act of worship necessary for righteousness before God. This must be settled in this controversy, and only then can we decide whether it is necessary for the true unity of the church that human traditions be alike everywhere. (AP 7–8:33–34)

What was at stake at Augsburg was the unconditionality of the gospel. The issue was whether there could be salvation outside the Roman church. Melanchthon, following Luther, argued that "church usages" are not necessary for salvation (AC 15:2). When the Roman Confutation condemned AC 15, he declared, "We gladly keep the old traditions set up in the church because they are useful and promote tranquillity, and we interpret them in an evangelical way, excluding the opinion which holds that they justify" (AP 15:38). Such traditions as liturgical orders, feast days, and ecclesiastical law in general are "adiaphora"—things which make no difference in regard to the question of salvation—or "things in the middle." Melanchthon and his colleagues were quite willing to negotiate with Roman theologians about the status of adiaphora in the church for "the greatest possible public harmony, without offense to consciences" (AP 15:52). But the question of the unity of the church could not be tied to ecclesiastical law and order. Lutheran confessional ecclesiology ties the issue of unity to the question of the gospel, the unconditional promise of the god who justifies the ungodly. A church which faithfully proclaims that promise in the world is "catholic"; a church which places conditions on that promise, by legislating rites of uniformity, is not.

The Community of Saints and Sinners

Luther's keen sense of Christian realism permeated not only confessional arguments concerning the *unity* of the church, but also its *reality*. The church, like the individual Christian, is "simultaneously righteous and sinful" (*simul iustus et peccator*). Ecclesiastical purity is not a moral but a functional phenomenon: as long as the church is guided by the Holy Spirit, mediated by word and sacrament, it will remain pure in its earthly purpose to be the instrument of God's promise of salvation without the merit of good works.

> Creation is past and redemption is accomplished, but the Holy Spirit carries on his work unceasingly until the last day. For this purpose he has appointed a community on earth, through which he speaks and does all his work. For he has not yet gathered together all his Christian people, nor has he completed the granting of forgiveness. Therefore we believe in him who daily brings us into his community through the Word, and imparts, increases, and strengthens faith through the same Word and the forgiveness of sins. (LC II, 61–62)

In its pilgrimage on earth, the church is the incomplete body of Christ, a "mixed body" of saints and sinners. "In this life many false Christians, hypocrites, and even open sinners are mixed in among the godly" (AC 8:1). This is the objective reality of ecclesiastical existence, even though moralists, puritans, and idealists in general may desire a "pure church." The Augsburg Confession rejects these groups as manifestations of the ancient heresy of Donatism (a North African group of rigorists who denied the efficacy of the sacraments when administered or received by immoral persons) (AC 8:3). "The sacraments are efficacious even if the priests who administer them are wicked men" (AC 8:1). The objective, *historical* reality of the church as a "mixed body" is balanced by the unconditional, *divine* efficacy of the sacraments as the "visible" word of God.

Luther's distinction between "true" and "false" church was misunderstood both by friends and by foes. Was the true church "hidden" because of the immorality of men? "Left-wingers" such as Caspar Schwenckfeld asserted that the true community of saints was invisible and did not need the external word and sacraments. Their "spiritualist" ecclesiology represented the complete opposite to the "materialist" position of Rome, which defined grace as "holy substance" independent of human subjectivity. Anabaptists such as Conrad Grebel in Zurich taught that the church must strive for moral purity. Their "moralistic" ecclesiology produced a community which tried to separate itself from the world—especially the political world—in order to embody the biblical principle of suffering discipleship. The Augsburg Confession rejected Anabaptists, Schwenckfelders, and Anti-Trinitarians as "heretics and sectarians," since they violated ecumenical teaching (FC 12).

Rome, on the other hand, distinguished between a "church in name only" and a "church in fact": the wicked are part of the church only in name and not in fact, while the godly are part of the church in fact as well as in name (AP 7–8:10–11). Although Melanchthon basically agreed with this position, he found it wanting in theological depth. Like Luther, he argued that the church is called to do battle on the side of God against the devil, and that the exact distinction between good and evil cannot be determined as long as the battle rages.

> If the church, which is truly the kingdom of Christ, is distinguished from the kingdom of the devil, it necessarily follows that since the wicked belong to the kingdom of the devil, they are not the church. *In this life, nevertheless, because the kingdom of Christ has not yet been revealed, they are mingled with the church and hold office in the church. . . .* Christ is talking about the outward appearance of the church when he says that the kingdom of God is like a net (Matt. 13:47) or like ten virgins (Matt. 25:1). He teaches us that the church is hidden under a crowd of wicked men so that this stumbling block may not offend the faithful and so that we may know that the Word and sacraments are efficacious even when wicked men administer them. (AP 7–8:17, 19; emphasis added)

Melanchthon insisted that what counts in Lutheran ecclesiology is God's promise of salvation, the gospel, not the measurable effect of the gospel in terms of an exact distinction between those who are and those who are not true Christians.

> We maintain that the church in the proper sense is the assembly of saints who truly believe the Gospel of Christ and who have the Holy Spirit. Nevertheless, we grant that many hypocrites and evil men who are mingled with them in this life share an association in the outward

> marks, are members of the church according to this association in the outward marks, and therefore hold office in the church. (AP 7–8:28)

The church is purified not by a Puritan discipline but the continuous encounter between the word of God and the word of men. The distinction between God and devil becomes visible in this *encounter*; and God promises in the gospel that he and not the devil will stay in charge of the church. To this extent, the church can never stand still, or identify any of its traditions with the word of God. It will always have to be "re-formed" in the faithful heralding of the Word which promises salvation to ungodly men. For the Word is the final arbiter in the enduring struggle between the two "realms" determining life on earth—the realm of God and the regiment of the devil. The church, therefore, is a body in conflict. The struggle between the two rules goes through the church rather than around it. As Luther put it, in his 1522 treatise "Sincere Admonition to All Christians to Guard Against Insurrection":

> Christ himself has already begun an insurrection with his mouth, one which will be more than the pope can bear. Let us follow that one, and carry on. . . . The devil has for a long time feared the coming of these years. . . . Get busy now; spread the holy gospel, help others spread it; teach, speak, write, and preach that man-made laws are nothing; urge people not to enter the priesthood, the monastery, or the convent, and hinder them from doing so. . . . Tell them that a Christian life consists of faith and love. (LW 45, 67–68)

B.

The Gathering

The church is "the gathering of all believers, in which the gospel is purely preached and the holy sacraments are administered in accord with the gospel" (AC 7:1). These stipulations do not make a complete theological definition of the church, but they provide essential parts of one; and they contradict all medieval and most postmedieval thinking on the matter. The Augsburg Confession, by speaking of a "gathering" and "believers," denies from the first the medieval understanding of the church as an *institution* for the supply of blessings. In classic medieval theory, all human life depends on a small number of institutions; as the legally structured peasantry supplies food and the state supplies order, the church supplies grace. In the Augsburg Confession a few words undo this whole structure. But neither does the Augsburg Confession make the popular modern assertion it is often thought to make, that "the church is people." The church, it says, is a "*gathering*" of people; the church is not the persons simply as such, but something that happens with them, as the concrete occurrence of their reality as a community. Neither a class of persons nor a structure is the church; the church is an event.

Thus the Lutheran Reformation had from the start an actualist understanding of the church: the church is something *going on* in the world. It does not follow that it had an occasionalist understanding: as if the church came and went when certain persons assemble and disperse. What goes on between believers as the event of their coming-together does not start and stop with any particular invocation and benediction. Yet, because the gospel is actual human discourse, neither does believers' mutuality occur apart from the kind of meetings that can indeed have an invocation and a benediction. A purely "spiritual" inner communion has little part in the reality of the church as Lutheranism conceives it.

Therefore "all" does not here mark a class of persons; the church is not simply the dispersed totality of all humans having such-and-such characters. The "all" rather means both "all such gatherings" and "of whatever believers come together on any occasion." Its point is anti-hierarchical: *whatever* believers come together around the gospel make the church. Their gathering does not need validation by the presence in it of any certain kind of believers—priests or charismatics; and therefore also all gospel gatherings of believers are church-gatherings, whether or not they are authorized by any other or superior institution. Quite apparently such freedom is as foreign now, to our ordinary ways of thinking about the church, as it was in the sixteenth century.

The Marks of the Gathering

The church-gatherings are not the only ones that happen in the world; they are some of an indefinite swirl of meetings and separatings that make up human history. If a definition of the church is to be of any use, it must enable us to *identify* the church, to pick it out from the melee of human concourse; the definition must say *which* gathering is the church. The remainder of AC 7 attends to this. It does not do so by specifying characters of the persons who can make the gathering in question, but by specifying characters of the gathering itself. This means that the presence in the gathering of persons who, for whatever reason, ought not to be there does not disqualify the gathering as church; the church is a "mixed body," although in a sense somewhat different from the traditional.

Two identifying characters or marks of the church are given in AC 7, but the first contains the whole: the church is wherever "the gospel is preached." The church is that gathering that happens where and when it is the particular communication, the gospel, that makes a common reality for two, three, or a thousand people. Not every morally or religiously laudable gathering is the church, not even every gathering that, in a variety of reasonable senses, might be called "Christian." Nor is even a gathering of believers necessarily the church, if what they are up to is something other than preaching the gospel—as they may often rightly be. The church is what it is: the gathering of the gospel.

The Augsburg Confession says further that the church is where the gospel is "*rightly*" or "purely" preached. This additional stipulation is often misunderstood. It is, in itself, tautological; for it follows from the very nature of the gospel that if it is proclaimed at all, it is thereby rightly proclaimed. There can be no such thing as an "impure," almost-unconditional gospel. "Purely" is, like "all," polemic. As soon as the proclamation of the gospel becomes a process within history, it is inevitable that messages other than the gospel will be proclaimed in the church, and will just so claim to be the gospel. The Lutheran reformers believed themselves to live in a time when most of what was claimed to be gospel had not *really* been gospel; it is that "really" that the "*rein*" (pure) of the German text, or the "*recte*" of the Latin text enforces. A gathering is not the church just because it claims to be, or because there is much talk of "Jesus," "grace," or "love," or other gospel-words; there are *tests* of what utterance is gospel, and the church is the gathering of such utterance as could stand the tests.

An ancient misinterpretation of "the church is . . . where the gospel is purely preached" attends wrongly to these tests, to make it mean "the church is that ecclesiastical body, or sum of these ecclesiastical bodies, with a right doctrinal position." There are indeed right doctrinal positions, and they are important in various connections, some of them organizational. But AC 7 is not at all about the doctrinal status of any organization; it is about what happens or does not happen in some gatherings of people. If we are looking for the church, this article does not instruct us to survey the doctrinal stock of denominations or territorial churches; it instructs us to visit gatherings and to ask whether it is in fact the gospel that gathers them, or something else.

The list of dogmas or proposed dogmas that an ecclesiastical body commends to or enforces upon its members is no guarantee that it is the gospel that gathers those persons. Nor is an inadequate or even perverse doctrinal stock an absolute barrier to the true proclamation of the gospel. The classic Lutheran definition of the church should suggest a very considerable ecumenical relativism: authentically Lutheran ecclesiastical bodies ought not automatically to refuse fellowship to other bodies merely because they disapprove of their official doctrinal status; nor should they extend fellowship merely because they approve. This relativism does not mean that an ecclesiastical body's doctrinal position is unimportant; the Augsburg Confession itself is, after all, a nascent ecclesiastical body's reckoning of its own doctrinal position.

The second mark of the church is that it is the gathering in which "the sacraments" are rightly "ministered." The sacraments appear here as visible words, the acting-out form of the gospel. Therefore the whole of the above is simply repeated for this form of proclamation: the sacraments are to be ministered "in accord with the gospel." And our whole discussion can also simply be taken as repeated; the issue is whether what is in fact done in a gathering is performance of the gospel or of something else. The mark of the church is that the canonical commands to "Do this . . ." are in fact obeyed, and so obeyed that the more-than-verbal act of obedience is a communication of the gospel rather than of the law.

The question, therefore, is not about an ecclesiastical body's formal doctrine of the sacraments, but about its practice of them. All Lutheran bodies, obviously, have official doctrines of the sacraments that are for Lutheran thinking satisfactory; but what happens in a great many Lutheran congregations at the Lord's Supper—when quantities of holiness are speedily created by "the consecration" and are dealt out by the most expeditious and sanitary methods—is a mark of non-church. Such eucharists say, as performances, that by certain manipulations we can conjure into our substantial control the blessing of God. Vice versa, Roman Catholic doctrinal pronouncements about sacraments are to this day mostly regrettable; but what actually happens in many Roman Catholic parishes is powerfully evangelical and a clear mark of the true church.

The Article of Standing and Falling

All this, of course, leads to the question of how one can tell when the gospel is "really" being preached and the sacraments ministered in accord therewith. Article 7 of the Augsburg Confession does not itself provide an answer. The whole confession was the attempt to do that, the attempt of the Lutheran territories and congregations to solve the matter of church fellowship, to state the criteria by which they recognized and claimed to be recognized as true church. The remaining confessional documents simply continued the effort. And with the attempt to *state* criteria, for the purposes of the actual life of the church within history, we are indeed with organizations and their formal doctrinal positions, with dogma and its authority.

There is no doubt where the Lutherans drew the line between church and non- or antichurch. They reaffirmed the ecumenical dogmas as stipulations of the gospel's content. These were not then in dispute. They then laid down the article of "justification by faith alone" as the test by which preaching and sacramental practice "stand or fall." To repeat: it is not the reiteration of the formula that they demanded, but that the teaching, preaching, and rite be such as to open the justification that is by faith rather than the justification that is by works.

Clearly, this criterion of church and nonchurch is as unheard-of now as it was in the sixteenth century; and even the most modest attempt to regulate church life by it would be as disruptive now as it was then. This criterion's revolutionary force is only masked, especially within Lutheran denominations, by the deterioration of its language. Most of us will accept the formula, but we are able to do so only because we have come to use "justification" for the relatively trivial matter of excuse for past offenses, and have made "faith" mean religiosity or sincerity. If, having reminded ourselves of the original meaning of the formula, we visit the churches, and ask if anything happens in them that could by this criterion be called "the gospel," we will have to answer, "Rarely." It is this chapter in which it must explicitly be said: *the church is now in at least as desperate need of reformation as it was in the sixteenth century, and by the very same criterion as then.*

A chief reason for the deteriorated ecclesiastical force of the doctrine of justification is that its connection to the ecumenical creeds, taken for granted in the Augsburg Confession, can no longer be taken for granted. The doctrine of justification was a metalinguistic stipulation about a *particular* message, stipulated as to content by the creeds. It said: when you talk about Jesus and his meaning for us, as the creeds instruct you to do, make that talk unconditional promise. It did *not* say: any talk about something that might be called "faith," and about the benefits of such an attitude, is the gospel. It did not even say: any and all apparently "unconditional" promises are the gospel. But when the antecedent commitment to the story about Jesus and his Father has itself been lost, then, if the formula is retained, it must come to carry some such generalized recommendation; and then its linguistic trivialization into a doctrine about us and our inner agitations is only a matter of time. We need not rehearse again how the doctrine that results is the precise opposite of the Reformation doctrine.

The whole of this book is, in one way, an attempt to restate the doctrine by which the church stands or falls, in order to make its ecclesiastical force effective again. Restated yet again, to make the connection to the gospel's content *explicit*, the marks of the church can be summed up in this formula: the church is where those promises are made and performed that can be sanely made if and only if the particular man Jesus of Israel is indeed risen from the dead.

The Church's Organization

As a community extended through time, the church will be organized, whether it wants to be or not; groups within the church that have denied this have either behaved inconsistently or behaved consistently and vanished. Someone will at least be assigned to call the next meeting; and from there to the Roman curia is only a matter of degree. The question is not *whether* we are to be organized, but *how* we are to regard our organization. A very great deal of the Reformation polemic and reforming activity was devoted to these matters.

The Lutheran Reformation saw the church as event; merely thereby much of the medieval organization was taken for inappropriate, and the entire medieval understanding of organization was taken as false. The Reformers did not deny that the church will be—and rightly so—institutionalized, but they did deny that the church itself is an institution. To formulate the difference somewhat crassly: medieval thinking said that God created an organization, the church; the Lutheran Reformation said that God gathers people and that this gathering, the church, creates an organization in order to carry out its mission. This does not make the organization unimportant. On the contrary, it makes the organization of the church the field of believers' free historical judgment and responsibility, and so makes it precisely as important as we are. It is a perverse sort of self-denigration that says, for example, that if it is we and not God who decree an episcopal organization of the church, then it does not make much difference whether we have bishops or not. In the insight of the Lutheran Reformation, the church is "always to be reformed." This does not mean that the church is always in such horrible shape that a new Luther is needed–though it often enough is–but that in every new day organizational imagination and wisdom are needed to effect the church's mission, and that it is the privilege of believers to provide them.

In the sixteenth century, the Calvinists, Anabaptists, and other groups took the primitive church, insofar as it is visible in the New Testament, as a permanently valid pattern for the church's reformation. The Lutherans were more radical. For them, if the organization of the church is our free historical responsibility, then there can be no permanently mandated pattern of organization, only a permanently mandated mission for which to organize. Then also the organizational decisions of the apostolic church are not apostolic command but only apostolic wisdom, to which we should pay all attention, but which will not necessarily provide answers to the organizational questions of our own time. Both because Lutherans have sometimes exercised this right of free judgment, and because they have sometimes failed to do so, Lutheran territorial churches and denominations now exemplify every historical form of churchly organization: some are radically congregational free churches, some are episcopally governed state churches, and some are at every point of the spectrum between.

Lutheranism's asserted organizational freedom has been both an ecumenical blessing and an ecumenical problem. It has made Lutheranism at once entirely open to the organizational concerns that have been so important to other movements in the church, especially to the various branches of the English Reformation; and utterly resistant to the claims that often accompany those concerns, such as that a non-Presbyterian, or non-Episcopal, or established, or disestablished order is not "really" as God would have it.

Chapter 10

Christian Life—Brave Sinning

Readings:
SC and LC I, III
SC VII–IX
AC 6
AC and AP 16, 20

A.

The Starting Point

Lutheran ethics is intimately linked to the chief article of faith: God saves ungodly man without the condition of human merit. Luther signaled a revolution in the history of Western Christian ethics when he proposed that righteousness before God is the result of confidence in divine mercy rather than the reward for good works performed in fear of divine wrath.

Luther's view of moral life is inextricably linked with his understanding of man "before God": "good" is that which is done in good faith—that is, out of the relationship God himself has established—rather than on the basis of the merit man has to earn to be accepted by God. Christian life is life "in the sight of God." It is life in constant encounter with God, and it is the encounter with God which makes man morally accountable. To live "before God" means to exist in a relationship which is dynamic rather than static, incomplete rather than complete, earthly rather than heavenly. Man's righteousness will only be completed in his resurrection from death. Luther put it succinctly in his debate with the "Antinomians" (those who wanted to abolish moral laws and live only by the gospel):

> While we are cradled here in the arms of the Father, clad with the finest garment, our feet stick out from under it, and Satan bites them

> whenever he can. Then the child wriggles and cries, for it is still made of flesh and blood. The devil is still there, tormenting men until they become completely holy and are extracted from this void and wicked world. So we are saints and children of God, but only in the spirit, not in the flesh. We live under the shadow of the wings of our mother hen, cradled by grace. Our feet still need to be washed and, because they are unclean, must be bitten and plagued by Satan until they are clean. For unless you withdraw your foot under the garment, you will have no peace. (WA 39 I, 521–22)

Life is a struggle between the forces of good and evil; the church is a body of conflict, participating in the duel between God and Satan in this world; and history is God's carnival, filled with masks that reveal clues for moral behavior, but no guarantees of eternal rewards. Christian ethics is life in eschatological tension—interim existence between the departure and the second coming of the risen Lord. Luther believed that the best Christians can do in this life is to achieve a balance between good and evil, "equity," a measure of justice, reasonable compromise. God's grace provides glorious liberty; reason, enlightened by faith and grounded in love, creates brotherhood. But neither the experience of freedom before God, nor the creation of equitable brotherhood, saves man from sin or earns him salvation. Freedom before God and love among men only disclose suffering existence, the "ethics of the cross" which rest in the faith that the most realistic vision of life is based on the death of God in the Jesus of Israel. This was Luther's message to Pope Leo X in his open letter entitled "On the Freedom of the Christian" (1520):

> A Christian is a perfectly free lord of all, subject to none. A Christian is a perfectly dutiful servant of all, subject to all. . . . Although the Christian is thus free from all works [for salvation], he ought in this liberty to empty himself, take upon himself the form of a servant, be made in the likeness of men, be found in human form [Phil. 2:5–11], and serve, help, and in every way deal with his neighbor as he sees that God through Christ has dealt and still deals with him. This he should do freely, having regard for nothing but divine approval. (LW 31, 344, 366)

Faith active in love means to be a Christ to the neighbor—that is, to embody the relationship between God and man created in the life, death, and resurrection of Jesus. To love one's neighbor is not a "good work" which earns salvation; to love, in this world, is, at best, "bold sinning." That is Luther's ethical option. As he put it to Philip Melanchthon in 1521, at the height of the political turmoil following his appearance at Worms:

> If you are a preacher of grace, then preach a true, not a fictitious grace; if grace is true, you must bear a true and not a fictitious sin. God does not save people who are only fictitious sinners. Be a sinner and sin boldly, but believe and rejoice in Christ even more boldly, for he is victorious over sin, death, and the world. As long as we are here we have to sin. This life is not the dwelling place of righteousness but, as Peter says [2 Pet. 3:13], we look for new heavens and a new earth in which righteousness dwells. . . . Pray boldly—you too are a mighty sinner. (LW 48, 281–82)

Confessional Elaborations

Luther's ethical stance of "bold sinning," based on the conviction that man is simultaneously righteous and sinful (*simul iustus et peccator*), determined his catechetical and confessional statements about the Christian moral life. The first commandment, "You shall have no other gods," means to have faith in a God who is the source of all good. True sin is idolatry—the lack of faith and trust in God (LC I, 13–15, 22). "Where the heart is right with God and this commandment is kept, fulfillment of all the others will follow of its own accord" (LC I, 48). The Decalogue teaches men what they ought to do; the creed tells what God does for, and gives to, men. "No human wisdom can comprehend the Creed; it must be taught by the Holy Spirit alone" (LC II, 67). The Holy Spirit "sanctifies"—that is, "makes holy"—by forgiving sins and granting eternal life to the members of Christ's body, the church (SC II, 6). There is no "justification" without "sanctification." Faith creates a new and clean heart, and good works follow faith. "If good works do not follow, our faith is false and not true" (SA III, 13:3). The word creates faith. Faith creates the church. The church embodies forgiveness. "Forgiveness is needed constantly, for although God's grace has been won by Christ, and holiness has been wrought by the Holy Spirit through God's Word in the unity of the Christian church, yet because we are encumbered with our flesh [literally: it is around our neck] we are never without sin" (LC II, 54). The Christian moral life is the ethics of justification—the living out of faith in the God who makes the ungodly righteous.

Philip Melanchthon put into cool doctrinal language what Luther had affirmed in hot prophetic proclamation. The Augsburg Confession was meant to be ecumenical, conciliatory, and dialogical without, however, sacrificing Luther's basic evangelical insights. Thus Melanchthon located the Lutheran confessional assertion about the Christian moral life between the articles on "ministry" and "church": God acts in his promise of salvation; and man proclaims God's action. Proclamation leads to a new relationship with God. Ethics is defined as "new obedience":

> It is necessary to do the good works commanded by God. We must do so because it is God's will and not because we rely on such works to merit justification before God, for forgiveness of sins and justification are apprehended ["received"] by faith. . . . The same is also taught by the Fathers of the ancient church. (Latin AC 6:1–3)

"Good works" are the result of "justifying faith":

> When through faith the Holy Spirit is given, the heart is moved to do good works. . . . For without faith and without Christ human nature and human strength are much too weak to do good works, call upon God, have patience in suffering, love one's neighbor, diligently engage in callings which are commanded, render obedience, avoid evil lusts, etc. (AC 20:29, 36)

Good works, therefore, are done in faithful obedience to God's word rather than by choice of will. Although man possesses "some measure of freedom of the will to make choices among the things reason comprehends," he cannot choose his salvation (AC 18:1). He is saved by faith, rather than by good works. Melanchthon, relying on Augustine's anthropology, wanted to make it clear that God alone is the cause of "good," and the devil is the cause of "evil" (AC 19). To sum up the position of the Augsburg Confession:

(1) Good works must happen, not for merit before God, but for his praise. They are never a condition for justification; rather, they are the natural result of a grateful heart filled with the power of faith in the God who loves the ungodly.

(2) The new obedience is the call into a struggle between the "old" and the "new" Adam. Although sins are forgiven and sons of God are adopted, the conflict between good and evil has not yet come to an

end. The Christian lives in an *interim* situation—between the ascension and the second coming of Jesus. "Faith"—the relationship of absolute trust in what God did in Christ—determines what is "good" in this situation. Consequently, there are no absolute, eternal, or ethical norms by which the Christian is adjudged good or evil. There is only faithful obedience to God through concrete acts of love in the world.

(3) Lutheran "situation ethics"—moral existence before God in anticipation of a new world—implies the use of reason when faith is active in love. Since Lutheran theology teaches the proper distinction between "law" (the work of God the Creator) and "gospel" (the work of God the Redeemer), there is an ethical dialectic between reason and faith: reason is able to create a limited "civil righteousness," as long as such righteousness is not confused with "spiritual righteousness." As Melanchthon put it:

> We are not denying freedom to the human will. The human will has freedom to choose among the works and things which reason by itself can grasp. To some extent it can achieve civil righteousness or the righteousness of works. It can talk about God and express its worship of him in outward works. It can obey rulers and parents. Externally, it can choose to keep one's hands from murder, adultery, or theft. Since human nature still has reason and judgment about the things the senses can grasp, it also retains a choice in these things, as well as the liberty and ability to achieve civil righteousness. . . . But so great is the power of concupiscence that men obey their evil impulses more often than their sound judgment, while the devil, who as St. Paul says (Eph. 2:2) is at work in the ungodly, never stops inciting this feeble nature to various offenses. For these reasons even civil righteousness is rare among men. . . . Although we concede to free will the liberty and ability to do the outward works of the law, we do not ascribe to it the spiritual capacity for true fear of God, true faith in God, true knowledge and trust that God considers, hears, and forgives us. . . . Therefore we may profitably distinguish between civil righteousness and spiritual righteousness, attributing the former to the free will and the latter to the operation of the Holy Spirit in the regenerate. . . . This distinction is not our invention but the clear teaching of the Scriptures. (AP 18:4–5, 7–10)

The relationship between justification and sanctification was hotly debated in the sixteenth century. "Gnesio-Lutherans" and "Philippists" or "Crypto-Calvinists" battled each other over the proper understanding of this relationship. Finally, the Formula of Concord established basic guidelines for the proper theological debate of the issues of "good works" and "law" during the Majoristic and antinomian controversies.

The Crucible: Life in Two Kingdoms

Luther's view of government, fundamentally stated in his 1523 treatise "Temporal Authority—To What Extent It Should Be Obeyed," and the Lutheran confessional position on the Christian's attitude to the state, stated in AC 16 on "civil affairs," have been hotly debated and fiercely criticized ever since. Since Luther himself forged his political ethic in the face of specific historical circumstance and frequently applied it to specific situations (such as the peasant rebellion of 1525), the question of whether or not he was bold enough in his sinning is often raised. Was he less bold when facing the relationship between personal faith and sociopolitical evil manifested in medieval feudalism? After all, he had become famous for such bold sins as his advice to the Landgrave Philip of Hesse to engage in polygamy, or his stance at the Diet of Worms. Did he teach and practice civil disobedience, the right to resist? Since he himself had disobeyed the Edict of Worms by continuing to propagate his ideas, should Lutherans resist tyrannical political decrees such as the imperial edict of January 20, 1522, which condemned Lutheran religious practices and urged bishops and princes to punish those who disobeyed? Or should Lutherans obey on the basis of the biblical injunctions "Do not resist one who is evil" (Matt. 5:39) and "Let every person be subject to the governing authorities" (Rom. 13:1)?

Luther's salient points with respect to the Christian's attitude toward "temporal authority" are:

(1) His theory of two kingdoms is set forth in the context of the Augustinian distinction between the spiritual and temporal dimensions of human existence. God ordained the spiritual kingdom by which the Holy Spirit produces righteous people under Christ; and he also ordained the temporal kingdom by which the wicked are restrained and outward peace is maintained (LW 45, 91). Totally committed Christians do not need the external restraint of law and sword, for they live in harmony with others on the basis of love. But since there is always the temptation to sin, Christians need to assume positions in temporal government so as to prevent the collapse of law and order. "No Chris-

tian shall wield or invoke the sword for himself and his cause. On behalf of another, however, he may and should wield it and invoke it to restrain wickedness and to defend godliness" (LW 45, 103). Christians must participate in both realms.

(2) Luther set limitations on temporal government. Although princes hold offices ordained by God for the sake of political order, they have no power over conscience. Neither faith nor heresy can be imposed or deposed by force. "Faith is a free act to which no one can be forced" and "heresy is a spiritual matter which you cannot hack to pieces with iron, consume with fire, or drown in water" (LW 45, 108, 114). What should Christians do when faced with persecution? He had some concrete advice to Lutherans in Saxony, Brandenburg, and Bavaria, where courts had ordered the confiscation of his translation of the New Testament:

> This should be their response: they should not turn in a single page, not even a letter, on pain of losing their salvation. Whoever does so is delivering Christ up into the hands of Herod, for these tyrants act as murderers of Christ, just like Herod. If their homes are searched and books or property taken by force, they should suffer it to be done. Outrage is not to be resisted but endured; yet we should not sanction it, or lift a little finger to conform or obey. For such tyrants act as worldly princes are supposed to act, and worldly princes they surely are. But the world is God's enemy; hence they too have to do what is antagonistic to God and agreeable to the world. (LW 45, 112–13)

(3) He defined the true office of a Christian prince and the ways in which he should use his power. Undoubtedly, Luther was thinking of his own prince (Elector Frederick, dubbed "the Wise") when he listed only positive features (LW 45, 120–26). On the whole, Christian rulers are to make their decisions in terms of reason, love, and the common good. Luther concluded his treatise with an example of true Christian statesmanship:

> A certain nobleman took an enemy prisoner. The prisoner's wife came to ransom her husband. The nobleman promised to give the husband back on condition that she lie with him. The woman was virtuous, yet wished her husband free; so she went and asked her husband whether she should do this thing in order to set him free. The husband wished to be set free and to save his life, so he gave his wife permission. After the nobleman had lain with the wife, he had the husband beheaded the

> next day, and gave him to her as a corpse. She laid the whole case before Duke Charles [of Burgundy, who actually was involved in such a case]. He summoned the nobleman and commanded him to marry the woman. When the wedding day was over, he had the nobleman beheaded, gave the woman possession of his property, and restored her to honor. Thus he punished the crime in a princely way. (LW 45, 128–29)

This story points up Luther's motivation for his formulation of what has become known as "the two-kingdoms ethic": he wished to avoid the complete anarchy that could result from his reformation, which was eroding the foundations of the monolithic medieval establishment, the fusion of church and state; and he wanted to present a theological rationale that would enable evangelical Christians to maintain a positive relationship with a troubled world without succumbing to the perennial temptation of either becoming spiritualists and otherworldly romanticists, or advocating the total Christianization of political order, as Puritans, theocrats, and totalitarian ecclesiocrats did.

To sum up Luther's political views: Christians are citizens in both kingdoms. They may use the sword for the sake of a neighbor in danger of losing his life. They must suffer injustice when their own faith is endangered by political tyranny. "Legitimate government"—noblemen and magistrates, by medieval feudal standards—may use the sword against tyrants who violate their call to be equitable and just. A Saxon Christian prince is a legitimate revolutionary when he uses his sword against an emperor who advocates tyranny over conscience. Just and defensive wars are legitimate instruments of divinely ordained government.

When Emperor Charles V and Pope Leo X let it be known that their armies might march against Lutherans, Luther used an academic disputation by one of his students in 1539 to call for armed resistance against these potential invaders of Lutheran territories (WA 39^{II}, 55–66) The invasion never occurred. But Luther had reached the point where his two-kingdoms ethic called not only for obedience to a legitimately instituted government, but also for resistance to such a government when it has become tyrannical.

This dialectic of Christian obedience and resistance, in matters of political government, was still used by Melanchthon in his confessional formulation, even though his distinction between civil and spiritual righteousness tends to be dualistic:

> The Gospel does not teach an outward and temporal but an inward and eternal mode of existence and righteousness of the heart. The Gospel does not overthrow civil authority, the state, and marriage, but requires that all these be kept as true orders of God and that everyone, each according to his own calling, manifest Christian love and genuine good works in his station of life. Accordingly Christians are obliged to be subject to civil authority and obey its commands and laws in all that can be done without sin. But when commands of civil authority cannot be obeyed without sin, we must obey God rather than men (Acts 5:29). (AC 16:4–7)

There was no intra-Lutheran debate in the sixteenth century about the proper distinction between "civil" and "spiritual" righteousness in the context of political ethics. The debate was limited to anthropological dimensions in the context of individual salvation. Luther's two-kingdoms ethic intended to avoid an interpretation of "Christocracy" in either strictly institutional terms (an "ecclesiocracy" along medieval Roman Catholic lines) or in exclusively moral categories (a "theocracy" along Protestant Puritan lines). Lutheranism has misused and misinterpreted Luther's political ethics whenever it has regarded it as a mandate to separatist quietism or pietistic patriotism.

B.

The Secularization of Morality

The Lutheran confessions contain a great deal of ethical discourse, of argument about what should and should not be done. Much of this, but not all, is about what should and should not be done about the government and organization of the church itself. The Lutheran confessions contain noteworthy texts of moral commitment and examination: the catechisms' "explanations" of the Ten Commandments. They develop a historic discussion of the relation between morality and the ground of life, in the various developments of the theme of "justification" and "good works." And there is an explicit doctrine of political and social morality—the two-kingdoms ethic. These discussions do not make a complete formal analysis of ethical discourse and choice, and Lutheranism has never espoused any one such analysis. But these discussions do clearly display certain characteristic Lutheran attitudes toward ethical discourse and choice.

The first and foremost Lutheran point is the simple obverse of "justification by faith apart from works": works must then have their goodness and badness otherwise than by justifying us. If I feed my hungry neighbor, I need seek in this act no justification of my life, his life, or even of our life together. My life is undoubtedly a better one if I feed him than if I do not, on several scales of "better" and "worse." But my life is no more justified. To the question, "What is your excuse?" I have no more answer if I feed him than if I do not.

This is the assertion at which most of modern Protestantism has been offended, and retreated from the Reformation. But also morally, the offense is ill-advised; for just so the article of justification by faith cuts the nerve of moral egocentricity. *Why* should I feed my hungry neighbor? In obedience to the article of justification, I must simply answer: in order that his belly may be filled. I may, of course, make a chain of more remote reasons: in order that his family may have a more vigorous father, in order that the country may have a more creative citizen, and so on. There is no end to the possible extension of the chain; but if my justification is by God's grace alone, the chain can never jump to any reason of this sort: in order that *I* may be justified in my life.

Most ethical theories and all sensible persons have known that a good act cannot appropriately be done for an ulterior egocentric reason. If I feed my hungry neighbor in order that I may acquire stars for my crown, I thereby lose the claim to any stars. But the mere injunction, "Do good to your neighbor for his sake, not for yours," does not itself make a way out of our egocentric predicament. If, in order that *I* shall not be egocentric and so lose the value of my deed, I try to act purely for my neighbor, this is only a new egocentricity. The radically proclaimed gospel frees me from moral egocentricity in that it does not merely tell me I *ought not* try to get anything out of my act for my neighbor, but that I *cannot* get anything out of it, that I will not in fact be rewarded at all. Only the word, "You have nothing whatever to gain from your efforts on behalf of your neighbor's belly," frees me to attend to his belly. To the question, "Why should I do good?" the radical gospel replies, "If you put it that way, no reason." Just so the radical gospel frees me to do good in the only way in which good can—by the unanimous testimony of human wisdom—be consistently done at all.

Egocentric reasons for action can be of two kinds. I might say: I feed my neighbor in order to gain stars for my crown. Or I might say: I feed my neighbor in order to gain a voter for my party's slate. Everyone will classify the second reason as *a*moral; if that is why I feed my neighbor, the question of moral value lifts from my act altogether and settles elsewhere—perhaps as a question about the policies and abilities of my party. Unless bribery and corruption are involved, everyone will be happy that my recipient has a square meal, and I am unlikely to claim any moral credit for providing it. With this sort of egocentric reason, the identification of the goodness of my act with my own goodness is so implausible that it does not tempt. The egocentric temptation is only plausible with reasons of the first sort: where the line between my act and my reward runs by way of God or his equivalent. Here it is plausible because of the ease of the steps: "What is the good?" "What God commands." "Why should I do the good?" "Because God commands it." "Why should I obey God?" "Because he has my final good in his hands." In normal, law-enforcing religion, these steps are inevitable; for the very function of "God" in such religion is to guarantee virtue's reward. The unconditional gospel speaks peculiarly about God in that it announces that he refuses to fill this function, insisting on settling our final worth by his own considerations independent of our works. This cuts the chain. Thinking from the gospel, we will answer the question, "Why should we obey God?" with, "If you must ask, no reason." And then we will answer the question, "Why should we do the good?" with, "Because it is good."

Thus the doctrine of justification by faith effects a particular *secularization* of morality. On my side, the chain of reasons cannot reach past the temporal consequences of the act into eternity or the eschaton. If I feed my neighbor in order to gain a vote for my party, there is nothing the matter with that, if it is legal. And I can go on: in order to bring my party to power, in order to enact my party's social-welfare program, and so on—but if the gospel is true, the chain can never legitimately reach to any supernatural or eschatological reasons. On the neighbor's side, there is no such restriction. My reasons may well extend into the eschaton: "Why should I feed my neighbor?" "In order that his belly may be filled." "Why should his belly be filled?" "To make a sound body for God's resurrection!"

The Two Judgments

The judgment of my act from the side of its goal in my neighbor is one judgment, and the judgment from the side of its origin in me is another; the two differ precisely in the way in which *God* enters as the final judge. Here is the point of the distinctions between "two kingdoms" or "two hands of God," or "two forums of judgment" that run through Lutheran discussions of man's works. An act has *moral* value only in some interpersonal forum over against other persons to whose judgment it is submitted. Confessional Lutheranism distinguishes radically between two such courts of judgment: using Luther's own language, each of our acts is done simultaneously "before God" and "before men."

In the one forum, our deeds are what they morally are as God finds them good or bad for his purposes, as he accepts and uses them. As it is, God's purposes are those established in that Jesus is risen; he accepts all created realities, including our deeds, as objects and matter of the promises of the gospel. Our deeds are, in other courts, some good and some bad; in this court, they are *all* the matter of the promise. In this forum we therefore can only turn over our deeds as raw materials of the gospel's eschatological fulfillment. Our evening prayer is, "Lord, here are the acts of my day. Keep them for the kingdom, for Jesus' sake."

We are what we do. "Before God," therefore, we are what God will make of our acts—we are children of God. The Lutheran term for the moral self posited in God's eschatological affirmation was "faith." This self is transcendent to all negative moral judgments, for it exists by God's unconditional affirmation; as this self, I am "free lord of all," subject to no person's critique, not that of other humans, not the devil's, not even my own. If God says I am his dearly-beloved child, then I am that, no matter what you may—even justifiably!—call me.

In the other forum, our deeds are what they morally are as they find their goal in the neighbor. Here, my relation to God, to what establishes my final worth, is quite irrelevant. Here the only relevant question is: is the neighbor in fact benefited? In this forum, I cannot plead that I meant well; and it also cannot be held against me that I meant ill, unless my ill will becomes public and so itself a deed upon my neighbor. Not even faith has relevance here; the unbeliever's bread is good and the believer's mere wishes are evil. If the neighbor's belly is full, he will affirm that this is good; and that ends the discussion in this court. If I filled that belly, my deed is good in this court. In this court, God makes no private judgments; he ratifies the judgment of my fellows.

Again, we are what we do. "Before men," therefore, we are what we work out as in the history of the communities to which we belong. The Lutheran word for the moral self posited in the forum of humanity was "servant." "Before men" I am "bound servant of all," subject to the cold and practical judgment of all my fellows, and justified only by my actual contribution.

The self before God and the self before men do not necessarily coincide. That I shall be one self, the same before God and before men, is what I await from the last Fulfillment. Now I hang between my two selves, "crucified" in my moral self-fulfillment. I can never surely grasp myself as moral subject, for I am in the eschatological making. I cannot guarantee "what I *really* am," "why I really do what I do," my "authenticity," or any other item of that litany; I can only "sin bravely"; I can only act in hope and trembling.

In the subsequent history of Lutheranism, these various polar distinctions have tended to degenerate into sorting principles. Trying to decide on an action, the Lutheran religionist's standard first move has been to ascertain in which court his choice would be judged. Is the contemplated act a piece of politics or business? Then it will be judged by man's standards, and "religion" need not be brought into it. Is it a piece of piety? Then we need not ask how it will affect our neighbors. The distinctions between "kingdoms" or realms were originally ethically activating, in that they prevented a completed grasp in the present of the moral self and so undid all possibility of self-satisfaction; but their degenerate forms as sorting principles produced a deadly ethical quietism. All eschatological disquiet is sealed off in a stable and private relation to God; the realm of men becomes an undisturbable status quo. Evidently, this degeneracy must be most disastrous in political ethics, and Chapter 13 will deal with this.

Reason

The secularization of morality places ordinary ethical discourse within the sphere of what the Reformers called "reason." We do not discover what is to be done "before men" by special revelation, or by deduction from Scripture, or by "praying about it" and obeying the next impulse from within. We discover what is to be done by rational consideration of the situation and of the neighbor's possibilities in it. "Reason," in this older usage, did not mean "intelligence" only. "Reason" is the whole effort of man to deal with the circumstances of his life. If we now say that someone has "good judgment," this is very close to what the sixteenth century would have meant by calling him "reasonable." Reason, moreover, is judgment exercised within a *tradition* of judgment. A true mere individual, who really was a sort of moral atom, would have no faculty of moral judgment at all; "reason" occurs as each person participates in the historical human effort to make sense of common life. Thus when Luther sometimes turned from praising reason as an ethical principle to denouncing it as a theological principle, he had the particular Western tradition of theological judgment, shaped by Aristotle, in mind.

If reason is the whole effort of man to deal with the circumstances of his life, then reason must also include *vision.* It must include an anticipatory and adventurous projection of the possibilities of the human enterprise, or judgment will be empty. This aspect of the matter came very short in the Reformers' analyses of reason—though not in their practice of it—and was nearly absent in subsequent Lutheranism. Though the Reformers' own judgments were in the highest degree historically creative, their discussions of judgment little emphasized its creative character. Again, it has been in political ethics that this lack has proved disastrous for the Reformers' followers.

That we act "before men" by reason, and "before God" by faith, does not mean that we follow two different laws. Lutheranism, alone among major theological movements, has insisted that the policy of action to which reason will lead us is the very same love that faith finds between God and his children. Or, in another connection, that the love which is reasonable between all men is the very same love which faith opens in the believing community. The man who works his best judgment on the necessities and possibilities of his circumstances over against other men will discover that "Do unto others as you would have them do to you" is his best maxim of action; he will not need to read it in the Bible. Most theology has said that "Christian love," whether for God or the brethren and sisters, is "higher" or more demanding or in some way different from the love that reason dictates as the best policy. Lutheranism has denied the distinction, not to the dishonor of Christian love, but to the honor of secular love and the reason that mandates it.

Both the "realm on the left hand" and the "realm on the right hand" are under the law of love, because the same God rules in both. Man's reasonableness is not a faculty he possesses of himself; it is a pattern of behavior elicited by God's rule of the circumstances and temporal sequences of man's world. Thus the connection between faith and moral action in the world lies in God, not in us. The "evangelical" solution, that faith makes good people who then "go out" into the world to do good, and that these people are the connection between the realm of faith and the realm of common morality, is not in the line of Lutheran understanding. There is no need to "go out" and "bring" anything at all into the world; God already rules in the world quite as well as in the believing community. The task is rather to live responsibly under God's two rules, finding the ways in which the one possibility of love works out in each realm, and suffering the clashes between love and love which, short of the eschaton, must come.

Freedom

Yet Lutheranism *has* posited some difference between believers' reason and unbelievers' reason. The difference is never analyzed in the Lutheran confessions, and has been variously stated by later Lutheran theologians. We suggest an analysis that seems to us to lie in the direction of original Lutheranism.

Reason is not an ahistorical faculty; it is man's effort as a historical person to deal with his historicity, with the sequences of events that make his life, and with the choices they pose. If I am a believer, my historicity is that which is granted by the gospel-promise. This promise has specific content about what I may await from life. This must make a difference in what I will take to be reasonable. Put quite naively: a believer, like anyone else, tries to reckon reasonably with the facts, but he will also include *those* facts which obtain only if the gospel is true, and which unbelievers will not count. If the Lord Jesus is indeed alive in spite of death, and therefore due to triumph, even the coldest rationality will judge situations of risk and personal threat quite differently than would otherwise be plausible. If God is in any case, for example, going to make opportunities for Christ's love out of all human differences, if the kingdom is going to be full of all colors precisely for the sake of their variety, then I might just as well get used to the blacks (or whites) moving into my neighborhood. Or, if I suppose that Jesus' father is God, I will judge prayer a perfectly reasonable undertaking on behalf of my neighbor and myself.

The first Reformation treatise on human life bore the title "On the Freedom of the Christian." The Lutheran Reformation saw the chief moral problem not as finding criteria for telling good from bad, but as finding freedom to face and try to tell the difference. Most usually, if we will only ask what ought to be done, the answer is all too clear; and when it is not, the obscurity often cannot be resolved by any available criteria. Our real problem is that we are both afraid to ask and afraid to act in obscure cases. "Freedom" is the Reformation one-word slogan for the existential difference which faith can make in reason.

The gospel is a message of freedom from inhibitions to questioning and to action. These are not necessarily psychological. To continue an example, there are objective risks in affirming a racial change in my community, but if the Lord is coming, these risks need not deter me. A believer, we may say, is someone who knows he does not need to care for himself, since God will do that, and so has all that time and energy left to care for other people. Such freedom is not given all at once and forever. Believers are not necessarily, in any sense of a continuing characteristic, "freer" than others. And yet, in a situation where I must seek the good, if someone tells me the gospel as a word about that situation, the required little crack of freedom opens. More we do not need.

Chapter 11

Predestination—The God of Promise

Reading:
FC 11

A.

The Temptation of Theo-Logic

Luther, like many a medieval man, was plagued by the fear of God's wrath; since he could not accumulate enough "good works" for his salvation, he feared that God willed his damnation. "Though I lived as a monk without reproach," Luther wrote in a brief autobiographical sketch in 1545, "I felt that I was a sinner before God, with an extremely disturbed conscience. I could not believe that he was placated by my satisfaction" (LW 34, 336). Luther flooded his confessor Staupitz with his *Anfechtung* over predestination. How could one be certain that God willed salvation rather than damnation? As Luther put it in 1525 during his debate with Erasmus on "The Bondage of the Will":

> Admittedly, it gives the greatest possible offense to common sense or natural reason that God by his own sheer will should abandon, harden, and damn men as if he enjoyed the sins and the vast, eternal torments of his wretched creatures, when he is preached as a God of such great mercy and goodness, etc. It has been regarded as unjust, as cruel, as intolerable, to entertain such an idea about God, and this is what has offended so many great men during so many centuries. And who would not be offended? I myself was offended more than once, and brought to the very depth and abyss of despair, so that I wished I had never been created a man, before I realized how salutary despair was, and how near to grace. (LW 33, 190)

Luther experienced the God who saves the ungodly without human merit. *This* God, the god of mercy, was the god revealed in Jesus Christ; and he was the center of the Christian god-talk which Luther labeled "theology of the cross." Luther recognized the temptation of "theo-logic": to solve the mystery of the relationship between the God hidden in creation and the God revealed in the gospel through syllogisms. Medieval textbooks of theology and philosophical diatribes by Christian humanists had attempted to construct arguments showing the logical connection between the work of God as creator and redeemer. God was defined in terms of "attributes" which indicated his "supernatural" control over human life: since he "foreknew" the sin of Adam, he simultaneously "permitted" and "remitted" this sin in Christ, etc. Luther called such logical casuistry a "theology of glory" which no longer distinguishes between the hidden and the revealed God.

> We have to argue in one way about God or the will of God as preached, revealed, offered, and worshiped, and in another way about God as he is not preached, not revealed, not offered, not worshiped. To the extent, therefore, that God hides himself and wills to be unknown to us, it is no business of ours. . . . God must therefore be left to himself in his own majesty, for in this regard we have nothing to do with him, nor has he willed that we should have anything to do with him. But we have something to do with him insofar as he is clothed and set forth in his Word. (LW 33, 139)

Luther rejected the traditional medieval doctrine of predestination because it tempts one to focus on one's own ego rather than on God. Faith clings to the God who promises to save without human merit. Luther's doctrine of predestination, therefore, is Christocentric: whatever God might have planned, or is still planning for the world of men, is known in the gospel, the cheering news that the Jesus of Israel is our destiny. One can always worry about the hidden God—what he might do in his great majesty. But to such questions as, "Where was God before the creation of the world?" Augustine's answer is appropriate: "God was making hell for those who are inquisitive" (LW 54, 377).

Whereas Luther and his most ardent disciples, the Gnesio-Lutherans, refused to develop a syllogistic doctrine of predestination, John Calvin and Calvinists like Theodor Beza did. Operating with the category of "prescience" in the final version of his systematic theology, *The*

Institutes of the Christian Religion (1559), Calvin concluded that man's relationship with God is based on an eternal decree known as "double predestination":

> By predestination we mean the eternal decree of God, by which he determined with himself whatever he wished to happen with regard to every man. All are not created on equal terms, but some are preordained to eternal life, others to eternal damnation; and accordingly, as each has been created for one or the other of these ends, we say that he has been predestined to life or to death. (Inst. III, 21:5)

Calvin formulated the doctrine of double predestination in order to safeguard the freedom of God: God alone is in charge of human destiny, be it salvation or damnation; and even Satan's "contrarity and opposition depend on the permission of God" (Inst. I, 14:17). But Calvinists were soon tempted by the logical desire to distinguish in earthly life between the state of salvation and the state of damnation. Are there "signs" by which I can know to which group I belong—to the "elect," or to those who are damned? Generally, the virtues of the "Puritan ethic" (work, frugality, sobriety, etc.) were regarded as signs of God's favor, while disregard for Puritan virtues signaled divine reprobation. While Calvin himself refused to focus his mission in Geneva on the question of "Who's Who in the kingdom of God," many Calvinist Puritans did. Frequently, their theocracies (or ecclesiocracies) produced tyrannical governments, bloody crusades, and joyless worship.

When Lutherans and Calvinists tried to develop formulae of concord during the 1560s in Strasbourg, the Palatinate, and Lower Saxony, radical predestinarians and conservative Gnesio-Lutherans refused to cooperate. Jerome Zanchi, a former Augustinian friar turned Calvinist, attacked the Augsburg Confession because it lacked a doctrine of predestination. Tilemann Heshusius, an ardent Gnesio-Lutheran professor at various German universities, refused to have any fellowship with the disciples of Calvin and Beza. Although he agreed with Calvinist predestinarians that God predetermined the destiny of mankind with respect to salvation and damnation, he attacked them for teaching that God caused the fall of Adam and the betrayal of Judas. Some Gnesio-Lutherans, therefore, became "semi-" or "crypto-" Calvinists; some formulated a doctrine of "single predestination" (God predetermined salvation, but not damnation); others stressed the mystery of God's inscrutable will which is beyond human investigation. The doctrines of predestination and of Christ's presence in the eucharist had become the chief obstacles to Lutheran and Reformed unity in the sixteenth century.

Toward Christocentric Restraint

Although there was no "public, scandalous, and widespread dissension among theologians of the Augsburg Confession concerning the eternal election of the children of God" (FC 11:1), the Lutheran confessions established basic guidelines for a theological and pastoral discussion of the doctrine of predestination. In FC 11 there is an affirmation of a "single predestination," based on the unconditional promise of God's love in Christ:

> The eternal election of God or God's predestination to salvation does not extend over both the godly and the ungodly, but only over the children of God, who have been elected and predestined to eternal life "before the foundation of the world was laid," as St. Paul says, "Even as he chose us in him, he destined us in love to be his sons through Jesus Christ" (Eph. 1:4, 5). (FC, SD 11:5)

The certainty of salvation is not to be found in special "signs" of Puritan or other "works," but in faith that God keeps his promises even against the "gates of Hades" (Matt. 16:18); when we are in Christ, predestination is "a cause which creates, effects, helps, and furthers our salvation and whatever pertains to it" (FC, SD 11:8). Whenever theologians discuss the doctrine of predestination, it is helpful to distinguish between "foreknowledge" and "election." God's "foreknowledge" extends to all of creation—"He sees and knows in advance all that is or shall be, all that happens or will happen, both good or evil" (FC, SD 11:4); God's "election" extends to all of re-creation or salvation—the promise of the gospel (FC, SD 11:14–22). Speculation about the relationship of predestination and sin ("Is God the cause of original sin?") or the relationship of divine election and human freedom ("Why did God harden the heart of Pharaoh?") is to be avoided as a temptation to go beyond the promise of the Word of God (FC, SD 11:7, 85). Luther's and Paul's advice is to be followed:

> Concern yourself first with Christ and his Gospel so that you learn to know your sins and his grace. Then take up the warfare against sin as Paul teaches from the first to the eighth chapter [of Romans]. Afterward, when in the eighth chapter you are tested under the cross and in tribulation, the ninth, tenth, and eleventh chapters will show you how comforting God's foreknowledge is. (FC, SD 11:33)

God's will is sufficiently revealed in Christ. "We should not explore the abyss of the hidden foreknowledge of God" (FC, SD 11:33). If a careful distinction is made between what God has expressly revealed in his Word and what he has not revealed, the doctrine of predestination is indeed "a useful, salutary, and comforting doctrine, for it mightily substantiates the article that we are justified and saved without our works and merit, purely by grace and solely for Christ's sake" (FC, SD 11:43, 52). If there are people "who hear the Word and do not come to faith . . . it is their own fault" (FC, SD 11:78). Speculation about why this might be so works contrary to the pastoral intention of a Christocentric doctrine of predestination.

> Hence if anyone so sets forth this teaching concerning God's gracious election that sorrowing Christians can find no comfort in it but are driven to despair, or when impenitent sinners are strengthened in their malice, then it is clearly evident that this teaching is not being set forth according to the Word and will of God but according to reason and the suggestion of the wicked devil. (FC, SD 11:91)

B.

The Place of the Doctrine

Whenever the Lutheran doctrine of justification—or any serious attempt to specify God's grace as response to our radical questionability—is expounded, someone will ask in alarm: "But if the promise is all that unconditional, does that not mean *predestination*? What then of human freedom?" Therefore, we must discuss the matter in some depth, even though it plays a relatively small role in the Lutheran confessions.

The Lutheran doctrine of justification certainly does imply a doctrine of predestination. Indeed, within any Reformation theology, a doctrine of predestination is merely the article of justification stated with respect to God. Justification-language has passive-voice sentences with man as subject; if we say the same thing using active-voice sentences and God as subject, we have the language of predestination.

As to whether predestination denies human freedom, this depends entirely on the sort of God to whom destining is attributed, or—which comes to the same thing—what sort of human freedom one has in mind. There is no one concept of predestination. Indeed, "predestination" is already too specific a label; "post-destination" would be more descriptive for some versions of Reformation doctrine; and most medieval theologies fill the slot with theologoumena having little to do with "destiny," being rather about a timeless ground of being.

No even remotely Christian discourse can avoid predestinarian statements. If we are to talk of a God in any real way, we thereby talk about some sort of "predestination." For the word "God" is only our label to mark the point, in whatever faith or theology we live by, where the buck stops: God is by platitudinous definition absolute. If, with the Greeks, we apprehend reality as a marvelous construction, posing a puzzle-challenge to the intelligence, "God" names the buck-stopping explanation. If, with the Bible, we apprehend reality as time, "God" is the buck-stopping will in history, the last word. Alarm at predestination is simply alarm at having to deal seriously with the reality of God.

The Logic of Reformation Doctrine

There are two places in Reformation discourse where God-as-really-God, that is, God-as-absolutely-destining, comes to word. The one place is assertion of the unconditionality of the gospel-promise; the other is a necessary corollary of the first—the assertion that the promising God rules all events whatsoever.

That God's promise to us is unconditional, or that his favorable decision about us is both unmotivated and final, obviously come to the same thing. If the matter is put the second way, we make the root affirmation of predestination within Reformation discourse. The Reformation talked of predestination to assert the pure promise-character of the gospel, to say: "If God says your life and mine will be good parts of the human fulfillment, then they will be—because he says so, even if no other reasons can be adduced and despite all reasons adduced to the contrary."

It is characteristic that only this sort of predestination-doctrine is explicitly discussed in the Lutheran confessions. Indeed, the Formula of Concord attempts to treat this part of the matter as the whole, thereby involving itself in considerable logical difficulty.

This first and main sort of Reformation predestination-doctrine is not an attempt to explain why some men are saved and some lost, or all saved, or all lost. It is not an *explanation* of anything at all; and it is vital to understand that. As the reverse of the doctrine of justification, this doctrine also is instruction to gospel-speakers. It instructs us: to whoever will listen, promise fulfillment regardless of his "works"; say, "It will be yours simply because God wants it that way."

Of course we argue: "But if we are to say this to whomever we speak, and if we are to speak to all, are we not saying that all will be 'saved'?" Some may find this argument comforting and want to answer yes; others will be offended by such an answer because it seems to contradict parts of the Bible. Most Reformation theologians were at least mildly offended, and looked for formulae to blunt the argument—this search is reflected in the slippery bits of the Formula of Concord. But the real point to be made is that the argument is without application. It slides out of the place where this part of Reformation discourse has its meaning: it has ceased to be instruction to me, speaking gospel to you, and has become instead speculation about mankind in general. Such speculation is no sin, but its results can have no churchly importance; "universalism" and "particularism" of this sort must equally remain strictly private opinions.

This first step of Reformation predestination-doctrine attributes destiny to a specific God: God deep in the flesh of Jesus. The doctrine is not about an abstract deity "picking" from outside time; transferred to such a context it does not even make sense. It describes that God whose reality and will are to be sought only in the occurrence of the speaking of the gospel, who indeed *is* the Absoluteness of the gospel. Therefore, the question of a contradiction to human freedom, even over against God, does not arise. On the contrary, the absoluteness of the gospel is the absoluteness of that very word the hearing of which, and only the hearing of which, is the event of our freedom before God.

As you must liberate me to whatever functioning freedom I am to have for you, by your promising and accepting words to me, so God liberates us for himself by his promising and accepting words of the gospel. There is, of course, this difference: you are not my creator. Therefore, I have freedom granted by others than you; and since this also is freedom before man, it is a freedom like that you grant me, antecedent to it, and therefore in various ways preparatory to it.' All your words of promise and acceptance must be conditional on the choices already made in this antecedent freedom; if they are not, they become tyrannical. Not so with God's gospel-address to us; for he is our Creator, and has no prior sharers in the kind of freedom we have for him.

If the gospel is not understood as God's creator-word itself, the analogy between freedom for you and freedom for God becomes perfect. It is the fundamental difference between medieval and Reformation theology that medieval theology reckons with a human freedom that (1) is antecedent to the freedom opened by the gospel-address, (2) is of the same kind as the gospel's freedom, or at least overlaps with it, and (3) must therefore be allowed for in the speaking of the gospel, by means of reservations and conditions. Medieval theology reckons with such antecedent freedom because it does not experience the gospel-address itself as God's creating word; instead, it thinks of God's creating of human beings as done once-for-all at some past moment, so that whatever freedoms are proper to human beings, every human must, when hearing the gospel, already possess in some measure. Reformation theology, on the contrary, thinks of man as in the making by the Word of God, and so of man's freedom before God as in the making by the preaching of the gospel.

We come to the second kind of predestination-language. If the gospel-promise is indeed unconditional, it must tell the outcome of *all* events, of the entire created enterprise. If any reality of life is outside the gospel's affirmation, there is a "Yes, but . . ." with which I can and must respond to the gospel, and to which the gospel-speaker will have no cogent reply. In terms of God, if the gospel-promise is unconditional and true, the will which is real in that promise must encompass every event whatever. Whether we like it or not, it is a strict implication of the doctrine of justification: whatever happens, happens by God's will.

Even so, this second sort of predestination-doctrine does not in itself deny human freedom. Medieval theology, working here in a more congenial field, had already worked out the logic. If all things happen within the will of God, then, if God wills some events to be exercises of creaturely freedom, that is how they will happen. Precisely *because*

God is Creator and his will is absolute, there is, so to speak, no competition between his will and ours; and therefore the utter freedom of his will is not reciprocal to an unfreedom of ours—*unless,* of course, the "freedom" we seek is the right of self-justification, the freedom to abandon our human possibilities and assume God's. So long as these metaphysical reflections are not put to justifying a gospel-type freedom antecedent to the gospel, the Reformation could and did adopt them.

The Problem and a Choice

By itself, neither of these affirmations of predestination is a theological problem, though both may pose philosophical questions and both are certainly existential problems for our unwillingness to face God. The theological problems arise *between* the two, for there a rift opens in our image of God. The God who is the absoluteness of the gospel is pure love. But the will behind all events is by no means easily apprehensible as pure love or even as pure justice—if we judge merely by what happens around us, we must deny either God's existence or his goodness. How are we to deal with this split in our image of God? That is the theological problem of predestination. There are four possible moves; each has been tried in the history of Reformation theology.

(1) We can take one of the two absolutenesses of God as basic, and interpret the other in its terms. This can work one of two ways. We can take the general absoluteness of God's will as the definition of his deity, and interpret the absoluteness of his gospel-will as an *instance* of this general omnipotence. This is the Calvinist move. All things, the Calvinists said, happen by the sheer unmotivated decision of God; if, as the gospel promises, we are to be saved, this too is by his sheer decision. Thus the absoluteness of the gospel is affirmed, and there is no rift in the image of God. But this systematic simplicity is purchased at high cost. In God's general rule of creation, it is clear that some are doomed and some are blessed; if election to the blessing promised by the gospel is a special case of this general rule, then the observable fact that some do not believe must mean that the gospel is true only for some people. Lutherans must ask: if I cannot be sure that it is meant for me when I hear it, how can it be *gospel*?

(2) We can take the gospel's declaration of God's absolute love as basic, and try to interpret his rule in all events as a realization of this love. This is, by and large, the way of Neo-Protestantism, the post-

Reformation Protestantism of faith in progress and morality. Again, a unified image of God is obtained, and the gospel seems to be honored. And again there is a price. The gospel is transformed from a personal message into the enunciation of a general truth about the world. And since the world certainly does not seem to be the expression of a universal love, we must try to show how, "really," at some "deeper level," it is not what it seems—this has proven to be a long and arduous task.

(3) We can compromise the two absolutenesses of God. This was the medieval expedient; and one Lutheran tradition adopted it with the doctrine of "*intuitu fidei.*" According to this doctrine, God wills salvation for all men, but includes in this will the call to freely chosen faith, so that God more specifically chooses those whom he in his omniscience foresees will in fact believe the gospel when it is preached to them. This is an ingenious teaching; like the two previous ones, it reckons with but one unified divine will, but avoids their problems by construing this will neither as mere general omnipotence nor as unqualified gospel-affirmation, but as a benevolence subtly constituted in a dialectic between both. The price is, however, already stated: the gospel-predestination is qualified, "if you believe it."

(4) The "*intuitu-fidei*" Lutherans claimed that their position was inside the bounds marked by the Lutheran confessions. The final possible way is also within those bounds, and seems to have been Luther's own. This is to abstain on principle from all attempts to resolve the division in our image of God. On the one hand, we see God as the ambiguous will behind all events good and evil—that there is a will behind all events, the gospel itself compels us to affirm. On the other hand, we hear the gospel of God as pure and universal love. Given our reason for believing in the world-Will in the first place, we must affirm that these two images are of one God. But we do not try to say or imagine *how* they are one—this "how" is that one fundamental truth about God reserved for the revelation of the last day, it is the cognitive aspect of the eschatological limit. Creation is not yet at its fulfillment, and therefore also our knowledge is now "in a glass, darkly." The missing "how" is the darkness.

We prefer the fourth way. Arguing from the Lutheran confessions, the advantage of this way is that its understanding of faith seems to be more like that of the confessions as a whole. Faith is man's situation over against a surprising message that contradicts his otherwise reasonable judgments about what is to be hoped and feared, and so detaches him from security and despair alike, including cognitive security and despair. That is exactly the situation in which we remain, if we eschew systematic unifications of our image of God. On the first two options "faith" becomes the holding of certain firm opinions about the world, and, on the third, faith becomes that satisfactory attitude toward God which justifies him in justifying us.

PART FOUR

UNFINISHED WORK

Chapter 12

Unity—How Much Is Enough?

A.

Reformation Objectives

On November 28, 1518, Luther solemnly appealed to Pope Leo X to summon a general ecumenical council to debate the reform of the church. In the presence of a notary and two witnesses in the Wittenberg Corpus Christi Chapel, he declared in a carefully drafted statement:

> I do so with the expressed and solemn assurance that I shall do nothing against the one, holy, catholic church, which I regard as the master of the entire world and thus as supreme, or against the prestige of the holy apostolic see, or against our most holy lord, the pope, if he is well informed. If, however, I should utter something that is not right or is said with irreverence, prompted by my opponents, I am quite willing to correct and to change it. (WA 2, 36)

Subsequent experience taught Luther that such appeals to conciliar authority were of no avail. First by excommunicating Luther at Worms in 1521, then by tedious diplomatic moves, Rome rebuffed all attempts to call "a free, general, Christian council." Still, the adherents of the Augsburg Confession were willing to participate in such a council since they, on their part, would "not omit anything, in so far as God and conscience allow, that may serve the cause of Christian unity" (AC, Preface 13, 21). When the conciliatory papal emissary Paul Vergerio visited Germany after the Diet of Augsburg to secure Lutheran participation in a possible council, the Smalcald League agreed to attend, under four conditions: (1) it must be a free, not a papal council; (2)

Lutherans must be invited as full participants, not as heretics; (3) its decisions must be based on the authority of Holy Scripture and not on that of the pope; and (4) it should be held in Germany, if at all possible (CR 2, 962). Needless to say, Rome did not accept these conditions. "Dear Lord Jesus Christ, assemble a council of thine own," Luther prayed bitterly, in the midst of strife and physical pain, "and by thy glorious advent deliver thy servants" (SA, Preface, 15).

By 1539 Luther had buried all hopes for any reconciliation with Rome through an ecumenical council. In his treatise "On the Councils and the Church" (1539), he wrote:

> These desperate tyrants, whose evil forces us to despair of a council and of a reformation, must not drive us also to despair of Christ or leave the church without counsel and help; we must instead do what we can, and let them go to the devil as they wish. (LW 41, 11)

Yet, despite the tragic events of the sixteenth century, the Lutheran movement is committed to strive for Christian unity. The Lutheran confessions are based upon the three ancient creeds (labeled "ecumenical" in the Latin version of BC I); they consistently affirm "that one holy Christian church will be and remain forever" (AC 7:1); and they regard faithful witness to the gospel as the only norm for the true unity of the Christian church (AC 7:2). The Lutheran movement ties the question of unity to the principal article of faith: justification by faith apart from works of law. At issue is the radical difference between gospel and "human traditions" (AP 7–8:34). The gospel commits the Lutheran movement to seek Christian unity without tyrannical uniformity, and to confess the eschatological provisionality of all forms of doctrine and ecclesiastical life.

This does not mean that the gospel of Jesus Christ is proclaimed without specific assertions at specific times in specific places. On the contrary, the Lutheran confessions themselves are attempts to establish norms for orthodoxy and orthopraxy in the church. The church, as the creature of the gospel, must make clear distinctions between unifying "articles of faith and doctrine" (AC 1–21) and separating "abuses" (AC 22–28). For the gospel of Jesus Christ is witnessed in the conflict between God and Satan, good and evil, life and death; and the church needs to be constantly reformed for the sake of its unity and mission.

> It must not be thought that anything has been said or introduced out of hatred or for the purpose of injuring anybody, but we have related only matters which we have considered it necessary to adduce and mention in order that it may be made very clear that we have introduced nothing, either in doctrine or in ceremonies, that is contrary to Holy Scripture or the universal Christian church. (AC, Conclusion, 4–5)

Dialogue for Unity

Orthodoxy

When Luther and John Eck debated the primacy of the papacy at Leipzig in 1519, Luther advanced the view that the church of Christ extends far beyond the narrow confines of the Roman church. "I brought up the Greek Christians of the past thousand years," he told his friend George Spalatin shortly after the debate, "and also the ancient church fathers who had not been under the authority of the Roman pontiff, although I did not deny the primacy of honor due to the pope" (LW 31, 322). During their conflict with Rome, both Luther and Melanchthon hoped to win the support of the Orthodox Eastern churches, but contacts during the sixteenth century were sporadic. Melanchthon cited the Greek practice of communion in both kinds to support the Lutheran position (AP 22:4), and he praised the Greek canon of the mass for its emphasis on thanksgiving rather than satisfaction for the pains of purgatory (AP 24:93). He may even have translated the Augsburg Confession into Greek (although the translation is sometimes attributed to Paul Dolscius of Plauen).

After Melanchthon's death, Tuebingen theologians kept in contact with the patriarch Jeremiah II; the first Lutheran archbishop of Upsala, Laurentius Petri, and the Finnish reformer Michael Agricola visited Macarius, the metropolitan of Moscow, to show their interest in Eastern Orthodoxy; and in the eighteenth century, the Lutheran Pietist center at the University of Halle labored for a theological rapprochement between German Lutheranism and the Russian church through publications in Slavonic languages. Although no practical results emerged from these sporadic contacts between Lutherans and Eastern Orthodox churchmen, sufficient ecumenical foundations exist to pursue official theological conversations in our own time.

The Hussite Brethren

Luther's recognition of the Hussite Bohemian Brethren as part of the ecumenical church generated a climate of mutual respect and hospitality. The Brethren regarded the Wittenberg reformer as the "John Hus of Saxony"; Luther met five times with Brethren delegations in Wittenberg between 1522 and 1524; and he published the confession of faith which the Brethren had presented to Margrave George of Brandenburg and to Western theologians in 1532 to show their ecumenical orthodoxy.

Although the Bohemian Brethren and the Lutherans drifted apart after Luther's death, due to political developments in Europe, Luther's respect for John Hus as a respectable father of the church laid a good foundation for later contacts (LC IV, 50). When a large group of Bohemian Brethren found refuge on the lands of the Lutheran count Nicholas Zinzendorf at Herrnhut, they established close ties to Lutheran Pietism. Their bishop, Daniel Jablonski, consecrated Zinzendorf bishop of the Herrnhut Brethren in 1737, to assure "apostolic succession" (a Hussite doctrine); and the Herrnhut Brethren signed the unaltered Augsburg Confession in 1748.

The Reformed

The chief obstacle to Protestant unity in the sixteenth century was the deep disagreement, on the interpretation of the Lord's Supper, between the Lutheran and Reformed movements. But while Luther preferred disagreement to compromise, Melanchthon strove for ecumenical reconciliation. He hoped that a doctrinal rapprochement between German and Swiss reformers would create a united political Protestant front against Rome. His first attempts were not successful. The colloquy at Marburg in 1529, sponsored by the Lutheran prince Philip of Hesse, demonstrated that Lutherans and Zwinglians were very far apart in their understanding of the Lord's Supper. The Marburg Articles, signed by ten theologians, list agreement on fourteen doctrinal points and confess disagreement "as to whether the true body and blood of Christ are bodily present in the bread and wine"; they close with the ecumenical mandate that

> each side should show Christian love to the other side, insofar as conscience will permit, and both sides should diligently pray to Almighty God that through His Spirit he might confirm us in the right understanding. Amen. (LW 38, 88–89)

Martin Bucer of Strasbourg, a member of the Zwinglian team, pressed for further dialogue after the Marburg colloquy. In 1530, when the Diet of Augsburg refused to accept Bucer's compromise statement on the Lord's Supper, which he had submitted in a confession of faith by four German cities (the "Tetrapolitana"), he contacted Luther and Melanchthon. While Luther was cautious, Melanchthon agreed to work on a possible compromise. By 1534, he and Bucer had drafted a doctrinal formulation that Luther accepted as a basis for further negotiation: "the bread and wine are signs which, being given and received, the body of Christ is at the same time given and received." After two years of further negotiations, a delegation of Swiss and German theologians agreed to meet at Wittenberg to draft a formula of concord about the presence of Christ in the eucharist. On May 22, 1536, Luther and Bucer signed the Wittenberg Concord which states that

> with the bread and wine the body and blood of Christ are truly and essentially present, distributed, and received. . . .
> that it [the validity of the sacrament] does not depend on the worthiness or unworthiness of the minister who distributes the sacrament or of him who receives it. (FC, SD 7:14, 16)

Ten Reformed and six Lutheran theologians signed the statement along with Luther and Bucer. The Lutheran delegation seemed convinced that the Wittenberg Concord was faithful to the doctrine on the eucharist contained in the Augsburg Confession and the Apology—a conviction shared by the authors of the Formula of Concord in 1577 (FC, SD 7:12–16). The Wittenberg Concord of 1536 did not create the hoped-for unification of the Lutheran and Reformed churches, but it did pave the way for fruitful dialogue and occasional altar and pulpit fellowship in various parts of the world (for example, several territorial "union churches" in Germany, the Austrian Evangelical Church of the Augsburg and Helvetic Confessions, and some Pennsylvania congregations).

Roman Catholic

Lutheran dialogue for unity faces its greatest challenge in the encounter with Roman Catholicism. From the Reformation until the conclusion of Vatican II in 1965, no substantial ecumenical consultations took place between Lutherans and Roman Catholics. The decrees of the Council of Trent (1545–63) initiated a counterreformation on the part of Rome; and the Lutheran confessions were fated to become the arsenal for a Lutheran anti-Roman Catholic polemic. There were, to be sure, frequent attempts by courageous ecumenists to reach compromise or even agreement, albeit without the sanction of ecclesiastical judicatories. Emperor Charles V initiated sporadic colloquies between Lutheran and Roman Catholic theologians at Hagenau and Worms in 1540, and at Ratisbon in 1541. But, although some agreements were reached on various theological points, no common ground could be found on the significant problems of teaching authority (papacy) and eucharistic ministry (transubstantiation).

Erasmian humanism, rationalist philosophy, and the Age of Enlightenment prompted some Lutherans and Roman Catholics to seek unity through dialogue. The humanist George Witzel, the irenical Lutheran orthodox theologian Nicholas Hunnius, the Pietist Philip Jacob Spener, the abbott of Loccum Gerhard Molanus, the philosopher of the Enlightenment Gottfried Wilhelm Leibniz, the founder and architect of the popular German Christian Fellowship John August Urlsperger—all were Lutheran voices for dialogue in the wilderness of Christian repristination. Lutherans and other Protestants had to wait until Pope John XXIII opened the windows of Rome to let in the breeze of ecumenism which had for some time been generated by an international ecumenical movement. Vatican II acknowledged, for the first time in the conciliar history of Roman Catholicism, the positive value of the Protestant ecumenical movement—which had its formal origin in an ecumenical council at Upsala in 1925, 1600 years after the first ecumenical council in Nicaea.

In the wake of Vatican II, official consultations between Lutherans and Roman Catholics took place in the United States (Lutheran–Roman Catholic Consultation, sponsored by the U.S.A. Committee of the Lutheran World Federation and the Bishops' Committee for Ecumenical and Interreligious Affairs) and on an international level (Lutheran–Roman Catholic Study Commission on "The Gospel and the Church," sponsored by the Lutheran World Federation and the Secretariat for Promoting Christian Unity). Lutherans can no longer afford to assess their own position in the modern world without looking closely at Vatican II and its impact on Roman Catholicism. Luther's old reformation and Pope John XXIII's new reformation are irrevocably intertwined in the mystery of God's time.

Lutheran dialogue for unity has been propelled by the mandate of the Lutheran confessions to struggle for the best way to witness to the gospel at various times and in various places. Lutheran ecumenical efforts since the Reformation have been burdened by sociopolitical constellations, intra-Lutheran quarrels, and lack of stamina under the pressure of grace. But the history of the Lutheran dialogue for Christian unity also discloses a pioneering spirit, hard theological work, and a sense of freedom under the gospel. Samuel Simon Schmucker's vision of an "apostolic Protestant church of America," in his *Fraternal Appeal to the American Churches* of 1838, is a significant reminder to contemporary Lutherans that even the Augsburg Confession can be revised in the name of Christian unity—albeit not with such new doctrines as the divine obligation of the Sabbath or baptismal regeneration which Schmucker espoused in his "Definite Synodical Platform" of 1855; and Archbishop Nathan Soederblom's meticulous, realistic construction of a worldwide organization for the promotion of dialogue on all significant issues of church life is an example of Lutheran dedication to witnessing to the gospel in the midst of the vicissitudes of history—albeit not by succumbing to the temptation of interpreting the Lutheran confessions by mystical insights into the history of religions. Lutherans can work for Christian unity on the basis of the confessional mandate that *it is sufficient* to be a faithful witness to the gospel of Jesus Christ who is the guarantor of Christian unity.

B.

Since the whole effort of the Augsburg Confession was to reestablish the threatened unity of the Western church, the confession contains an explicit statement of the nature and requirements of churchly unity:

> For it is sufficient for the true unity of the Christian church that the Gospel be preached in conformity with a pure understanding of it and that the sacraments be administered in accordance with the divine Word. It is not necessary for the true unity of the Christian church that ceremonies, instituted by men, should be observed uniformly in all places. (AC 7:2–3)

These propositions functioned in three contexts. We shall discuss the three functions in sequence.

The Definition of Unity

In the first place, the confessional propositions try to define the unity of the one catholic church, whose existence is unquestioned and to whose existence unity essentially belongs. The definition is accomplished by listing certain unities, the lack of which marks the division between church and nonchurch, and certain other unities, the lack of which can be encompassed within the one church. Since the church occurs as that gathering of persons which is distinguished from other gatherings in being constituted by the preaching of the gospel and the celebration of the sacraments, any gathering not so constituted is outside the church. "Ceremonies," on the other hand, may vary.

The term "ceremonies" should be taken as widely as possible. The provision asserts the historicality of the gospel: that the liturgical, hierarchical, legal, and dogmatic arrangements for the preaching of the gospel and performing of its sacraments are the responsibility of free human creativity, and that therefore they will legitimately vary from time to time and place to place. Thus, for example, the unity of the church is not broken by liturgical variations short of such as make it doubtful that the sacraments are being performed at all.

We have already reached a decisive point: in the Lutheran view, if Christians can have mutual recognition and acceptance of "preaching" and mutual recognition of, and acceptance at, the eucharistic table, we thereby achieve all that must necessarily be achieved between us. For a Lutheran understanding, *communio in sacris* ("fellowship in holy things") is the main ecumenical goal, and is not necessarily the beginning of any further organizational or legal unification.

The essential unity of the church, for Lutheranism, is neither an inward and invisible "spiritual" unity nor an institutional unity, but unity in proclamation and sacramental action. This unity is necessary for the church; and where it is lost, we must work to recover it. The work involved will ordinarily be institutional work, and will create various organizational unities; but these latter are by-products.

The Conditions of Unity

Our situation is one of lost unity; we turn to the Lutheran confessions above all for help in the work of achieving renewed unity. But there is a hermeneutical gap between the confessions and our situation.

The confessions know nothing of the denominational system. They certainly know nothing of our present decadent denominationalism. That is, they know nothing either of the structure of our disunity or of the organization through which work for unity must now be done. Our reading of the confessions is and must be *interpretation* in the proper sense; we cannot simply "apply" them to ourselves. What follows is a proposed *exegesis* of AC 7.

The plural "churches" at one point in the German text assumes not denominationalism but the general experience of churchly plurality: between territorial churches as they had existed in varying independence through medieval history, between confessing groups of the Reformation period, or between the Eastern and Latin churches. The Augsburg Confession further assumes that insofar as churchly plurality interferes with communion in the holy things, this interference should be overcome—unless, of course, it should develop that one party had ceased altogether to be church. What follows "It is sufficient" are the simultaneously maximum and minimum demands of the Lutheran parties in such endeavors. There are two.

The first demand is that it be possible to preach the gospel *together*, with understanding of how this is to be done. This is not a demand for dogmatic unity; as the German text makes especially clear, the required unity is in actual preaching of the gospel, not in confessional statements or systematic theologies. Nor does "It is sufficient" single out some set of essential doctrines on which there must be agreement, as against other less essential doctrines on which there need not be agreement. Rather, "It is sufficient" contrasts "gospel" with "ceremonies" as conditions of unity. When the gospel can indeed be preached *together* by a group of persons, any party within the group must recognize other parties therein as actualizations of the one church, and so as entitled to the full communion of holy things, despite whatever "ceremonial" (including dogmatic!) controversies may otherwise divide them.

This does not mean that theology, dogma, and "ceremonies" generally are irrelevant to the unity of the church. For the judgment must be made whether it is in fact the gospel that is spoken by a community, or some other word pretending to be the gospel. It is this latter possibility which the demanded "purity" of preaching raises and condemns.

The gospel will in fact be preached by a community only if it is preached "in accord with pure understanding," that is, if the community is committed to the theological enterprise and having some success with it. The theological enterprise is the continuing effort to understand how to preach the gospel in each new situation; and where this enterprise flags, we may expect the gospel to be perverted. Dogmatic formulation is a recurrent step in the church's theological enterprise, marking especially significant crises, especially such as threaten the unity of the church; the Augsburg Confession itself is just such a theological act.

Article 7 of the Augsburg Confession does not permit Lutherans, faced with a question of fellowship, to evade judging whether the word by which the other group coheres as a group is indeed the gospel or is something else. Nor does AC 7 allow us to make that judgment by anything so pleasant as a sense of fellowship, or an intuition of eschatological unity. Lutherans have to ask: When the Episcopalians or the Baptists or others speak as a community, what do they *say*? Is what they say the gospel?

The theological and liturgical collapse of much of contemporary denominational Christianity makes it so hard to answer the first part of the question that, were Lutherans permitted to make traditional assumptions, we might be tempted to forego ecumenical endeavors. But the assumptions Lutherans have traditionally made about their own theological status can no longer be made. For despite the Lutheran denominations' greater official fervor for their dogmatic tradition, the Book of Concord has little greater communal effect among them than do the Thirty-Nine Articles among Episcopalians or papal decrees among American Roman Catholics. The Lutheran denominations live—or do not live—by the same mixture of fundamentalism, helplessness before every wind of doctrine, tag-ends of denominational tradition, and occasional saving theological and proclamatory miracles as do the other American denominations. We will make progress only when we recognize that what we have to do is to make interim arrangements between segments of a disintegrating form of the church, to try to make the birth of a new form of the church a little easier.

Therefore the question which separated Christians have to ask about each other can be no stronger than, Is there enough of the gospel alive in our various groups to make it likely that they will prepare the way for a rebirth of the church better *in* communion than *out* of communion? This is still AC 7's demand for judgment, but in the form appropriate to our present situation. It cannot be answered by any comparisons of documents, or by intelligence operations conducted from afar, but only by painful mutual explorations, under the judgment of the Bible.

The second demand is "that the sacraments be administered in accordance with the divine Word." This is not a demand for an agreed-upon doctrine *about* the sacraments; it is a demand upon the *performance* of the sacraments. The "Word of God" in question is simultaneously the canonical command in obedience to which we perform these actions, and the gospel which is the meaning of the actions (as is clear from the parallel "according to the Gospel" of the previous paragraph). Therefore what is demanded is that what the canonical command says to do be in fact done, and that it be so done that its meaning as a communication is the gospel and not the law.

All current denominations may rightly have some suspicions about the others on these scores—the issue, again, is not what is said in sermons, catechetical instruction, or confessional formulae *about* the sacraments, but what is said and done as the actual celebration. The divisive problems are mostly about the eucharist. Lutherans may rightly suspect other denominations' styles of eucharistic celebration which, despite all disavowals, make the deed fundamentally a petitionary and doxological work of those present, or liturgical formulations which make the blessing dependent on the attitude of the recipient. Other denominations may rightly suspect Lutheran patterns of eucharistic celebration which make it dubious that the canonical command is being obeyed at all, as when, instead of sharing wine from a common cup, some Lutherans receive the wine (or in some cases, grape juice) from individual glasses, or, although commanded to "give thanks" do no such thing, or perform the eucharist so infrequently or even lugubriously as to transform the sacrament into a substitute for penance.

With respect to this demand, our situation is much the same as with the first. Can we judge that, despite everything, the sacraments do, by and large, happen in another denomination? If any two denominations can make an affirmative judgment of genuine sacraments in both, the second demand of AC 7 would be satisfied—insofar as we now could think of satisfying it at all.

The Lutheran Sticking Point

"It is sufficient" not only specifies the demands which Lutherans must make on others, it also limits the demands which Lutherans can allow to be made on themselves. Most bluntly stated: if other parties can affirm that the gospel is preached acceptably among us, and the sacraments celebrated acceptably, they have no right to demand further uniformities as conditions of communion. Indeed, Lutherans have generally regarded any tendency by another party to make further demands for uniformity as prima facie evidence that the gospel is not being preached rightly in that quarter.

Here is the point where unity negotiations around the world have regularly broken down. Most denominations with which Lutherans are led to negotiate define themselves by some organizational peculiarity, that is, by something the Lutherans must regard as a "ceremony." Roman Catholics define themselves by the juridical primacy of the bishop of Rome; the various branches of the English Reformation define themselves by *episcopacy*, *presbyterial*, or *congregational* government; the Methodists define themselves by a "method" of holiness; and the sects are just that. For Lutherans, all these matters are negotiable; but for the bodies in question they are not. Great ecumenical proclamations often represent them as negotiable, but when it comes to actual proposed steps to unity, the contrary is regularly discovered. And as soon as it is discovered that, for example, congregational autonomy is *constitutive* for the unity of the church as some group proposes to establish it, Lutherans are bound to resist.

We approve this Lutheran stubbornness, yet the situation is logically peculiar, and failure to keep it straight may be one cause of previous difficulty. If another group were able to recognize Lutheran proclamation and sacraments, on *whatever* theological or practical basis, this would be in itself all the recognition of their ministries that Lutherans, within *their* theology, need or should demand. There are, therefore, no Lutheran conditions to be met at this point; or rather, if others can at all approve communion, that in itself satisfies the only Lutheran condition in this connection.

If, *after* the establishing of communion, two denominations wished to move toward further organizational unifications, the issues that would arise would all be subject to negotiations, as far as Lutherans are concerned. Precisely because communion in the holy things defines churchly unity for Lutherans, once this is achieved Lutherans can lose their sensitivity about conditions. Once communion in the gospel and its sacraments is given, then juridical, liturgical, hierarchical, and dogmatic conditions are obviously appropriate to juridical, liturgical, hierarchical, and dogmatic unifications; and Lutherans would probably discover a few conditions of their own. This does not mean Lutherans should regard these subsequent issues as unimportant; on the contrary, as the matter of our free historic responsibility for the gospel, they are precisely as important as we are.

At this particular epoch of history, however, those guided by the Lutheran confessions may well be somewhat skeptical of further traditional ecumenical negotiations. Putting two or three present denominations into a new big organization of the same sort would be no great accomplishment. Perhaps all we can hope for denominations, as we know them, is to get them a bit out of the way of whatever God may have in mind for the future of his church. What God has in mind will surely involve upheavals and creations far more drastic than any further institutional ecumenism. If we can make our institutions help believers get together in the word and the sacraments, rather than hindering them, our old denominational forms will have done yet one good thing. Past that point, we should expect God to work some surprises.

Chapter 13

Politics—Two Kingdoms?

A.

The Lutheran Neuralgia

The political ethic of the Lutheran confessions, based on Luther's "two-kingdoms ethic," has caused a painful neuralgia for twentieth-century Lutheranism. The rise and fall of Hitler, two world wars, and the murder of millions of Jews in concentration camps have led many interpreters to the conclusion that Luther and Lutherans are much to blame for what happened in Germany. Luther research has been affected by a scapegoat hermeneutic. The controversy between the German scholars Karl Holl and Ernst Troeltsch is symptomatic for subsequent disagreements: Holl and his disciples regarded Luther as the progressive reformer who gave the decisive impetus to the development of the modern "cultural, political community"; Troeltsch and the Troeltschians saw in Luther the regressive defender of the medieval state, tolerating injustice and demanding feudalistic obedience (especially during the peasant rebellion of 1525). The controversy was sharpened when the Swiss Reformed Karl Barth blasted Luther as the fountain of Hitlerism, and the Lutheran Dietrich Bonhoeffer accused Luther of reducing New Testament ethics to a morality of quietistic innerworldliness.

Troeltsch's basic criticism of Luther became popular in the United States after World War II. Reinhold Niebuhr labeled Luther's political ethic perverse and tyrannical. Staunch defenders of the two-kingdoms ethic argue that Luther's political ethic is the best alternative to Christian extremism. Other analysts of the two-kingdoms ethic call for a balanced revision in the light of the article on justification and of the contemporary problems which separate us from Luther. In 1941 the Norwegian Lutheran bishop Eivind Berggrav told his constituency that their resistance against Nazi occupation was in total harmony with Luther's doctrine of the two kingdoms; rebellion against a diabolical tyrannical power, Berggrav argued, is an act of faith rather than sin.

The critique of Luther's two-kingdoms ethic can be summarized in terms of two objections: (1) Luther limits the lordship of Christ by deriving from the gospel only a new *attitude* to the world of political order, but not the Christian's *task* to work for the renewal of such order to make it conform to Christ's kingdom; and (2) Luther violated the teaching of the New Testament by viewing the two kingdoms in terms of static coexistence rather than eschatological tension.

With regard to the first objection, it can be argued that Luther did not see the lordship of Christ at work in *orders* or structures such as family, government, or economics. Rather, he saw Christ at work in *persons* or fellowships such as parents, princes, or congregations. Luther meant by "government" a ruler's exercise of political power for the sake of equity, which is best achieved by the combination of reason, law, and faith. He did not know the impersonal, bureaucratic, and demonic Machiavellian state with its secularized banality of evil; at most, he sensed it behind Rome's tedious medieval diplomacy, rather than in the benevolent, supportive government of Frederick the Wise. Besides, Luther never lived anywhere but in sixteenth-century Saxony! He reckoned that even the ferocious Turks were able, by some kind of "natural law," to deal justly with their subjects. He simply could not imagine that legitimate government—the hierarchy of feudalism, with its sixteenth-century variations—could be worse than the rebellious peasants. For while the former had the promise of the "first use of the law," namely, to have been "instituted" by God (Rom. 13), the latter had only the promise of the gospel, namely, to suffer in passive disobedience—but do no more. Rebellion on the part of the "common man" was against the will of God. Only legitimate government could rebel against injustice. Luther fiercely condemned the peasant rebellion in 1525; but he sanctioned the armed resistance of German princes against pope and emperor.

> Rebellion is a crime that deserves neither trial nor mercy, whether it be among heathen, Turks, Jews, Christians or any other people; the rebel

> has already been tried, judged and condemned, and sentenced to death, and everyone is authorized to execute him. (LW 46, 81–82)
>
> The pope seeks out the souls of all humanity, that is, he desires, above all, to subject each soul to his blasphemies, so that they go to hell for his sake. Hence it is necessary to march and rally against all the armies which fight under his command, even though it means insurrection. . . . If he [the emperor] wants to protect the werewolf [the pope]—this cannot be tolerated. Instead he must be opposed. (WA 39, ii, 55–56. 65–66)

The question is, who committed the braver sin? The peasants who rebelled against feudal landlords and were slaughtered by infinitely superior armies, or Luther and his followers who disobeyed imperial law at Worms and elsewhere and called for rebellion against pope and emperor?

With regard to the second objection, it can be argued that Luther developed his two-kingdoms ethic in two stages. When first faced with the question of how to deal with evil in the political order, Luther told his followers in "Temporal Authority: To What Extent It Should Be Obeyed" (1523) that there is a basic conflict between the kingdom of God and the kingdom of this world, between the believers in Christ and the adherents to the Antichrist. "This world" meant sinful existence under Satan; the ruler's law is needed to prevent total chaos. Consequently, God instituted political order to recognize and prevent massive sin (according to Paul and Augustine). Christians do not need the law, for they do voluntarily what the law requires: justice, civility, decency, etc. If all men were Christians, there would be no need for secular government. But when Luther was asked how to deal with good created order, such as marriage and property, he concluded that such order dates back to paradise rather than to the Fall. Adam and Eve did not need the law because they were without sin. They lived by the law of God's good created order, expressed in marriage and economics. Consequently, Luther distinguished between the realm of Satan, the realm of law (in the sense of good created order), and the realm of the gospel.

The Christian can live in the realm of law and order as well as in the realm of word and sacrament. Both realms are the work of God: creation and redemption. Although Satan may tempt Christians in both realms, he cannot take over. The "kingdom of this world" is no longer under the lordship of Satan; it is under the power of God who works behind the "masks" of the created order and of the re-created fellowship of gospel. The "law" has two functions: it orders the creation and it reveals the sin of God's creatures. The "gospel" functions in terms of word and sacrament. The law preserves the old order and the gospel promises a new order; Christians need both.

In 1529 Luther no longer held the view that Christians could live without secular authority. For secular authority is not only the state, but also marriage, property, and other matters which express the goodness of God through, and apart from, the state (the first article of the creed and the fourth petition of the Lord's Prayer, SC II, 1–2; III, 12–14). While Luther, in 1523, saw a close correlation of the New Testament conflict between the kingdoms of God and Satan to the conflict between church and state in his own time, by 1529 he no longer viewed the relationship of church and state in terms of an eschatological conflict. He could still summon Christians into the battle against Satan, but this battle should not be understood as a battle against the state. Does this mean that Luther regarded the state as an "order of creation"? Was this the reason that he viewed any rebellion against the state as apostasy from the gospel?

An Old Mandate and New Realities

Luther tried hard to provide pastoral guidance to people threatened by persecution for their membership in the Lutheran movement. He did not construct a systematic Christian political ethic, but addressed only the question of civil obedience and its limitations. In wrestling with the question of civil disobedience, or the right to armed resistance, Luther provided three clear answers:

(1) Individual violent resistance is justified, in order to protect oneself and the neighbor. Such violence is a form of faith active in love. Self-defense and defense of a neighbor in the face of extreme danger are to be viewed as mandates of the law of creation and the gospel of redemption.

(2) Political violent resistance is justified when legitimate government carries it out. Thus the right of political rulers to engage in acts of violence, such as defensive war, capital punishment, and even revolution, is but an extension of the personal right of self-defense, and is an obligation to keep order in the world.

(3) It is the vocation of the Christian in this world to suffer political violence rather than to resist it forcefully (unless he is a political ruler). This is the point at which Luther's two-kingdoms ethic, anchored in Augustinian pessimism about the world and influenced by his personal experiences with Frederick the Wise, dampens his view of Christian action as "bold sin." Why, one is driven to ask, is a Christian revolution against tyrannical oppression not a bold sin, especially when engaged in for the sake of the neighbor who has become a victim of political tyranny?

Luther's two-kingdoms ethic should be viewed within the framework of medieval theology and political theory; it should not just be criticized from the viewpoint of modern democratic ideals. Luther tried to overcome the confusion between the realm of Christ and the realm of the world, created by the medieval church's sacerdotal-juridical interpretation of the Christian faith and the spiritualist-moralistic speculations of left-wing reformers. The two-kingdoms ethic avoids the extremes of institutional Christocracy (ecclesiocracy) and moralistic theocracy (Puritan ethic). But, in his attempt to steer clear of papal authoritarianism and utopian sectarianism, Luther tended to separate the two kingdoms so sharply that their fundamental unity—anchored in the eschatological tension between law and gospel—was obscured.

Post-Reformation Lutheranism frequently dissolved the original tension between Luther's two kingdoms and arrived at an ethical dualism. Seventeenth-century Lutheran orthodoxy and eighteenth-century Pietism stressed a "religion of the mind" and a "religion of the heart" which could behave one way in private and another way in public. The history of Lutheranism discloses a tendency on the part of Lutherans to be quietistic rather than revolutionary in the face of political tyranny. "Liberal" Lutherans in the nineteenth century ignored the two-kingdoms ethic altogether, and spoke only of an ethic of the self. Lutheran state churches in Europe were not consistently the critical consciences of the state. American Lutherans generally ignore the old mandate of the Lutheran confessions to seek a healthy balance between God and Caesar. A pietistic patriotism or a quietistic separatism have prevailed as a substitute for a Lutheran confessional political ethic.

To be sure, there were always Lutherans who followed the apostolic injunction to obey God rather than men (Acts 5:29 and AC 16:7). But, in the matter of civil disobedience, very few brave sins have been committed by the Lutheran movement. Between Luther's resistance to pope and emperor and the resistance of the German "Confessing Church" to Hitler there is a long history of degeneration. Lutherans must rethink the old mandate of the article on justification in light of new political realities; for not only must faith be active in love, but love also must be active in justice.

B.

The doctrine of the "two kingdoms"—or "realms"—cannot be directly applied to modern problems of political ethics, for the political entities it discusses no longer exist. The great political question is always, Who shall rule? The Lutheran reformers' answer, that since revolution always makes matters worse, those shall rule who now rule, is no help to us; for the revolution they feared was the kind typified by the French Revolution, which has in the meantime happened despite them—for better or worse. What must be done is to interpret the two-kingdoms doctrine as a historical expression of Lutheranism's call for radical faith, and of Lutheranism's basic ethical attitudes, and to build a new Lutheran political ethic in this interpretation.

The Political Corollaries of Justification

Whatever happens, happens within the will of God. This immediate corollary of the doctrine of justification, combined with observation of what actually happens, may well drive us to unbelief. But if our faith is so sustained by the proclamation of Jesus' crucifixion that it can live in such testing, no part of life and the human world can then be indifferent for it. "Politics," in modern language, is the whole of those processes by which are established the rules of a community's future shared life, that is, it is the human world's relation to its own future. As encounter with this endeavor must clearly be a chief test of faith, so it must be a chief exercise of faith.

The Reformation's radical proclamation of God has at least four consequences for faith's political exercise. First, all questions posed by the impact of external, public reality are questions posed by God; so, therefore, are all political questions. There are two political questions: By what rules will our community, so as to be a community, live in the future? And who shall decide? A community's answer to the second question is fundamental; for it is the choice of communal values, and so creates the ethical language in which the first question can be deliberated—for notorious example, totalitarian "democracy," republican "democracy," and direct "democracy" are not the same thing at all.

Every answer to an actual historical choice of the second sort confesses some God or other. If God is *the* Sovereign, there must be reciprocal appropriateness between different identifications of God and different ideals of where sovereignty is to be located among us. The gospel can surely be preached within every possible sort of polity. It does not follow that Luther's choice between underclass populism and personal rule, or ours between forums in which the citizens are only represented and forums in which they appear personally, are theologically neutral choices.

Second, the believing community must participate in politics whenever it has the chance. The tests of faith are the occasions of faith; for believers to let the political world go its way is therefore merely unbelief—if, of course, we have a choice. More in the terms of traditional Lutheranism, an opportunity of political participation is an opportunity of service to the neighbor and therefore is commanded by God. If an allegedly Christian groups finds that its religion dispenses it from political action, the God of that group is not the gospel's God.

Third, to confess God by our political choices over against the realities of this world's history is to abandon all hope of a unified explanation of God's works. It is to accept the contradictions of historical experience as definitive short of the Fulfillment. God rules this world by created ministers; we believe that he is one and rules for the triumph of the one love of the one Lord Jesus. But we may not expect theoretically or experientially to unify the works of his ministers by that belief. God's right hand will know what his left hand has been doing when both are stretched out to receive the fruit of his creation; until then, to confess God really, politically, is to accept struggle and polarity.

Fourth, although we may not synthesize the contradictions of God's rule over this world, we may *interpret* them, by the dialectic of law and gospel. God's rule of creation is not a mere forceful compelling of events; it is done by his word, it is his self-communication. All events are his deeds *insofar* as they are in their total sequence his self-communication to his creatures. But God's word is law *and* gospel. Therefore we may interpret the antinomies of his omnipotence by this duality, though we will never see through them. God rules his creatures by the preaching of the gospel, by this particular future-granting communication among humans. He also rules his creatures by *all* communication among them, insofar as all communication *somehow* opens the future. The two modes of God's self-communication open creatures to God's future in very different ways; but it will be the same future. Our hope in this identity does not lift us above the antinomies that rend our image of God; but it does let us live in them.

From God's Action to Our Sorting

The two-kingdoms ethic was, to begin with, a law-and-gospel interpretation of the sixteenth century's political struggle. The Reformation was a decisively and massively "political" action, in our sense of the word, however Luther and his followers may have eschewed what they called "the power of the sword." The Reformers demanded and brought about radical changes of public organization and policy; and their struggle was in large part fought in assemblies of state power. The two-kingdoms ethic was, in its time of authenticity, politically energizing and a guide for action; those who lived by it defied an empire, bent princes to their purposes, invented new forms of international alliance, mobilized public opinion for the first time in history, and even created new polities to suit.

Yet modern American Lutherans regularly suppose that Lutheranism's great achievement was "separation" of "religion and politics." Such a separation did indeed occur in the eighteenth century, from a variety of causes; but none of them was Lutheran—or Calvinist—theology, except by way of reaction. Insofar as Lutheran language about "two kingdoms" became involved in the separation, and even became our after-the-fact justification for it, the language suffers a dislocation which neatly reverses its function.

If the unsolvable tensions of life under God's rule come to our consciousness, they may destroy us; but if they do not, they free us unconditionally for action, allowing neither self-satisfaction nor despair. The two-kingdoms ethic was a particular, historically conditioned, consciousness of those tensions; and that it set free a torrent of creative political action is observable fact. Those caught between God's rule by the princes and his rule by preaching could never cease from action, wherever and whenever action for God or the neighbor became possible. But this energizing character of two-kingdoms ethics depended on lively apprehension that God's two modes of rule have but one goal, the fulfillment promised by the gospel; that is, it depended on lively eschatological faith. The moment eschatological awareness weakened, the two-kingdoms ethic began to function quite differently.

If christological faith ceases to be attention to promises made now, and becomes meditation or theorizing only of what Christ, back then, made available, if it loses its eschatological reference, the unity of God's two "kingdoms" is lost; for this unity lay in a common final goal. The two kingdoms then cease to be poles of historic unrest and become instead static compartments of interest. The two-kingdoms ethic becomes a sorting principle. Just this happened in post-Reformation Lutheranism. Faced with a moral choice, the traditional Lutheran's first move has been to determine to which compartment to assign the matter in question: if it turned out to be a public matter, the gospel would not need to be dragged in; if it was a religious matter, the neighbor's needs would not be relevant.

In most of Lutheranism the two kingdoms thus changed from modes of God's actions to compartments of man's concerns. Ethical discourse *so* structured necessarily promoted political incompetence. For faith in the future, located in the religion-compartment, was simply sealed out of the politics-compartment. Thus bereft of political hope, most Lutherans have either withdrawn from public responsibility or accepted it with a "realism" barely distinguishable from heathen cynicism.

Our Present Situation

Our political situation is very different from that to which the Reformers addressed their counsel. First, the once self-evident difference between rulers and ruled has collapsed. We indeed have ruling classes more entrenched in privilege than any sixteenth-century princes; but the members of these classes no longer derive their *claim* to power merely from their membership. The most arbitrary and hated tyrant must claim to govern by the "just consent of the governed." Sovereignty, as distinct from mere power, is universally located with the people; all states claim to be "true" democracies. If, therefore, the ministers of God's rule are those in whom human sovereignty is vested, we all are those ministers. If as the Reformers' addresses to the princes apply now, they do so only insofar as they can be applied to all of us.

Since the French and American revolutions have made us all "princes," there cannot now occur any such thing as the revolution which the Reformers feared. There can be nihilist terror, on the model of many currently "radical" movements; and to this Luther's fulminations entirely apply, such antipolitics being precisely the anarchy to which he expected all revolution to lead. But a revolutionary movement with stateable goals and considered methods must now be considered a political act *within* the arena of sovereignty, since it is conducted by "princes." Whether a particular revolutionary impetus is a justifiable act or not cannot now be decided merely by its being revolutionary; rather, this depends on what its goals and methods in fact are. Also, the question of violence attendant on revolution can no longer be settled generally. Sovereignty cannot be exercised in this world without violence; but each execution, imprisonment, abortion, or compulsory "therapy" must be justified by considered criteria. Post-French Revolution, revolutionary violence is in the same category.

Second, a separation has indeed been made between politics and religion. The above proposition, that we are all, as rulers, ministers of *God*, will be accepted by few. In the United States, for example, Jefferson indeed traced the sovereignty of the people to an endowment by the "Creator," but the Creator he had in mind was religiously quiescent, a deity whose presence or absence would make no difference to the practical conduct of affairs. Insofar as modern states appeal to deity, they appeal to a deity invented especially for the purpose of not interfering. The God who *would* make a difference to public affairs is explicitly banished from them by the founding ideologies of all modern states. Thus James Madison insisted on religious freedom *in order to* "multiply sects," the purpose of the multiplication being so to balance them against each other that none could achieve public influence.

Lutheranism cannot approve this arrangement. In Lutheran theology, all exercise of human sovereignty is ministerial service to the *same* God worshiped by "sects," that is, by those who acknowledge a God active in human events. A system that banishes institutionally the people's lively relation to God from the decision processes of their common life is institutionalized atheism, which sooner or later must penetrate personal faith. And if God really is, such a system flies in the face of reality, and therefore must lead also to political disaster.

What Lutheran theology should have predicted seems to be happening. In all Western secular states, the expulsion of faith from the political realm is gradually destroying faith. Expelled from the arena in which we make shared choices, faith becomes a "private matter." But the "private" in this sense shrinks to a dimensionless point; for once the individual is set *against* the community, the individual loses reality. The individual's religion loses application to actual life, which is lived in communication and community.

Thus American Protestantism once dreamed of the American commonwealth as a new Zion prepared for the returning Christ. Then Protestantism abandoned the commonwealth itself to the inactive Creator of Jefferson and Madison, and the collapse to the dimensionless point began. First Protestantism set out to create, instead of a holy state, a holy *people* for the Lord *within* the state; the great movements of reform and revival in nineteenth-century American Christianity are the successive waves of this effort. Then, around the turn of the century, Protestantism abandoned the attempt to convert the people, and limited itself to "saving" enough individuals to make a holy leaven *among* the people. Now, finally, it is accepted doctrine that religion is "private," that for communal purposes it does not matter what I believe so long as I believe something. As is manifest to all observation, this "private" religion is precisely that religion which can be counted on not to interfere with any actual action or communication of its possessor, all of which are necessarily in some fashion public. This religion is pure self-delusion.

Just as the separation of religion and politics is bringing modern Western communities to religious deprivation, so it is bringing them to political dehumanization. The inactive deity of American state religion was never of much practical use: he never functioned as a guide to the commonwealth's decisions or as an energizer of its undertakings. But so long as Protestant Christianity could be counted on as the religion of the people, the state religion's vacuousness was not noticed; statesmen could always appeal to that other God when they really needed to lead moral choice or summon sacrificial dedication to the community. Now that Jefferson's "Creator" has to go it alone, his incapacity is manifest; and the moral cohesion and common purpose of the American people visibly decrease from day to day. The "patriotism" that supported our Indo-Chinese aggressions was the last empty form of American communal morality; the antiwar movement was its last formless content. Now that both have been disappointed, we are becoming nihilists.

Believing communities within Western states should take the collapse of the modern religious settlement not merely as a disaster, but as the opportunity to replace it with something better. In this endeavor—which history is anyway forcing on us—Lutheranism could be uniquely advantaged. Its adherents could be freed and sustained for reconstruction by the knowledge that all labor for the public good is service to God, even when it leads into profound moral ambiguity; and that no such labor will lack its fulfillment, the God thus served being the same God who promises to bring all things together into his final Community.

Moreover, the Lutheran interpretation of political obedience to God, by the dialectic of law and gospel, could provide indispensable clarity for the work of religious-political reconstruction. The great problem has always been to meet God in the political without deifying the state. Religious history is an oscillation between the idolatry of politics and disgusted withdrawal from them. Political history offers mostly a choice between polities that make themselves absolute for their citizens and modern polities that avoid this by altogether banishing faith from citizenship. In democracies, this choice either absolutizes some mystic and therefore tyrannical "common will" of the people, or banishes faith from all of life.

But if *one* God rules through all powers but in *more than one* mode, then he meets us in the political arena and there tests and exercises faith, without having to be identified with the sovereignties through whom he rules. And if *we* are now those sovereignties, we may understand this too in such a way as perhaps to avoid democracy's seeming choice between tyranny and nihilism.

Much thinking and rethinking lie between us and an authentically Lutheran political ethic. But the enterprise is not hopeless. Should it succeed, there would be great benefit to the church, and perhaps also to the world.

Chapter 14

Adiaphora—Freedom or Bondage?

Readings:
AC and AP 15
SA III, 15
FC 10

A.

Gospel, Freedom, and Human Tradition

In his treatise "The Freedom of the Christian" (1520), Luther distinguished two classes of men: "unyielding, stubborn ceremonialists" who insist that human precepts are means to salvation and justification; and "simple-minded, ignorant men, weak in the faith" who have been misled by wicked pastors but who are willing to be liberated from the snares of idolatrous traditions (LW 31, 373–74). The former may be beyond pastoral care, but the latter need love, patience, and instruction.

> Although we should boldly resist those teachers of traditions and sharply censure the laws of the popes by means of which they plunder the people of God, yet must we spare the timid multitude whom those impious tyrants hold captive by means of these laws until they are set free. (LW 31, 374)

The true Christian must steer a middle course between legalism and antinomianism. As long as this world exists, "ceremonies," "human traditions," and "works" are needed to witness to Christ in faith and in love toward the neighbor.

> As wealth is the test of poverty, business the test of faithfulness, honors the test of humility, feasts the test of temperance, pleasures the test

> of chastity, so ceremonies are the test of the righteousness of faith. . . . Hence ceremonies are to be given the same place in the life of a Christian as models and plans have among builders and artisans. They are prepared, not as a permanent structure, but because without them nothing could be built or made. When the structure is complete, the models and plans are laid aside. . . . Thus we do not despise ceremonies and works, we set great store by them; but we despise the false estimate placed upon works in order that no one may think that they are true righteousness. (LW 32, 375–76)

There is, then, a difference between the gospel which brings salvation, and human traditions which do not. To know the difference means to be a truly free Christian.

Luther's views were challenged by ardent disciples in the fall and spring of 1521/22 while the reformer was absent from Wittenberg. Luther's colleague Andreas Bodenstein von Carlstadt and an apostate Augustinian monk named Gabriel Zwilling took over the reform movement in Wittenberg. They were uncertain of Luther's fate, even though Melanchthon knew that the reformer had been "kidnapped" by order of Frederick the Wise, and secretly brought to the Wartburg for his own safety. Carlstadt and Zwilling publicly asserted that the time had come to remove images from the churches, to dissolve the hierarchical order of Romanism, and to realize the common priesthood of all believers by allowing laymen to celebrate the eucharist. Many Wittenbergers, led by students and apostate monks, stormed and pillaged churches and monasteries; during the 1521 Christmas season, radicals from the Saxon town of Zwickau proclaimed the end of all externals and the end of the world. The sociopolitical order of Wittenberg began to crumble under the pressure of a "radical reformation."

Since Melanchthon seemed unable to restore peace, Luther himself returned to Wittenberg on March 6, 1522, and, after analyzing the situation, preached eight powerful Lenten sermons at the parish church between March 9 and 16, one each day. The sermons dealt explicitly with the difference between "things which must be" and "things which are left to our free choice by God."

> All works and things which are either commanded or forbidden by God, and thus have been instituted by the supreme Majesty, are "musts." Nevertheless, no one should be dragged to them or away from them by the hair, for I can drive no man to heaven or beat him into it with a club. . . .

> In the things that are free, such as being married or remaining single, you should take this attitude: if you can keep it without burdensomeness, then keep it; but it must not be made a general law; everyone must rather be free. (LW 51, 79)

Luther's pastoral advice on images, fasting, communion in both kinds, and oral confession stressed that common sense, patience, and concern for the weak should prevail. Images should be kept for aesthetic edification, but should not be worshiped; fasting is a good discipline, as long as it does not lead to works-righteousness; the laity may take the host in their hands and receive the chalice, but if some are not used to touching the host, let them not do it in public so that there is no offense; as long as oral confession helps Christians survive in the struggle with evil, it is a good practice and should be kept. In short, these things have proven themselves beneficial in the history of the church and should not be abolished unless any one of them is confused with the gospel. The enemy is idolatry: the temptation to make "matters of choice" "musts" for salvation. "True worship" lets God be God; "false worship" makes conscience seek salvation in its own works, keeping count of how often it has fasted, prayed, and confessed (LC I, 22). Luther could accept much of the Roman tradition as good and useful for service to the gospel—even bishops, so long as they were "true bishops" and it was understood that they are "for the sake of unity, but not of necessity" (SA III, 10:1). But the Roman teaching "that human traditions [such as the episcopacy] effect forgiveness of sins or merit salvation" he considered un-Christian and meriting condemnation (SA III, 15).

Melanchthon shared and solidified Luther's position on the difference between gospel and human tradition (in the *Loci Communes* of 1521, the first Lutheran systematic theology, and in AC and AP 15). "Church orders" and/or "ecclesiastical rites" do not belong to the gospel but to "human tradition" (CR 21, 510–14). Such matters as ecclesiastical constitutions and liturgies "contribute to peace and good order in the church," but are "not necessary for salvation." Any teaching which claims that they are instituted for the purpose of propitiating God and earning grace is "contrary to the gospel and the teaching about faith in Christ" (AC 15:2–3). Melanchthon defended AC 15 as an ecumenical position grounded in Scripture and the tradition of the church fathers (especially Thomas Aquinas and John Gerson) (AP 15:24,

28). He hoped for reconciliation on such matters as monastic vows and episcopacy, which he labeled "adiaphora" (AP 15:52). But the label "adiaphora" (from the Greek *adiaphoron,* meaning "a thing that makes no difference") for what the medieval church called "ecclesiastical law" did not please Roman Catholics at Augsburg. Although medieval textbooks used the ancient Stoic term "adiaphoron" to describe what the Christian is "allowed" rather than "commanded" to do (based on 1 Cor. 6:12 and 10:23), they did not teach an adiaphorist understanding of any aspect of the ecclesiastical hierarchy, certainly not of episcopacy. Thus it is not surprising that the Roman Confutation of Augsburg stated that "it is false that human ordinances instituted to propitiate God and make satisfactions for sins are opposed to the Gospel" (BC 215, n. 4). The several meetings between Lutheran and Roman Catholic theologians, initiated by Emperor Charles V in the wake of the diet, only revealed the radical differences about the relationship between gospel and adiaphora. "Now we leave it to the judgment of all pious people," Melanchthon ended his statement on episcopacy, "whether our opponents are right in boasting that they have really refuted our Confession with the Scriptures" (AP 28:27).

The Adiaphorist Controversy

Political events in Germany, after Luther's death and the defeat of the Lutheran Smalcald League in the spring of 1547, presented the Philippists with an opportunity to reach interim agreements with Rome. Although the new ruler of Wittenberg, Elector Maurice, had sided with the emperor, he was willing to tolerate Lutheran doctrine in his territory—a move motivated by a mixture of political ambition, humanist leanings, and clever diplomacy. Melanchthon, who had left Wittenberg in fear of persecution, returned to work for the rehabilitation of the university as the center of the Reformation, even though Maurice (later dubbed the "Judas of the Reformation" because of his treacherous relationship with the emperor) could not be fully trusted. The Gnesio-Lutherans viewed Maurice as an enemy of the gospel and retreated to Jena, which they hoped to build up as the center of the Lutheran movement (with the help of the sons of Elector Frederick, who had been imprisoned by the emperor after the defeat of the Smalcald League).

Both Maurice and Emperor Charles V hoped that the Philippists could be persuaded to arrive at some compromise with Rome in order to save the unity of the empire. In the spring of 1548, the emperor appointed a committee of three well-known intellectuals to prepare a doctrinal interim agreement between Lutherans and Roman Catholics until a general ecclesiastical council could make a final decision. The Lutheran John Agricola, the Erasmian philosopher Julius von Pflug, and the historian Michael Heldin were to draw up a statement which would secure agreement in essentials (the gospel) and let the government dictate nonessentials (adiaphora). When the interim statement was published at Augsburg on May 15, 1548, both Gnesio-Lutherans and Philippists rejected it, since it conceded very little—the eucharistic cup for the laity, clerical marriage, and the restitution of confiscated property to Lutherans (CR 6, 865–74).

Although the emperor managed to enforce the Augsburg Interim Agreement in most of the southern German territories, the northern territories, led by the city of Magdeburg, refused to abide by it. Afraid of civil war, the two electoral princes Maurice of Saxony and Joachim of Brandenburg urged Melanchthon to revise the Augsburg Interim in such a way as to reflect the most conciliatory Lutheran position. Melanchthon agreed to do so after a series of meetings with political consultants and some theologians. The princes made it clear to him that peace with the emperor had to be achieved at the cost of reducing Lutheran doctrine to bare essentials and conceding as much as possible to Rome. The result was the Leipzig Interim of December 17, 1548. It affirmed justification without meritorious sacrifice as the inviolable Lutheran article of faith, but it conceded the validity of seven sacraments and agreed to regard most medieval ecclesiastical practices as useful adiaphora (CR 7, 260–64).

A stormy controversy followed the publication of the Leipzig Interim. Lutheran theologians from Hamburg, Berlin, and Jena accused Melanchthon of betraying his own Augsburg Confession and Luther's Smalcald Articles. Melanchthon defended himself by asserting that Christian liberty consisted in the free confession of the gospel and not in the rejection of adiaphora. But Gnesio-Lutherans, led by Matthias Flacius, were convinced that Melanchthon and the Philippists had reverted to papal abomination.

Flacius' essential arguments are contained in two major treatises published in 1549: *Against the Interim (Wider das Interim)* and *Con-*

cerning True and False Adiaphora (De veris et falsis adiaphoris). While the first treatise attacked primarily the Augsburg Interim rather than that of Leipzig, it advanced the basic Flacian and Gnesio-Lutheran thesis that in a period of persecution adiaphora cease to be indifferent; as long as imperial edicts compel Lutherans to restore medieval ceremonies and rites, their rejection is mandated by the gospel. Flacius' second treatise undergirds this position by arguing that divine commandments (to preach, to baptize, to celebrate the eucharist, and to forgive sins) are accompanied by divinely instituted ceremonies. Liturgy reflects doctrine; since Roman Catholic liturgy reflects Roman Catholic doctrine, it must be rejected as being contrary to the gospel.

The point at issue between Gnesio-Lutherans and Philippists was the status of adiaphora in times of persecution. Philippists held that even in a period of persecution, when a confession of faith is called for (*in statu confessionis*), "one may still with a clear conscience, at the enemies' instant demand, restore once more certain abrogated ceremonies that are in themselves matters of indifference and that are neither commanded nor forbidden by God, and one may justifiably conform oneself to them in such adiaphora or matters of indifference" (FC, SD 10:2). Gnesio-Lutherans denied that (FC, SD 10:3). Melanchthon kept cool, despite Flacius' sharp invective. When Melanchthon finally defended himself, in an open letter to Flacius dated October 1, 1549, he declared that the core of Lutheran doctrine, the article of justification, had been preserved; that the Leipzig Interim had protected Lutheran churches and schools from wanton destruction; and that God should be trusted in the entire affair (CR 7, 477–82).

Although FC 10 tried to settle the controversy, it succeeded only in establishing confessional norms which tended to support Flacius and the Gnesio-Lutherans: (1) The position of AC 15 regarding the distinction between the word of God and adiaphora is upheld (FC, SD 10:5–8); (2) "ceremonies" can be changed according to the will of the church at different times in different places, as long as this is done "without frivolity and offense but in an orderly and appropriate way, as at any time may seem to be most profitable, beneficial, and salutary for good order, Christian discipline, evangelical decorum, and the edification of the church" (SD 10:9); and (3) "at a time of confession" (a Flacian phrase!) all Christians—especially pastors—must witness, in word and deed, to "the true doctrine and what pertains to it" and "not yield to adversaries even in matters of indifference." FC 10 stressed the dynamic connection between gospel and adiaphora in times of persecution, that is, when adiaphora are "imposed on consciences" (SD 10:13–15). However,

> churches will not condemn each other because of a difference in ceremonies, when in Christian liberty one uses fewer or more of them, as long as they are otherwise agreed in doctrine and in all its articles and are also agreed concerning the right use of the holy sacraments according to the well-known axiom [of Irenaeus against Victor of Rome] "Disagreement in fasting should not destroy agreement in faith." (SD 10:31)

The sixteenth-century adiaphorist controversy waned under the pressure of political events that led to the Peace of Augsburg in 1555. In 1552 Maurice had become the emperor's enemy; the treaty of Passau in August of the same year ended the Leipzig Interim; and the Lutheran princes (Elector John Frederick of Saxony and Landgrave Philip of Hesse) had been released from prison. Maurice's "turncoat" politics and Melanchthon's theological pussyfooting had saved the Lutheran movement from possible extinction.

The Problem of Teaching Authority

The Lutheran confessions did not establish a list of adiaphora for all time. What are adiaphora is a decision the church must make at various times in various places (FC, EP 10:4 and SD 10:9). Gnesio-Lutherans and Philippists struggled for a proper *doctrinal* definition of adiaphora in the sixteenth century, and Lutheran Orthodoxists and Pietists tried to come to terms with the *ethical* meaning of adiaphora in the seventeenth century. When the city fathers of Hamburg founded the now-famous opera, disciples of the Pietist August Hermann Francke denounced operatic performances as un-Christian and sinful. Francke's most ardent disciple, Joachim Lange, declared that all entertainment is against the will of God, invented by men to enjoy sin. He urged that visitors to the opera and other places of entertainment should not be admitted to the Lord's Supper, and welcomed the decision of the directors of the orphanage in Halle not to allow games for children. Pastors and theologians who defended the opera and other forms of entertainment as true adiaphora approved when the city fathers simply dismissed the most radical Pietists in 1697 and 1698. But the struggle for proper ethical definition of adiaphora continued in Lutheran and Reformed theological textbooks.

The question of adiaphorist freedom is intimately linked to the question of what constitutes Lutheran teaching authority or the Lutheran teaching office. Luther and the Lutheran confessions reaffirmed the ecumenical office of bishop or "superintendent" (the Latin translation of the Greek "*episkopos*," AC 28), but they rejected the medieval fusion of "jurisdictional power" and "teaching authority" (*magisterium*, AP 28:12–14). Consequently, the difference between theological confession and ecclesiastical constitution has not always been clear.

The earliest Lutheran church orders tried to prevent heresy, schism, and rebellion in a given territory. After the Peace of Augsburg in 1555, the "superintendent," "general superintendent," "dean (*Propst*)," and "bishop"—titles in vogue in Germany after 1580—became guardians and executors of doctrine, sharing these functions with the territorial prince. Frequently,."consistories" assisted the bishops and princes. In the nineteenth century, after a period of absolutism, the rise of constitutionalism reduced the power of the prince. The creation of an "evangelical ecclesiastical council" (*evangelischer Oberkirchenrat*) in Prussia in 1850 influenced later developments in Germany. The administrative model for a number of territorial churches, the council was no longer chaired by the prince but by a territorial bishop. At the end of the German monarchy in 1918, Lutheran bishops functioned in the teaching office.

The episcopal teaching authority became the subject of intra-Lutheran and ecumenical dialogue before World War II. In Germany, the struggle (*Kirchenkampf*) between "German Christians"—under the leadership of a national bishop (*Reichsbischof*) appointed by the Nazi regime—and the "Confessing Church" produced sharp differences over the interpretation of "spiritual" and "temporal" power in a territorial church. The 1934 Barmen Declaration ardently reaffirmed the ancient confessional norms: the gospel of Jesus Christ, Holy Scripture, and the creeds of the Reformation. It rejected as false teaching any view which holds that the church is subject to a special political leader. As a result, the postwar constitutions of Lutheran territorial churches in Germany emphasized the interrelation of clerical and lay authority.

This is why the Declaration of the United Evangelical Church in Germany in 1954 rejected the idea of an apostolic succession of bishops.

Scandinavian Lutheran churches took similar positions with regard to the question of episcopal authority. The Swedish Bishops' Assembly of 1922 and the archbishop of the Church of Finland, during ecumenical conversations with the Church of England, asserted that episcopacy should not be understood in terms of *ius divinum* but rather in terms of *ius humanum*.

Lutheran churches in the United States also need to concern themselves with theological and practical considerations of teaching authority. The principle of separation of church and state did not allow the development of territorial churches according to German models. Immigrant Lutherans, who distrusted Anglican episcopalianism, adopted a variety of synodical and congregational structures with nonchalant pragmatism. The highest Lutheran ecclesiastical authority in America is usually placed in a biennial convention consisting of an equal number of clerical and lay delegates. The Lutheran Church in America, for example, is chaired by the elected president of the church, and its doctrinal norms are featured in Article II of the constitution. The constitution generally follows the model of a business corporation.

A survey of confessional subscription among members of the Lutheran World Federation indicates that Luther's definition of authority as a hermeneutical process, in terms of the interaction of "word" and "faith," seems prevalent. While some churches engage in this hermeneutical process with great care and constantly attempt to sort out the difference between gospel and adiaphora at any given time and place, other churches exhibit authoritarian tendencies and aim for scriptural or parliamentary infallibility. Both processes reflect the shift in the definition of teaching authority, which occurred during the sixteenth-century doctrinal controversies leading to the Formula of Concord: while the Augsburg Confession *assumes* that human traditions are to be judged by Scripture, the Formula of Concord *asserts* that this must be so (FC, EP, "Rule and Norm," 1–2).

The relationship between gospel and adiaphora on the one hand, and the nature of the office of ministry on the other, are the two principal issues which have determined theological formulations of Lutheran teaching authority. The history of these theological formulations and their relation to sociopolitical developments discloses the perennial

Lutheran perplexity and open-endedness with regard to definitions of *magisterium*. If Lutheran teaching authority is faithful to the eschatological nature of the gospel, it will regard an ecclesiastical structure as the instrument through which the church reflects the mystery of its Lord, rather than the contentiousness of an institution. Lutheranism is under the perennial mandate to move from the heresy of institutionalism to the orthodoxy of ecumenism, for Christian truth and Christian unity are always in tension.

B.

The Adiaphora Concept

In medieval moral theology, an "adiaphoron" was a human act neither commanded nor forbidden by divine law. Whether or not there are any such acts depends, of course, on how divine law is given. A law continuously written on the heart by God's Spirit might command one specific possibility in every situation of choice; then there would be no adiaphora. Spiritualist movements therefore regularly reject any such concept. But to whatever extent divine law is an external phenomenon, to whatever extent it is a written or customary code, it will demonstrate the notorious character of all positive law, that it does not cover all cases and works best if it does not try to; then there will be adiaphora. Medieval theology found the divine law externally in Scripture and the rules of the church, was suspicious of claims for unbroken direct inspiration, and so had use for the notion of what is neither commanded nor forbidden.

Lutheran theology continued to use the adiaphora concept for its own purposes. For all Reformation theology, God's word is both law and gospel. For Lutherans specifically, the hermeneutic character of God's word is defined by the gospel, so that the law shares the gospel's essential externality; thus the Lutherans could also adopt the medieval concept that marked the externality of the law. Whether they were wise to do so is another question.

The Lutheran Use

Luther and Melanchthon used "adiaphora" as a label for what is "not necessary" to be done. "Not necessary" for what? Already there is difficulty. "Not necessary for the doer's salvation" cannot be the sense, even though it often seems to be. Nothing is necessary to be done by us for salvation, so that if this were the sense, *all* our acts would be adiaphora and the concept would be emptied. We must not, therefore, take the adiaphora concept as a comprehensive expression of the Reformation's concern for Christian liberty. When such an interpretation has been made, the resulting message is: "Only believe, and for the rest it does not matter what you do." To the considerable damage of the Lutheran movement, many of its opponents (including the Council of Trent, canon 19) have misunderstood the matter in this way.

If "not necessary" does not mean "not necessary for the doer's salvation," Lutheranism offers only two other possibilities: "not necessary for service of the neighbor" and "not necessary for disinterested obedience to God." And in fact Lutheran assertions about "adiaphora" can all be accommodated in these two contexts. Indeed, the observable context is still more restricted: "adiaphora" always turn out to be churchly practices of one sort or another. Adiaphora, therefore, are things "not necessary" to be done by the church in its task of doing good for the neighbor by proclaiming and enacting the gospel, or in its privilege of obeying God's contingent commands about that task.

But what *is* necessary to be done in the church's mission? After all we have heard about Lutheranism, we may suppose that the answer must be: whatever in a time and place is strategically required to bring the gospel to utterance. But that is not how the confessions in fact talk about the matter. Indeed, this answer would again dissolve the necessary/adiaphora distinction. We find the actual place of the distinction only when we observe yet another actual context: the original reforming use of "adiaphora" was *polemic*. Much which the medieval church called necessary, the Reformers called adiaphora, in order to lighten the burden of law on believers' consciences. For example: "Even though the bishops insist on the Lenten fast, you do not sin by following another custom if that other custom is edifying in itself, does not hurt other Christians, and is not contrary to Scripture." The means by which the polemic is accomplished is demonstration that something the established church calls necessary lacks scriptural authority.

The things "necessary" to be done or not done therefore finally turn out to be those commanded or forbidden in Scripture. But here a new difficulty appears. For purposes of anti-Roman polemic and evangelical pastoral care, perhaps this distinction between "scriptural" and "adiaphoral" usually worked well enough. But it will hardly do in principle, for long lists of Scripture's commands were in fact ignored by the Lutherans; the classic example is no less than the third commandment. Moreover, such scriptural commands have been ignored precisely on that principle of Christian liberty which the adiaphora principle was to protect. Thus, when sectarians have insisted that Saturday must be observed, Lutherans have called the particular day and mode of observance "adiaphora."

In fact, the Lutherans clearly used an additional principle in determining which churchly commands of Scripture establish necessary churchly acts, that is, really belong to God's law for us now: they are those that Scripture makes integral to its one great command to preach and enact the gospel—such as are the sacramental mandates. Those mandates of Scripture which establish the fundamental forms of the gospel impose acts about the doing or not doing of which we are not called to make any judgments. "Adiaphora" are all *other* matters, about which we are indeed called to judge.

Our faithful judgment, left to itself, might decide that in a time and place some other form and elements would work better than joint thanksgiving-prayer with shared bread and cup, or that a sacramental meal without thanksgiving-praise of God would less tempt to works-righteousness. Lutheranism protected the historical contingency and externality of the sacraments, and so the historical contingency and embodiment of the gospel itself, by commanding abstention from such judgments. Where Scripture specifically makes particular sacramental performances essential to the gospel-mission, Lutheranism bows to the contingency of the mandate. A word is needed for all those choices *not* included in this abstention; the Lutherans chose "adiaphora." Where they used the word in other than liturgical contexts, the use was, we suggest, an extension of this use, to achieve similar purposes.

Spiritualism openly dissolved the gospel's historicality and embodiment by making the authority of the contingent apostolic witness subject to the continuous correction of the interior Spirit. Medieval catholicism implicitly dissolved the gospel's historicality by extending the apostolic mandates' sort of authority to the whole continuously developing body of churchly law and custom. With the distinction between "biblically mandated" and "adiaphora," the Lutherans were able to contradict both positions.

The Pitfalls of "Adiaphora"

"Adiaphora" means literally, "what makes no difference." This literal meaning has been kept alive by the obvious Graeicism of the word, which always has to be translated. The resulting suggestion that what Scripture does not altogether remove from our judgment therefore makes no difference has been a disastrous temptation for Lutheranism.

Liturgically, talk of "adiaphora" has continuously tempted Lutherans to suppose that so long as sermons are preached, and water, bread, and wine are regularly present with the minimum "words," it does not really matter what happens otherwise; and Lutherans have hardly ever resisted the temptation. Naturally, one devotes little thought to what does not really matter.

The charge is not merely—as Lutherans usually suppose it must be—that bad liturgy is aesthetically unsatisfying or annoying to scholars of ancient tradition. Liturgy is the union of the audible and visible word, and is thus itself communication; and uncared-for liturgy is certain to say anything but the gospel, just as is uncared-for proclamation. In congregation after congregation, pastors and leaders ignore or abet liturgy that says we are saved by works, then wonder why their verbalizing about "grace" is so ineffective. They abet liturgy throughout which the people are rooted to one spot (mostly to their seats, as if at a lecture), then wonder why the word there spoken is not experienced as an energizing message.

In contradiction to what most Lutherans may suppose, the Lutheran confessions in no way support the general adiaphorizing of liturgical questions. Rather, they explicitly teach that some liturgical questions are never adiaphora. Thus, concerning the liturgy of the Lord's Supper, the Formula of Concord declares: "But . . . this recitation of Christ's words of institution by itself, if the entire *action* of the Lord's Supper as Christ ordained it is not observed . . . does *not* make a sacrament. But the command of Christ, 'Do this,' which comprehends the whole *action* or administration of this sacrament . . . , must be kept integrally and inviolably" (SD 7:83–84, emphasis added). What component actions are in fact commanded by a sacramental "This do" is, of course, an *exegetical* question, which can only be settled by work on the texts, not by systematic considerations directly, by historical preference, or even by reference to the confessions' opinions. But just such questions are also the chief *liturgical* questions, which are therefore not adiaphoral.

There is, for example, no mystery at all about the action ordained by the texts that mandate the Lord's Supper, nor any difficulty in obeying. We are to offer thanksgiving-praise to God the Father, remembering especially his acts in the death and resurrection of Jesus, sealing our joint thanksgiving by shared bread and cup of wine. The decision to obey once made, there are unlimited possibilities of how this may be done. This field of possibility is the arena of our obedient creativity through the history of the gospel. And here again, the literal meaning of "adiaphora" is misleading. To say that what happens in this arena does not really matter is to say that we and our freedom do not matter. Moreover, our creativity has a *goal* set not by us but by God: creation of a complex of audible and visible words appropriate to the mandated proclamation and sacramental enactment of the gospel.

In the matter of church polity, Lutheranism's history is perhaps even more dismal than is its liturgical history. Here again, our terminology has misled us into supposing that questions of polity are neutral with respect to the gospel, and may safely be left to those who enjoy organizing things. In consequence we have well-deservedly fallen victim to ecclesiastical tyranny after tyranny.

Questions of polity are in fact by no means theologically neutral. The people of God organize for one purpose only: to serve the gospel-mission. And nothing so determines whether the organization will in fact serve the gospel as whether the authority that is established in it is of the promise-variety that is appropriate to the gospel. That is, nothing so determines whether the organization will serve the gospel as the way in which the central *political* question is settled in it.

In analogy to the status of canonical sacramental mandates, there is at least one matter of polity that the confessions do not consider adiaphoral: the existence of an office of ministry to the gospel. The internal organization of the ministry, and to some extent its relation to other political structures of the church at a time and place, are the historically variable free responsibility of the believers; but the existence of the office, and its possession of whatever authorities are at a time and place necessary for its incumbents to fulfill their responsibility, are not.

The mandated place of the ministry within the church's polity means also that our historical—"adiaphoral"—freedom to make new arrangements does not lack a goal. It implies that administrative authority over congregations and pastors should normally be exercised by persons who first have the authority of speakers of the gospel, whose chief daily work is the immediate ministry to word and sacraments. Where this is, "exceptionally," not possible, Lutheran theology would seem to suggest that administrative authority be exercised by–genuine–laypersons. As it works out, Lutheran theology calls for a mode of government in the church much like the pastoral episcopacy of the most ancient church, or indeed of a small Anglican or Roman Catholic missionary diocese today.

Lutherans have rarely had such polity. Misled by our terminology, we have generally supposed that questions of polity were not to be argued by theological considerations, but by considerations of "efficiency." The result has regularly been that Lutheran polity has merely imitated–usually about fifteen years behind–the sort of organization currently dominant in society. Far from fulfilling the organizational freedom in the gospel which Lutherans claim, and which we have supposed our detheologized organizing to exemplify, we have thereby merely accepted that bondage to the world's example from which the gospel is supposed to free us.

In America, we have imitated the "managerial" methods of bureaucratized capitalism. A model more uncongenial to the work of the gospel is not conceivable. Our "bishops" and "presidents," with their multitudinous staffs, exercise a mode of authority opposite to that of a pastoral episcopacy. If they at all find time to preach, teach, baptize, and preside at eucharist, these acts lie on the periphery of their job descriptions; and immersion in other concerns soon makes them pastorally incompetent in any case–at which point, the legitimacy of their authority is, by genuinely Lutheran standards, in grave doubt.

The Legitimate Concern

There is nothing we "must do" to be right with God. If we will do good for our fellows, on the other hand, there is much we must do, including that we speak the gospel to them: therewith the church's mission is established. Within labor to do the church's mission, Lutheran theology introduced another distinction between what we must do and what we need not do. We have noted the problems created by the introduction of this distinction. Nevertheless, it served a function with continuing importance.

The church is set free in history to work out how at each time and place to fulfill its mission. Assertion of this freedom is an immediate consequence of the doctrine of justification by faith. But also, this freedom is not a mere abstract spontaneity, arising afresh from within believers of each moment; it is freedom achieved precisely in conversation with voices that speak—just as does the gospel itself—from outside the immediate place and time of those who are to choose. All the army of our predecessors says to us, "Go speak the gospel," articulating the command in all the variety of the total Christian tradition. Nor do our predecessors ever actually address us with the abstract formulation just quoted. Their command to preach the gospel sounds concretely, "Go, tell men they are atoned for," or "Go, establish monasteries," or "Go, settle America." It is in *conversation* with this rich flow of orders and advice that we can be freely responsible for the church's mission.

It belongs to freedom that various voices of the tradition speak with various authority. When we come to the apostolic witness, we hear final authority; we are no longer able to reply "Yes, but . . ." if we wish to remain in conversation with the *gospel*-tradition. Yet even here, a distinction must be made. Insofar as the apostles say to us, "*Speak* . . . , to be saying the gospel," our attempt to say "the same" as they said is the *interpretive* effort described in the first chapter of this book, and will not be fulfilled merely by repeating their forms of words. Insofar, on the other hand, as the apostles say to us, "*Perform* . . . , to be saying the gospel," there is no room for interpretation. For *visible* words belong to no language; they have no grammar or rule-determined vocabulary, and therefore they cannot and need not be translated, as must the audible sentences of language. As the body-side of the gospel-event, visible words guard the sheer historical contingency of what the gospel is and of where and when it became speakable; they are the factual body-continuity of Christ's presence in the gospel-event. Our attempt to obey apostolic mandates of the sort that create sacraments therefore involves only linguistic and historical exegesis; it does not involve existential exegesis, only obedience or disobedience to the command once read, and freedom of invention in fulfilling obedience once chosen.

Such are the manifold dialectics of believers' freedom in the mission of the church. Lutheranism's adiaphora concept kept space open for them. But in view of the dangers of the concept itself, it will probably in the future be better to accomplish this function with direct analysis of the dialectics, such as has been sketchily attempted in the preceding paragraphs.

Postscript

Lutheranism is a theological movement within the church catholic. At its center is the proposal of dogma which Luther and the Lutheran confessions cherished as the essential characteristic of the gospel: justification by faith apart from works of law. This article of faith commits the Lutheran movement to the cause of unity, which is to be pursued in ever new ways of doctrinal formulations as concrete evidence of ecumenicity.

> If no amicable and charitable negotiations take place between us, and if no results are attained, nevertheless we on our part shall not omit doing anything, in so far as God and conscience allow, that may serve the cause of Christian unity. (AC Preface, 12–13)
>
> The primary requirement for basic and permanent concord within the church is a summary formula and pattern, unanimously approved, in which the summarized doctrine commonly confessed by the churches of the pure Christian religion is drawn together out of the Word of God. (FC, SD "Rule and Norm," 1)
>
> We shall at all times make a sharp distinction between needless and unprofitable contentions (which, since they destroy rather than edify, should never be allowed to disturb the church) and necessary controversy (dissension concerning articles of the Creed or the chief parts of our Christian doctrine, when the contrary error must be refuted in order to preserve the truth). (FC, SD "Rule and Norm," 15)

The Lutheran confessions claim to be norms for the proper proclamation of the gospel in the church. As such, they are by no means above either the canonical Scriptures or the trinitarian creeds of the ancient church. Moreover, they are sixteenth-century documents reflecting the context of specific historical circumstances. Thus they are subject to human error and in need of correction on the basis of contemporary ecumenical mandates to the life and mission of the church.

Whether Lutheranism's proposal of dogma will ever be ecumenically accepted may remain a mystery this side of the eschaton. But as long as some Christians band together by subscription to the Lutheran confessions (in one way or another), they are committed to keep trying.

If we are to continue to propose "justification by faith" as ecumenical dogma, we must do so in the ecumenical theological arena. It will not do merely to reiterate the formula. That is not the way in which dogma is recognized in the church; nor does experience suggest much hope of success. Rather, we must share the ecumenical theological enterprise, doing so as persons who are controlled by the article on justification. In this manner, we can make whatever contribution seems necessary in the course of Christian history—as has indeed been the classic behavior of Lutherans in the past.

Throughout this book, we have noted items of theological work remaining for the Lutheran movement to do. Some are simple continuations of work begun and needing to be carried on, for example, the need to reflect further on the doctrine of ordained ministry. Some are cures for perverse developments, for example, the need to overcome Lutheranism's political quietism and cynicism. And some are explosive redoings of fundamental Western habits of apperception and action, implied in Lutheran positions but never yet quite carried through.

Of the last sort, we will mention two again. First, Lutheran positions imply an attitude toward the community, authority, and organization of the church which is nowhere now exemplified, least of all by Lutheran bodies. Second, Lutheran positions involve a radical challenge to our inherited ontology, made especially by Lutheran Christology and sacramentology. It seems to us that these remarkably match two great crises of our time: the manifest decadence of that form of the church which has obtained since the Reformation, and the collapse of Western communities' inherited values and shared apprehensions. It may seem suspiciously convenient for us thus to point to the four-centuries-old Lutheran heritage as a source of fundamental renewal. But the Lutheran movement has been, in ways both good and bad, an initiator and continuing motor of specifically modern apprehensions; it should not, therefore, be surprising if the Lutheran tradition can sometimes speak to them.

The Lutheran movement and its theology, grounded in the article of justification, may still open new vistas for ecumenical doctrine and life. It goes almost without saying that Lutheran denominations and territorial churches have not always existed by the confessional norms of the Lutheran *movement*. But a serious encounter with these norms, as they emerged in the struggle and controversy of the sixteenth century, can stimulate ecumenical answers to many pressing concerns of today. This, at least, is our conviction, after some years of such encounter. To confess the authority of the Lutheran confessions is to confess that they speak to living options. That confession is what this book, on every page, has been about.

Index

Names

Subjects

Subjects adequately located by the table of contents are not listed here.

Chronology

273 Death of Mani, founder of Manichaeism
325 Council of Nicea
411 Rejection of Donatism at Synod of Carthage; beginning of Pelagian controversy
418 Condemnation of Pelagianism at Synod of Carthage
429 Beginning of semi-Pelagianism
430 Death of Augustine
431 End of Pelagian controversy
529 Second Council of Orange; end of semi-Pelagian controversy
1109 Death of Anselm of Canterbury
1215 Fourth Lateran Council; doctrine of Transubstantiation
1274 Death of Thomas Aquinas
1308 Bull *Unam Sanctam* by Boniface VIII
1415 Council of Constance; doctrine of Concomitance; death of John Hus
1429 Death of conciliarist John Gerson
1483 Birth of Martin Luther
1507 Luther's ordination
1509 Luther's biblical baccalaureate
1512 Luther's doctorate
1512–13? Luther's "tower experience"
1517 Disputation against scholastic theology; Ninety-five Theses
1518 Heidelberg Disputation; Luther's appearance before Cajetan in Augsburg; Melanchthon's call to Wittenberg
1519 Leipzig debate
1521 Diet of Worms; Luther's condemnation by church and state; Melanchthon's *Loci Communes*; death of Leo X
1521–22 Luther at the Wartburg; Wittenberg unrest; Zwickau prophets; Carlstadt's leadership in Wittenberg
1522 Imperial Edict against Lutherans
1523 German knights' rebellion
1524 Diet of Nuremberg
1525 Death of Elector Frederick, succession by son John Frederick; Peasants' War; Leagues of Dessau and Gotha; Luther's marriage to Catherine of Bora; Luther's controversy with Erasmus over free will
1526 Diet of Speyer
1528–29 Visitations in Saxony; catechetical reforms
1529 Luther's Small and Large Catechisms; Marburg Colloquy; Schwabach Articles
1530 Diet of Augsburg; Augsburg Confession, Catholic Confutation
1531 Apology of Augsburg Confession; Smalcald League; death of Zwingli
1536 Wittenberg Concord; death of Erasmus
1537 Smalcald Articles; treatise on the power and primacy of the pope; antinomian controversy
1538 League of Nuremberg
1540 Altered Augsburg Confession; Philip of Hesse's bigamy; colloquies at Hagenau and Worms
1541 Colloquy at Ratisbon; Maurice of Saxony joins emperor
1545 Beginning of Council of Trent
1546 Luther's death; Smalcald wars
1547 Defeat of Smalcald League
1548 Augsburg Interim; Leipzig Interim; beginning of adiaphorist controversy
1549 Beginning of Osiandrian controversy
1551 Maurice of Saxony's attack on Charles V in Innsbruck
1552 Agreement of Passau; end of adiaphorist controversy; beginning of Majoristic controversy; death of Osiander
1553 Death of Maurice of Saxony
1555 Peace of Augsburg; beginning of crypto-Calvinist controversy
1556 Beginning of synergistic controversy; death of Charles V, succession by Ferdinand I
1558 End of Majoristic controversy; Frankfurt Recess
1560 End of synergistic controversy; death of Melanchthon; Weimar Disputation
1561 End of crypto-Calvinist controversy; dismissal of Flacius from Jena University; "middle party"
1563 End of Council of Trent; Heidelberg Catechism
1564 Colloquy at Maulbronn; death of Calvin
1566 End of Osiandrian controversy
1569 Church Order of Brunswick
1570 Death of John Brenz
1573 Union sermons of Jacob Andreae; Swabian Concord
1575 Swabian-Saxon Formula; death of Flacius
1576 Evaluation of Wittenberg theologians in Maulbronn; Torgau Book
1577 Bergen Book; Formula of Concord; Solid Declaration; Epitome
1580 Book of Concord
1586 Death of Martin Chemnitz
1590 Death of Jacob Andreae
1618 Thirty Years' War
1648 Peace of Westphalia

9 780800 612467

8146768R0

Made in the USA
Lexington, KY
13 January 2011